OUT OF THE SHADOW

ROSE COHEN

Rose Gollup Cohen, formal portrait, Underwood & Underwood studio, New York City, date uncertain.

OUT OF
THE SHADOW

A RUSSIAN JEWISH GIRLHOOD
ON THE LOWER EAST SIDE

BY
ROSE COHEN

WITH AN INTRODUCTION BY
THOMAS DUBLIN

ILLUSTRATED BY
WALTER JACK DUNCAN

CORNELL UNIVERSITY PRESS
ITHACA AND LONDON

A volume in the series
Documents in American Social History,
edited by Nick Salvatore

A complete list of titles in the series appears at the end of the book.

First published 1995 by Cornell University Press
First printing, Cornell Paperbacks, 1995

Printed in the United States of America

Library of Congress Cataloging-in-Publication Data

Cohen, Rose, 1880–1925.
   Out of the shadow : a Russian Jewish girlhood on the Lower East
Side / Rose Cohen ; with an introduction by Thomas Dublin.
   p. cm. — (Documents in American social history)
   Originally published: New York : Doran, 1918.
   Includes bibliographical references.
   ISBN 978-0-8014-8268-7 (pbk. : alk. paper)
   1. Cohen, Rose, 1880–1925.   2. Jews, Russian—New York (N.Y.)—
Biography.   3. Immigrants—New York (N.Y.)—Biography.   4. New
York (N.Y.)—Biography.   5. Lower East Side (New York, N.Y.)—
Biography.
I. Title.   II. Series.
F128.9.J5C673   1995
974.7'1004924047'092—dc20
[B]   95-15726

Cornell University Press strives to use environmentally responsible suppliers
and materials to the fullest extent possible in the publishing of its books.
Such materials include vegetable-based, low-VOC inks and acid-free papers
that are recycled, totally chlorine-free, or partly composed of nonwood fibers.
For further information, visit our website at www.cornellpress.cornell.edu.

Paperback printing   10 9 8 7

TO
LEONORA O'REILLY

Jacob Adler in "King Lear."

ILLUSTRATIONS

The Gollup family, New York City, ca. 1897. Front row: (from left) Abraham, George, Annie. Back row: Rose, Eugene, Rebecca, Sarah

Introduction to the 1995 Edition

"This is the story of a Russian Jewish immigrant girl who came to this country at the age of 12, and who, after years of hard work, privation, and perplexity, found a settled life. . . . It leads to no conclusion of arresting prosperity. It has in it few 'high lights' of any kind. It is just such a record as may be true of thousands of immigrant girls. Therein its greatest value lies."[1] So wrote one reviewer, describing *Out of the Shadow*, the 1918 autobiography of an otherwise unknown Russian Jewish immigrant, Rose Gollup Cohen. Encouraged by a night-class instructor, Cohen wrote a personal memoir that spoke to the broader experience of immigrants on New York's Lower East Side in the 1890s and early 1900s. The publication of *Out of the Shadow* thrust her briefly onto the contemporary literary scene. But her life and writing were both cut short, and her early death in 1925, when she was only forty-five, returned her to obscurity.[2]

More than seventy-five years after its original publication, *Out of the Shadow* has enduring value for readers. Cohen offers vivid recollections of Eastern European *shtetl* life, of her illegal exodus from Russia and her transatlantic voyage, of tenement life and sweatshop work in New York City, and of the influence of settlement-house work on the Lower East Side. She is a perceptive observer with an ability to make her experiences come alive for readers. Unlike the work of more celebrated immigrant writers, such as Mary Antin and Morris Raphael Cohen, hers is not a self-conscious success story tracing the Americanization of an immigrant Jew.[3] She offers a story of everyday events in the life of the Lower East Side unaffected by myth. We see the exploitation of the sweat-shop and the anti-Semitism of city streets with a clarity that is rare in immigrant autobiography.

Out of the Shadow speaks to experiences that were shared widely in the decades before the outbreak of World War I. Two million Russian and East European Jews emigrated to the United States between 1880 and 1914. Roughly a third of the Jewish population residing in western Russia and the Polish and Baltic provinces ruled by the tsar fled their home-lands in the face of mounting religious persecution and eco-nomic restrictions. Along with the Irish famine emigration of the mid-nineteenth century, this population movement was one of the great migrations of modern times.[4]

Most Russian and East European Jews in the period of mass emigration were confined to residence within an area known as the Pale of Settlement, which stretched from the Baltic Sea in the north to the Black Sea in the south. Within that area, Jews lived in larger cities, such as Vilna and Kovno, as well as smaller Jewish villages, called *shtetlekh* or shtetls. Not permitted to own land, Jews clustered in artisan trades, garment work, and trading. Beginning in the 1880s, growing economic disabilities and attacks on Jewish commu-nities made life increasingly unbearable for the Jewish mi-nority. The result was a mass exodus, despite restrictive laws forbidding emigration.

By 1920 fully 45 percent of Eastern European Jewish im-migrants to the United States resided in New York City, pri-marily on the Lower East Side. In 1910, this area of scarcely more than half a square mile provided homes for over 540,000 people. The population density of the Lower East Side exceeded 700 per acre, making it the most crowded neighborhood in the city, perhaps in the world. Its foreign and exotic atmosphere struck one observer, who wrote:

"The vast east side is scarcely New York. It is Europe,—with a touch of Asia." On the streets the visitor found "Yiddish signs, Yiddish newspapers, Yiddish beards and wigs."[5]

Historians have written vividly of the experience of Eastern European and Russian Jewish immigrants. From Moses Rischin's classic account *The Promised City* (1962), to Irving Howe's cultural history *The World of Our Fathers* (1976), to Susan Glenn's exploration of the female working-class Jewish experience in *Daughters of the Shtetl* (1990), a substantial body of research on the immigrant generation before World War I has emerged.[6] All these works have relied heavily on Yiddish and English-language memoirs and reminiscences, but few of these primary sources are accessible to a general audience today.[7] The publication of this volume is intended to address that need and open for contemporary readers a window onto shtetl life in the Pale of Settlement, the migration experience, and immigrant life on the Lower East Side. Rose Cohen offers rich views of one family's experiences during the 1890s in what are today Belarus and New York City.

Although clearly the work of an author who had only recently mastered the English language, *Out of the Shadow* is written with a strength that brings alive the characters and events it portrays. The autobiography is particularly useful because Cohen wrote it while she was still in her thirties and relatively close to the time period her narrative covered. Unlike most immigrant autobiographies, her story is not the product of assimilation and old age, but represents the first effort of a relatively young woman struggling to make a place for herself in a new world.

As valuable as the autobiography is, however, it proves frustrating to the historian trying to trace Cohen's life. She does not indicate her birthplace or date of birth; she does not name her mother, husband, or daughter, or indicate the dates of her marriage or her daughter's birth. Fortunately, additional sources offer glimpses of her life and permit us to place her autobiography within that broader context.[8]

Born Rahel Gollup on April 4, 1880, the first child in her family, Cohen grew up in a small village in western Russia, in present-day Belarus. Her father was a tailor and a pious Orthodox Jew, whose motivations for emigrating must have been much like those of thousands of others in the Pale of Settlement. As was common in Russian Jewish families, Rahel Gollup's father migrated first, leaving his family behind. Lacking proper papers, he was arrested and had to escape from custody before crossing into Germany and securing steamship passage to the United States in 1890. There he worked and got a foothold for himself in New York City, and after a year and a half sent two pre-paid steamship tickets to his family. In *Out of the Shadow*, Cohen describes the 1892 emigration of herself and her unmarried aunt, Masha. A year later, her mother, two brothers, and two sisters joined the rest of the family.

The autobiography describes in particular detail Cohen's work in garment sweatshops on the Lower East Side. She began in the shop where her father worked, but soon graduated to work on her own, stitching sleeve linings for men's coats. She recounts union organizing among the men of her shop, her own attendance at a mass union meeting, and finally joining the union herself. After the arrival of her mother and other siblings, her story continues with accounts of a brief stint as a domestic servant, her rejection of a prospective suitor, and increasing health problems. During one illness, she was visited by the noted settlement worker Lillian Wald, and Cohen soon discovered the world of the Nurses' Settlement on Henry Street. Through the settlement she was referred for treatment to the uptown Presbyterian Hospital, and there met wealthy non-Jews who sponsored summer outings for children of the Lower East Side. She worked during successive summers at a Connecticut retreat established for immigrant children and, like others, found herself torn between the world of her family in the immigrant ghetto and the broader American culture beyond its bounds.

The narrative trails off after the 1890s, but other sources permit a partial reconstruction of Cohen's later life. In 1897 Lillian Wald referred Rose Gollup to a cooperative shirtwaist shop under the direction of Leonora O'Reilly, later a board member of the national Women's Trade Union League. That work proved short-lived, but when O'Reilly began teaching at the Manhattan Trade School for girls in 1902, she recruited Rose as her assistant.

In 1900 Rose still lived with her parents, Abraham and Annie, at 332 Cherry Street. Her father continued to work as a tailor. Rose (called Rosie in the census) was 19, and she and her 17-year-old sister, Sarah, were both employed as tailoresses. Three younger siblings, Michael, Becca, and George, attended school while the youngest, Bertham, was not quite one. A 20-year-old boarder lived with the family.[9] With three family members working and income from a boarder, the family may have been able to save in this period, for in 1902 Abraham was operating a grocery on 1st Street.

Improving family economics may have led the Gollup family to thoughts of marriage for their eldest daughter and *Out of the Shadow* provides a fascinating account of Rose's courtship by a young grocer. Although Rose rejected the suitor, she eventually married Joseph Cohen and, upon the birth of her daughter, stopped working. She continued her education after her marriage and slowly overcame her self-consciousness about the English language. Attending classes at Breadwinners' College sponsored by the Educational Alliance and also at the Rand School, she came under the influence of Joseph Gollomb, a Russian Jewish immigrant who later wrote his own autobiographical novel, *Unquiet*. In a 1922 self-portrait she expressed gratitude to those who had helped on her journey to becoming a writer: "I owe much of what I know of writing to all my teachers, from the blue-eyed girl in the Thomas Davidson School long ago, who explained a sentence to me, to my present teachers."[10]

In addition to her autobiography, Cohen wrote at least five short pieces published in New York literary magazines between 1918 and 1922. In an autobiographical account addressed "To the Friends of 'Out of the Shadow,'" she summed up her motivation for writing: she sought to communicate her origins "among the Russian peasants," her recent past "among the Jews of Cherry Street," and her present life "among the Americans." Her autobiography captures that cultural journey with striking clarity.[11]

Her writing was received enthusiastically by contemporaries. A brief review of her book in *The Outlook* described it as an "autobiography that reads like a novel. How a Russian emigrant girl could write such a story as this is one of the mysteries of the thing we call genius." The *New York Times* offered a very positive review, noting: "The book is written simply and with sincerity." Lillian Wald, who had known Cohen for some time, wrote perhaps the most glowing review: "The story is told wonderfully well and cannot fail to interest deeply a good many different kinds of readers. I venture to predict that it will fascinate, but also prick and prod, and that it will be accepted as a social document transcending in value many volumes that have been brought forth by academically trained searchers for data on the conditions that the writer has experienced." The book appeared in two

European editions, translated into French and Russian.[12] Cohen's short story, "Natalka's Portion," was reprinted at least six times, including in the prestigious *Best Short Stories of 1922*.[13]

All this acclaim must have made quite an impression on the immigrant author, and Cohen began to travel in more exalted circles. In the summers of 1923 and 1924 she resided at the MacDowell Colony in Peterborough, New Hampshire. After a day's writing in her studio, Cohen would join other resident writers, composers, and artists for dinner and evening activities. There she met and enjoyed the company of the American impressionist painter Lilla Cabot Perry and the poet Edwin Arlington Robinson, both of whom she kept in touch with after her time at the Colony. She probably also met the philosopher Morris Raphael Cohen and the play-wright Thornton Wilder, also residents at the Colony in 1924.[14]

Yet perhaps the attention intimidated Cohen as much as it encouraged her. After her autobiographical sketch appeared in 1922, she published no more. A few scant clues offer hints as to what may have happened, but we cannot tell the story of Cohen's last years with any certainty. The *New York Times* of September 17, 1922, reported a suicide attempt by a "Rose Cohen, 40, of 25 Decatur Avenue, Brooklyn," who jumped into the East River from a landing at the New York Yacht Club.

Anzia Yezierska, another leading Russian Jewish writer, embroidered this account into a 1927 short story, "Wild Winter Love."[15] It depicts an immigrant woman driven by the need to write her life's story and alienated from her tailor husband in the process. Despite her struggles with the demands of a young daughter and domestic life, the protagonist, Ruth Raefsky, writes her book, *Out of the Ghetto*, and gains a measure of fame. Her success further distances her from her husband and ultimately leads her to move out on her own. After a brief, but ill-fated love affair with an older, married Gentile, the protagonist commits suicide. How much of Yezierska's story is fact and how much fiction we will never know.

Personal communication with several surviving children of Rose Gollup Cohen's younger siblings suggests that family members did not talk about Rose. One niece of Rose Cohen indicated that her mother had told her that Rose committed suicide, but others in the family did not recall that story. At this point we can say that Cohen's untimely death may have been a suicide, though we cannot be certain.

Although we are ultimately frustrated in reconstructing Cohen's personal life, her autobiography still portrays important aspects of Jewish immigrant life. Three of these elements deserve highlighting: the poverty and insecurity of Jewish families and the importance of wage earning by all family members; the cultural insularity of Jews; and the existence of influences that eroded this insularity and contributed over time to the assimilation of Jews into broader American culture.

As a newcomer, or "greenhorn," in the Lower East Side, Rahel Gollup was amazed at the evident wealth around her. At the same time, she was struck by her own poverty and the way work dominated her father's life. She pressed him one evening when he came home late from a day of stitching: "Father, does everybody in America live like this? Go to work early, come home late, eat and go to sleep? And the next day again work, eat, and sleep?"[16] But it was not long before Rahel joined her father in the tenement sweatshop stitching men's coats, often working the same long hours he did.

When her mother, brothers, and sisters arrived, the family moved into its own apartment. Father and daughter supported the family at first, but with the depression of 1893 work dwindled and the family had to take in boarders to supplement declining wages. Soon both daughter and father had been laid off. With no garment work in sight, Rahel's younger sister—then only eleven—began doing odd jobs around the neighborhood and Rahel took a position as a servant for a nearby family. Feeling the oppressiveness of their demands on her every waking moment, she soon left that job and found work once again in a garment shop. The nation recovered from the depression, but one senses that its hardships were etched deeply into the memories of members of the Gollup family.

Although family economic needs dominate much of the narrative in Cohen's autobiography, the restrictiveness of life on the Lower East Side resulted from more than economics. From the assaults on Jewish passersby on election night to the harassment of Jewish peddlers by saloon-goers on Cherry Street, anti-Semitism was very much in evidence, and Jews learned to stay among their own and to avoid strangers. The existence of Christian missionaries—some of them Jews who had converted—lent an additional force to the admonitions to stay within the boundaries of one's own kind. In this setting Rahel Gollup had very little contact beyond her family and her shopmates. She generalized upon her own experience, writing "the child that was put into the shop remained in the old environment with the old people, held back by the old traditions, held back by illiteracy." She wrote of Lower East Side life, "On the whole we were still in our old village in Russia."[17]

Had Rahel married the young man her parents had selected for her or had she simply remained healthy, this restricted Russian Jewish world might have been her lifetime lot. Her health broke down, though, under the pressure of her garment work, bringing her to the attention of settlement workers and opening up a world beyond. It was in an uptown Protestant hospital that she heard a very different English from the "Yiddish English" she had learned and began to glimpse a lifestyle very different from that of the Russian shtetl or the Lower East Side. Increasingly, the world of the social settlement entered Rahel's life. She struggled with Shakespeare in English, she checked out books from the free library at the Educational Alliance, and she grew distant from the Yiddish world of her parents in the process. Summer trips to a rural retreat in Connecticut operated by the Henry Street Settlement reinforced this distance.[18]

In her autobiography, Cohen offers an account of her "making herself for a person," in the words of Anzia Yezierska.[19] Cohen rejected the suitor her parents tried to arrange for her; as time passed she worked less and less to help support her family and focused her energies increasingly on her own development. But Cohen does not complete the story of her own individual growth. Her focus in the last section of the book again is on her family, not on herself, as she describes her father opening a store and her brother completing high school and entering Columbia University.[20] One really has no sense of where she herself has arrived as the story ends. She writes as an individual, precariously balanced between the old world and the new, not fully rooted in either culture, ambivalent about her life, and unable to wholeheartedly grasp her future. She has come "Out of the Shadow," but it is clear that she has not fully entered into the light.

In the end, Cohen's legacy is the autobiography she has written: a story of the struggle of her own life, whose outcome was still in doubt as she wrote. In the subsequent silencing of her author's voice, in the possible suicide attempt, and in the uncertainty surrounding her death, we sense the conflict and lack of clear resolution in one immigrant's life. *Out of the Shadow* is very much a reflection of Rose Gollup Cohen's life. In both the strength of its expression and the uncertainty of its conclusion, it speaks to us today as it did to readers when it first appeared.

For helpful research assistance, I thank my Binghamton students Eric Contreras, Melissa Doak, Laura Free, Soo Youn Kim, Michelle Kuhl, and Ivy Wong. My thanks also to Susan Glenn, Alice Kessler-Harris, Nick Salvatore, and Kathryn Kish Sklar for critical readings of earlier drafts of this introduction. This essay began as a biographical sketch for the forthcoming *American National Biography* (Oxford University Press). I acknowledge the permission of the American Council of Learned Societies to utilize portions of that sketch here.

THOMAS DUBLIN

Brackney, Pennsylvania

NOTES

1. *New York Times*, 1 Dec. 1918, sec. VII, p. 7. The original edition of the book is Rose Cohen, *Out of the Shadow* (New York: George H. Doran, 1918).

2. There is no obituary in the *New York Times* and apparently no death record in New York City's Municipal Archives. The only source that permits us to date Cohen's death is a notation on her rolodex record at the MacDowell Colony in Peterborough, N.H. For Cohen's birth, see Edward J. O'Brien, ed., *The Best Short Stories of 1922 and the Yearbook of the American Short Story* (Boston: Small, Maynard, 1923), p. 309.

3. Mary Antin, *The Promised Land* (1912; rpt. Princeton: Princeton University Press, 1969); Morris Raphael Cohen, *A Dreamer's Journey* (Boston: Beacon Press, 1949).

4. For an overview of Russian Jewish immigration to the United States, see Arthur A. Goren, "Jews," in Stephan Thernstrom, ed., *Harvard Encyclopedia of American Ethnic Groups* (Cambridge: Harvard University Press, 1980), pp. 579-88.

5. Goren, "Jews," p. 581; Moses Rischin, *The Promised City: New York's Jews, 1870-1914* (1962; rpt. Cambridge: Harvard University Press, 1977), pp. 79, 93. Quotes are from Bernardine Kielty, *The Sidewalks of New York* (New York: Little Leather Library, 1923), pp. 67, 72.

6. Rischin, *The Promised City*; Irving Howe, *The World of Our Fathers* (New York: Simon and Schuster, 1976); Susan A Glenn, *Daughters of the Shtetl: Life and Labor in the Immigrant Generation* (Ithaca: Cornell University Press, 1990). I thank Susan Glenn for introducing me to *Out of the Shadow* and for help in placing the work in a broader perspective.

7. Of the vast memoir literature, particularly useful for comparison with *Out of the Shadow* are Antin, *Promised Land*; Mary Antin, *From Plotzk to Boston* (1899; rpt. New York: Markus Wiener, 1986); Cohen, *Dreamer's Journey*; Emma Goldman, *Living My Life*, 2 vols. (1931; rpt. New York: Dover, 1970); and Elizabeth Hasanovitz, *One of Them: Chapters from a Passionate Autobiography* (Boston: Houghton Mifflin, 1918).

8. Rose Gollup Cohen, "To the Friends of 'Out of the Shadow,'" *Bookman* 55 (Mar. 1922): 36-40; O'Brien, ed., *Best Short Stories of 1922*, p. 309; U.S. Federal Manuscript Census of Population (1900), National Archives, microfilm T623, reel 1084, enumeration district 82, sheet 9, line 10. Likely links to Abraham Gollup, Rose's father, were found in New York City directories for 1895-96, 1898-1907, and 1915-16. Abraham Gollup worked as a tailor, ran a grocery store, and returned to work as a machine operator, occupations confirmed in *Out of the Shadow*. For a surviving Rose Cohen letter, see the Perry Family Papers, Colby College Library, Waterville, Maine.

9. U.S. Federal Manuscript Census of Population (1900), National Archives, microfilm T623, reel 1084, enumeration district 82, sheet 9, line 10. The family surname in the census is "Gulob," but there can be no doubt that this is Rose Gollup and her family.

10. Rose Gollup Cohen, "To the Friends of 'Out of the Shadow,'" p. 40.

For more on Breadwinners' College, see Adam Bellow, *The Educational Alliance: A Centennial Celebration* (New York: Educational Alliance, 1990), pp. 56-64. See also Joseph Gollomb, *Unquiet* (New York: Dodd, Mead, 1935).

11. Rose Gollup Cohen, "To the Friends of 'Out of the Shadow,' " p. 40. Her other writings include: "My Childhood Days in Russia," *Bookman* 47 (Aug. 1918): 591-608; "The Books I Knew as a Child," *Bookman* 49 (Mar. 1919): 15-19; "Sifted Earth: A Story," *The Touchstone* 7 (July 1920): 255-60; and "Natalka's Portion," *Current Opinion* 72 (May 1922): 620-28 (originally published in *Pictorial Review*, Feb. 1922).

12. *The Outlook* (Nov. 6, 1918): 382; *New York Times*, 1 Dec. 1918, sec. VII, p. 7; *Bookman* 48 (Nov. 1918): 385. The French edition was Rose Cohen, *A travers la nuit*, 3d ed. (Paris: La Renaissance du Livre, 1924), translated by Sophie Godet. The preface to the French edition was a translation of Cohen's autobiographical sketch, "To the Friends of 'Out of the Shadow.' " The Russian translation of the autobiography was *Skvoz' Noch'*, translated by N. Ia. Khozina, under the editorship of Osip E. Mandel'shtam (Leningrad: New Books, 1927).

13. MacDowell Colony, *Annual Report*, 1924, p. 10; O'Brien, ed., *Best Short Stories of 1922*, pp. 83-99.

14. Rose Gollup Cohen to Lilla Cabot Perry, 12 Nov. [?], Perry Family Papers. In the Edwin Arlington Robinson Papers, also at Colby College, is an autographed presentation copy of the French edition of Cohen's autobiography. For Cohen's times at the Colony, see MacDowell Colony, *Annual Report*, 1923, p. 7; 1924, p. 7. Courtesy of the MacDowell Colony.

15. Anzia Yezierska, "Wild Winter Love," *Century Magazine* 113 (Feb. 1927): 485-91. The story has been reprinted in Anzia Yezierska, *Hungry Hearts and Other Stories* (New York: Persea, 1985), pp. 316-35. My thanks to Anzia Yezierska's daughter, Louise Levitas Henriksen, for responding to my queries about the relationship between Yezierska and Cohen.

16. *Out of the Shadow*, p. 74.

17. *Out of the Shadow*, p. 246. It is striking here how Cohen's rendition of the Russian Jewish experience contradicts the influential interpretation offered by Oscar Handlin in *The Uprooted: The Epic Story of the Great Migrations That Made the American People* (New York: Grossett & Dunlap, 1951).

18. The settlement house had a strong influence on many new immigrants as they took their journey from old to new world culture. For others,

participation in trade unions, public schools, or urban politics served a similar purpose.

19. For a thoughtful analysis of this theme in Yezierska's writing, see Alice Kessler-Harris's introduction to Yezierska, *Bread Givers* (New York: Persea, 1975), p. xiii.

20. Both of these developments are corroborated by independent sources. New York City directory listings for Abraham Gallup (sometimes Gollup) confirm the Cherry Street residence and his period as a grocer. Rose's brother, Eugene Michael Gollup, received a B.S. in Educational Psychology from Teachers College in 1911. Correspondence with the author, 8 Mar. 1994, Dinesh Bhatt, Administrative Assistant to the Registrar, Teachers College, Columbia University.

PART ONE

Our home was a log house covered with a straw roof.

PART ONE

I

I was born in a small Russian village. Our home was a log house, covered with a straw roof. The front part of the house overlooked a large clear lake, and the back, open fields.

The first time I became aware of my existence was on a cold winter night. My father and I were sitting on top of our red brick oven. The wind, whistling through the chimney and rattling the ice-covered windows, frightened me, and so I pressed close to my father and held his hand tightly. He was looking across the room where mother's bed stood curtained off with white sheets. Every now and then I heard a moan coming from the bed, and each time I felt father's hand tremble.

Appearing and disappearing behind the bed curtains, I saw my little old great-aunt, in a red quilted petticoat and white, close-fitting cap. Whenever she appeared and caught father's eye, she smiled to him, a sweet, crooked smile. Finally, I recall hearing a few sound slaps, followed by a baby's cry and aunt calling out loudly, "It's a girl again."

About three years passed. With my little sister as companion, I recall many happy days we spent together. In the summer we picked field mushrooms at the back of the house or played near the lake and watched the women bleaching their linens. I was happiest in the morning when I first went out of doors. To see the sunshine, the blue sky, and the green fields, filled my soul with unspeakable happiness. At such moments I would run away from my little sister, hide myself in a favourite bush and sit for a while listening to the singing of the birds and the rustling of the leaves. Then I would jump up and skip about like a young pony and shout out of pure joy.

In the winter we cut and made doll's clothing. Father was a tailor, and as soon as we were able to hold a needle we were taught to sew. Mother taught us how to spin, grandfather made toys out of wood for us, and grandmother told us stories.

These were the pleasant days during the winter. But there were others, days that were cold and dark and dreary, when we children had to stay a great part of the time on top of the oven, and no one came, not even a beggar. But when a beggar did come our joy was boundless.

I remember that grandfather would hasten to meet the poor man, as we called him, at the door with a hearty handshake and a welcoming smile, saying, "Peace be with you, brother. Take off your knapsack and stay over night."

Mother would put on a fresh apron and begin to pre-pare something extra for supper. And grandmother, who was blind, and always sat in bed knitting a stocking, would stop for a moment at the sound of the stranger's voice to smooth the comforter on her bed. Her pale face, so indifferent a minute before, would light up as if with new life, while we children, fearing, if seen idle, to be rebuked and sent into a distant corner from where we could neither see nor hear the stranger, would suddenly find a dozen things to do.

On such a night after supper there was something of the holiday spirit in our home. We would light the lamp instead of a candle and place it on a milk jug in the centre of the table. Then we all sat around it, grandmother with her knitting, mother with her sewing, all of us listening eagerly to the stories the stranger told. But more surprised even than any of us children about the wonderful things going on in the world, was grandfather. He would sit listening with his lips partly open and his eyes large with wonder. Every now and then he would call out, "Ach, brother, I never would have even dreamt such things were possible!"

At bedtime grandfather would give up his favourite bed, the bench near the oven, to the stranger. Mother would give him the largest and softest of her pillows. And grandmother would give him a clean pair of socks to put on in the morning.

The next day after he was gone we felt as after a pleasant holiday when we had to put on our old clothes and turn in to do the every day things.

Yes, I recall happy days, and sad days—days of sorrow which then were very real.

Across the road from our home, about a quarter of a block to the left, was a cemetery. Over each grave stood a wooden cross, and about the middle of each one there were tied little aprons of red, green and yellow material. On windy days I loved to watch these fluttering in the wind and whenever I looked through half-closed eyes they took form and became like coloured birds hovering over the graves.

One windy day, at dusk, I went out to the middle of the road to watch the little aprons flying in the breeze and saw something red lying on the road near the cemetery. I guessed it to be an apron blown away by the wind.

How beautiful my doll would look in one of these, thought I. But how could I get it? I was in mortal fear of the cemetery. Although mother had often pointed out

how peacefully the dead slept and had said that she
wished the living were as little to be feared, I never went
near them.   But now I wanted the little red apron for
my doll. The longer I looked at it the more I wanted it.
Finally, I decided to risk getting it. Slowly, step by
step, I walked toward it, keeping my eyes on the graves
and repeating softly to myself, to keep up courage,
"There is nothing to fear; there is nothing to fear,"
until I reached it. When I had it in my hand I
stood still for a moment. The very thought of turning my back on the dead made my hair stand on end. I
walked backwards a few steps; suddenly I turned and
ran. As I ran I felt my heart beating violently against
my ribs; my feet were as heavy as lead and the distance
to the house seemed endless. But I ran fast; so fast,
that when I reached the door I could not stop. I fell
against it, it flew open and I fell headlong into the house.
Mother came running over to pick me up. When I regained my breath, I told her what had happened and
showed her the little apron which I still held in my hand.
As usual, sister, who wanted everything she saw and to
whom I was made to give in because she was younger,
came over and asked for it and, as usual, I refused. She
tried to snatch it from my hand but I pushed her away.
She fell and struck her head against a bench. Then
father came over with a strap and told us to kiss each
other or we should be spanked. Mother looked at me with
tears in her eyes, knowing, no doubt, what would happen,
and she left the room. Grandmother called to me to hide
behind her back, but I would not do that. My sister
looked at me, then at the strap, and came over to kiss me.
But I could not at such moments, neither would I let her
kiss me. So I was spanked and the little apron was taken
away from me and given to her.

II

WHEN I was about eleven years old there were five of us children. One day father went to town and came back with a stranger, who, we were told, would teach us to read and write. Our teacher was a young man of middle height, thin, dark and pale. He had an agreeable voice, and when he sang it was pleasant to hear him. When we did our lessons well his eyes brightened and his tightly closed lips would relax a little. But when we did poorly he was angry and would scold us.

As soon as I learned how to read I would sit for hours and read to my grandmother. Besides the Bible, we had a few religious books. I read these again and again, and became very devout. I read the morning, noon and evening prayers, and sometimes I fasted for half a day. Then I became less stubborn and the quarrels between sister and myself became less frequent.

One day father left home on a three days' journey. When he returned he did not look like himself. His face was pale and he seemed to be restless. During the three days that followed, father went out only at night. I also noticed that mother collected all of father's clothes, and, as she sat mending them, I often saw her tears fall on her work. On the third night I awoke and saw father bending over me. He wore his heavy overcoat, his hat was pulled well over his forehead and a knapsack was strapped across his shoulders. Before I had time to say a word he kissed me and went to grandmother's bed and woke her up. "I am going away, mother." She sat up, rubbed her eyes and asked in a sleepy voice, "Where?" "To America," father whispered hoarsely.

For a moment there was silence; then grandmother uttered a cry that chilled my blood. My mother, who sat in a corner weeping, went to her and tried to quiet her. The noise woke grandfather and the children. We all gathered around grandmother's bed, and I heard father explaining the reason for his going. He said that he could not get a passport (for a reason I could not understand at the time). And as no one may live in Russia even a week without a passport, he had to leave immediately. His explanation did not comfort grandmother; she still sat crying and wringing her hands. After embracing us all, father ran out of the house, and grandfather ran after him into the snow with his bare feet. When he returned he sat down and cried like a little child. I spent the rest of the night in prayer for a safe journey for my father.

III

As father's departure to America had to be kept secret until he was safe out of Russia, we had to bury our sorrow deep in our own hearts, and go about our work as if nothing unusual had happened.

Mother and I sat at the window, sewing, and grandfather found relief in chopping wood. All day long his axe flashed in the sun and chips flew far and near. And even grandmother's tears, which were always ready, were kept back now as she sat on her bed, knitting a stocking and rocking the cradle with one foot, while sister seemed to be everywhere at once. It was then and for the first time that I realised something of her real worth. Those soft grey eyes of hers seemed to see every one's needs. When grandmother put her feet down on the floor and felt about for her slippers, it was sister who would find them and stick them on her toes. The same little woman of eight kept a little brother of five and a sister of two playing quietly in a corner. And even when they were hungry she would not let them disturb mother, but would cut some thick slices of black bread, dip them into water, sprinkle them with salt, and taking a bite of her slice, she would close her eyes and say, "M-m-m—what delicious cake!" In the evening, after supper, when grandfather would sit down near the stove staring sadly into the fire, she would climb up on his knee and plait his long grey beard into braids. Soothed by her gentle touches and childish prattle, he would fall asleep and forget his troubles for a while.

IV

So the days passed.

One morning mother went to the postoffice and when she came back she looked as if she had suddenly aged. She took a postal card from her pocket and we all bent our heads over it and read: "I have been arrested while crossing the border and I am on my way home, walking the greater part of the way. If we pass through our village I shall ask the officer to let me stop home for a few minutes. Be brave and trust in God." At the news more tears were shed in our house than on the Day of Atonement.

That night after the doors were barred and the windows darkened, grandmother, grandfather, and mother, with a three weeks' old baby in her arms, sat in the niche of our chimney, making plans to defeat the Tzar of Russia.

The next day mother sent grandfather away on a visit. He was not a person to have around in case of trouble, for the very sight of brass buttons put him into such fright and confusion, that he would forget his own name. After he was gone mother went to town to see her brother and arrange for the escape. Then there was nothing left to do but wait for father's home-coming. I remember that I used to run out on the road many times a day to see if he were coming.

One afternoon we were all startled at hearing some one stamping the snow off her feet at our door. I ran to the window and looked out. It was only Yana, a woman known in our village to be very clever and religious, but unkind. I wondered at her coming for I knew that she and my mother were not on friendly terms. She came into the house and walking straight over to mother, who was bending over the cradle, she said in her usual voice, which was like a drake's, soft and hoarse, "Your husband is arrested; I just saw him on the road!" Mother became so pale and looked so ill that I thought she would fall, but the next minute I saw her straighten herself, and putting her arm over the cradle as if to protect it, she said quietly and distinctly, "Yana, I hope you will live to carry better news." When Yana passed me on her way out of the house I thought her face looked more yellow than usual, and her black, large teeth further apart.

After the woman was gone mother put on a cheerful face and busied herself laying the cloth and setting food on the table, and grandmother put on her best apron, father's last gift, and sat down near the table with her hands folded in her lap, waiting. We children stood at the window looking out. Soon we saw father open our gate. He was closely followed by Yonko, the sheriff, in his grey fur cap which he wore summer and winter, and grey coat tied with a red girdle.

Father was limping and when he came nearer I saw how greatly he had changed. His face was thin and weatherbeaten, and his eyes had sunk deep into his head. At sight of us near the window his lips twitched, but the next moment we saw his own old smile light up his whole face.

Our greeting and our conversation were quiet and restrained.

When father sat down at the table he said that he was very hungry but after taking a few mouthfuls he fell asleep. The peasant who sat near the stove resting his elbows on his knees and turning his cap between his

hands, rose and wanted to wake father. "Oh, let him
sleep a little while," mother entreated. "Impossible," said
Yonko, "the roads are bad and we have to be in the next
village before night falls." "Well, then just let him
sleep until I bathe his feet." The man consented. Father's
boots were worn and wet through, and were hard to get
off, but he never woke while mother tugged away at
them. At last they were off and the socks also.

"Thank God that his mother is blind," she whispered,
covering her face for a moment. Father's feet were
red, blistered, and swollen. As she lifted them into the
basin I saw her tears falling into the water. When I
looked at Yonko he turned away quickly and became
interested in a crack in the ceiling.

Our parting like our greeting was restrained. Father
embraced grandmother, then he smiled a quick farewell
from the door and was gone. Sister and I ran out on
the road and stood watching him until he looked a
black speck against the white snow. Then we ran back
to the house, she to help and I to pray.

V

WITH the exception of grandmother, I was the most pious and the most superstitious member of the family. In sickness or trouble, while the others turned to do practical things, I appealed to God for help.

So it was on the day when father was led away to the next village. Knowing that he was to attempt an escape that very night, I felt that there was no time to be lost. Better to concentrate my mind on my prayers I climbed up on the stove and sat down in the darkest corner, facing the wall. To shut out the children's voices I stuck my fingers into my ears and began to pray. But I could not put any heart into it. I felt, however, that if I only could pray with all my heart and soul, God would hear me. In despair, therefore, I let my mind dwell on my father. Again I saw him, weatherbeaten and care-worn, limping through the gate. Again I saw his lips twitch as when he tried to smile to us from the window. Then I recalled stories of cruelty to those who served in the army. I remembered Yonko, a strong young peasant, telling grandfather how he had been treated. One day, for some slight offence, he was struck such a powerful blow on the ear that he fell unconscious.

Father will never survive such a blow, thought I. Once he goes to the army we will never see him again. How dark and desolate our home will be!

With a pang of remorse I recalled how often I had been discontented. Only a while before I remembered having sulked for hours merely because I had no shoes of my own, and had to wear out old ones which were much too large and made an awful clatter as I walked.

How sinful I had been to be discontented when we were all well and father was with us. "Oh, God, if Thou wilt spare my father, I will never wish for anything again! Never complain!"

When I rose it was dark, the children were all in bed, and except for the squeak of the cradle as it swung back and forth, all was quiet. I knew that it was mother who sat up rocking the cradle. I longed to speak to her of the hope I felt but feared in case my feelings were deceiving me after all.

I think it was the next day that a message came telling us that father had escaped from the constable in the next village. That was joy indeed though limited, for father was still on Russian soil and could be recaptured any minute. And so while we were waiting, fearing, hoping, another week or so passed.

Two things I recall distinctly of that time. Grandmother, believing children to be prophets, often asked us to predict the future. One day she asked my brother, a little serious-faced, wide-awake boy of six, who looked upon himself as one of the future great Rabbis, "Tell me, my child, will father reach America safely?" "Yes," he said with so much conviction in his voice that her face lit up with hope. From that moment she was more cheerful. The second thing is that there was an awful storm and the snow lay piled up almost as high as our windows. But on Friday it cleared. The sun came out bright and warm. "It is a good sign that it cleared in honour of Sabbath," said grandmother, turning her pale, thin face hopefully to the window. That afternoon we saw the mistress of the inn and postoffice walking up to her waist in snow, coming toward our house. "Nothing but a letter would bring her here on a day like this," mother cried and rushed out of the house. When she came back she had a letter but she stood in the middle of the room holding it in her hand as though she feared to open it. "Look," said the post-mistress, pointing to the post mark. It was stamped Memel, Prussia.

Mother ran to grandmother and they embraced, and stood so long and so silently with their faces hidden from us, that we children were frightened and begged them to speak to us. Then mother turned and caught us all into her arms with a cry of joy, while grandmother raised her tear-stained face to Heaven in silent prayer.

VI

Spring came. The snow which lay high all winter began to melt, and here and there green spots appeared. Then the dandelions began to show their yellow heads, and the storks came flying back to build their nests in the old stump in the cemetery. Hens, followed by groups of black and yellow headed chicks, walked about scratching in the soft warm earth and cackling cheerfully.

As for us, mother and grandmother having lived in fear and anxiety about father for thirteen years, and then having come near losing him, found it hard to believe at first that he was really beyond the reach of Russia. But once they realised this fact they were as happy as they had never been before.

Mother, who never sang except when rocking baby to sleep, and then only hummed, sang now as she went about her work. And grandmother spoke about America from morning till night.

Having a lively imagination, she gave us her ideas of what she thought America was like, the kind of people father would be likely to meet, how soon he would find work, how much he would earn, and how soon he would be able to take his family over. Here she cried a good deal, saying, "If I had been told a year ago that my only son would go away to the other end of the world, and that I would continue to live knowing that I would never see him again, I would not have believed it possible. And yet it has come to pass and I am not only alive, but contented that he should be away. Ah, how strange is life and its ways!" Then she would dry her tears and begin to wonder how he would live without her care, who would look after his socks, and who would cover his feet on cold nights. But soon she consoled herself by saying, "Oh, but socks are cheap out there, as no doubt everything else must be, and they say that it is not as cold in America as in Russia."

And we children were as happy as if we had been released from a dark, damp prison cell. It seemed to us that the lake was never so clear and blue or sparkled so brightly, and the birds never sang so gaily before. We ran about visiting one familiar place after another, unable to stop long anywhere.

I came to my bush where I hid so often when I wanted to be alone. As I stooped and parted the branches so as to hide more comfortably among them, I saw a small, half finished bird's nest. I picked it up and as I stood looking at it, it occurred to me how very near our home came to being broken up. So I put the nest back carefully and went away.

When grandfather came home we were shocked at the change in him. His hair and beard, grey before, had turned white, and his eyes, they were the trustful eyes of a child, had a strange questioning look in them. He had become quite deaf. But otherwise he was as sprightly as ever.

Now the chief part of the support of the family fell to mother, and the rest of us helped. Grandmother knitted stockings for the women of the village. Of course the stockings had to be looked over, the lost stitches found and mended carefully. That was my work.

Grandmother also peeled the potatoes for the house. These, too, I had to go over, and cut away the peelings she had left. I disliked this work and dropped many a tear on the potatoes. Then mother would say, "What, crying? So much the better, we won't need to salt the potatoes." And grandfather, after bringing the wood, building the fire, fetching water from the spring, would go to the village to see if there were any pots to mend.

Grandfather had clever hands. He could do wonders with a penknife and a piece of wood. And in mending pots he was a perfect artist. And so whenever he walked through the village the women would call him into their homes, bless him for the pots he made whole, and fill his little bag, which he always carried upon his back, with potatoes, carrots, turnips or onions. On coming home he would look as happy as if he had a whole fortune in his bag. "Come, children, and see what I have," he would call out while still on the threshold. Then he would open his bag, take out a carrot, and holding it up high for our admiration, he would say, his face beaming, "Is it not a perfect beauty? And sweet and juicy! Just wait till you taste it!" Then he would scrape it, divide it among us and sit looking at us while we ate.

VII

AFTER Easter there was some pleasant outdoor work. Grandfather dug up the garden and we planted some vegetables. Of this work I liked planting potatoes best. I enjoyed walking after the plough in the cool moist earth with my bare feet. And while doing so, it pleased me to imagine that I was Yanko the sower. I took long even strides and swung my arm back and forth in a circle, as I took and dropped the potatoes.

Mother saw me and scolded, saying that I dropped them too far apart. "You are always playing," she said. "Your sister, almost three years younger, is already a little woman; look!"

Bent almost double under a bag of potatoes, sister was coming towards us, walking unsteadily under the weight.

When she reached us mother took the bag and asked, "Is it not too heavy?"

The love in her eyes, and tenderness in her voice made my heart ache with envy. And so as usual I went for consolation to my bush.

While walking along I determined never to play again. But as soon as I sat down, the twigs and flowers turned into fanciful girls and boys who adored me. I named each one of them and myself I called Dena. And then we went romping about in the fields.

I was extremely happy among these imaginary companions. But often they were the cause of punishment. For like real companions they lured me away from my work in the house, to play.

Among these companions there was one who at first was just a name I liked. But after a while at the thought

of the name I saw a vision of a tall, dark, handsome
youth.   And as I always wished for a big brother who
would take care of me, I adopted him.

So real did this imaginary brother become that when I
found myself alone in the dark, trembling with fear, I
would call out, "Oh, Ephraim, where are you?" Then I
seemed to hear him say, "Ah, you little 'fraidcat, I knew
you would want me. Here, take my hand." Then my
two hands would clasp each other and I seemed to feel
safer.

As soon as the warm weather came the women of the
village gave all their time and thought to the work in
the fields.   And so now we had no stockings to knit, no
sewing, and no pots for grandfather to mend.   He
would often come home from the village with his little
bag empty and sadness in his eyes.   Indeed, there were
many days when we had not enough even of potatoes.
But this hardship did not last long.   Soon a letter and
money came from father. This was the first letter from
America.   Father did not tell us much about his life
out there.   He just said that he was boarding with a nice
Russian Jewish family and that he was already working
and earning ten dollars a week.   The rest of the letter
was just good cheer and loving messages to each one
of us.

Grandmother kept the letter under her pillow and soon
the writing was defaced by her tears.

One day I managed to get hold of it.   I put it into
my pocket, slipped out of the house, then I took it out
and looked at it.

It seemed to me so wonderful that a letter posted in
America found its way into our little village.

"And this is American paper and here is an American
stamp! And no doubt father touched this very stamp

with his fingers!" When I thought of that, he did not
seem so far away.

When winter came mother bought feathers to pick.
Having three daughters she said she needed many pillows for their dowry. I liked picking feathers, as I liked
sewing, not so much for itself as because it left my mind
free to dream.

Sometimes mother would let sister and myself take our
bags of feathers and go to visit our neighbours. One
whom we enjoyed visiting most was Siomka. She was
a little, lonely, old widow who lived in a small hut not
far away from us. During the summer she lived by
working in the fields for neighbours and in the winter
she spun and wove.

To get to her living room we had to pass her out-
house. This was a large windowless room, a place I
used to run through when alone, with fast-beating heart.
But when sister was with me I was not so afraid.

Though she knew no fear herself, she always seemed
to understand. As soon as we would come to the out-
house door she would slip her little hand, which was
always warm, into mine and say, "Hold on to me!"
Then together we would run through. Often by the time
I found the latch I was in a cold perspiration. But once
within Siomka's smoke-covered walls, I was happy.

By means of a log of wood we would climb up on her
bed, which was just some boards knocked together and
covered with a sack of straw. And there we would remain all afternoon picking our feathers and watching
Siomka weave.

I loved to see the shuttle sliding between the threads,
and hear the rhythmical sound of the loom. Often
Siomka would stop her weaving and stoop down to pat
the pink snout of her wee pig. At her touch he would

blink his tiny eyes, wag his little tail, and grunt softly.

The first time we saw the little pig, Siomka told us that she received him for some spinning she had done and that she was feeding him up for Christmas. But Christmas came and went and we saw the little pig still following Siomka about the house, or lying curled up at her feet while she spun.

Then she told us that she would surely kill him for Easter. Easter noon while passing Siomka's window I saw her eating black bread and potatoes. Then she came out and sat down on the door step, and watched with smiling eyes the little pig rolling in the soft mud before the hut.

VIII

GRANDMOTHER had two children besides father, both daughters. The elder was happily married and lived about two or three days' journey from us. Whether through indifference or because of the distance, I do not know, but she never came to see her parents or wrote to them. Sometimes a traveller from her part of the country, passing through our village, would stop at our house and give us her greetings.

The younger was twenty-one years of age now and was working in Mintck, a large city. She left home when she was sixteen and being fond of children she became a nurse girl. As grandmother expected her to be a seamstress, this choice of occupation caused grandmother as many tears as father's becoming a tailor instead of a rabbi. For a nurse girl was thought to be as much below a seamstress as a tailor below a rabbi.

Father had been in America but a short time when grandmother realised that his emigration had lessened Aunt Masha's prospects of marriage. When she came to this conclusion her peace was gone. She wept night and day. "Poor Masha," she moaned, "what is to become of her? Her chances had been small enough without a dowry. And now, burdened with an aged father and a blind helpless mother, the best she can expect is a middle-aged widower with half a dozen children!"

Mother tried to comfort her by telling her that she would remain in Russia as long as grandmother lived, so that she would not have to live with Masha. But this only irritated her. "You talk like a child," she wept. "You stay here and wait for my death, while my son, at the other end of the world, will be leading a life of loneliness. And as for me, would I have any peace, knowing that I was the cause?"

Mother, seeing that she could do nothing to comfort her, silently awaited results.

One night I woke hearing a muffled sound of crying. I felt for grandmother, with whom I slept. But she was not beside me. Frightened, I sat up and peered into the darkness. The crying came from the foot of the bed. And soon I discerned grandmother sitting there. With her hands clasped about her knees and her face buried in her lap she sat rocking gently and weeping.

I called to her in a whisper to come and lie down, but she did not answer. For a while I sat trembling with cold and fear. Then I slipped far back under the warm comforter and tried to sleep. But the picture of grandmother sitting alone in the dark and cold haunted me. And so again I arose.

Creeping over to her quickly I curled up close to her and put my arms around her cold, trembling form. At first she did not take any notice of me. But after a few minutes she lifted her head and unclasping her hands, she drew me under her shawl, saying as she laid her wet face against mine, "Oh, you little mouse, how you do creep up to one! But you had better go back to your place or you will catch cold."

When I went back and as grandmother tucked me in, I asked her why she cried so. "Never mind, you little busybody," she said, "go to sleep." But I teased her to tell me. And finally she said with a sigh and speaking more to herself than to me, "It is about Masha. Go to sleep now, you will hear all about it to-morrow."

She sat down on the edge of the bed gently patting

my shoulder, as she had often done when I was a little child. Soon I fell asleep.

The next day the rings under her eyes were darker, and her eyelids were more red and swollen than usual. But otherwise she seemed more calm than she had been for a long time.

After dinner she said to mother, hesitating at every word as she spoke, "You know, I decided last night, that when you go to America Masha should go with you." This startled mother so that she almost dropped the baby whom she was swinging on her foot.

"What are you saying? Masha go to America and you left here alone?"

"Yes, alone," she sighed, "as if I never had any children. But so it must be. True, I have not had a happy life. But happy or not I have lived it. And now, it is almost at an end. But Masha has just begun to live, and in America she will have a better chance, for there are fewer women there, they say. As for me, I shall not be without comfort in my last days. When I am lonely, I shall think of her happily married and surrounded by dear little children like yours. And now listen to this plan. Of course I can not be left here alone, though my needs are few. And so before you start for America you will take me to my niece in the city. She is a very pious woman and so I am sure she will give me a little space in some corner of her house. Of course you will pay her for a year of my board. And after that perhaps you will send her money. But I hope it won't be necessary. Indeed, I feel that I won't trouble this world much longer."

Mother tried to dissuade her from this plan but she turned a deaf ear and insisted that we write to father at once. And we did.

About a month passed before we received an answer.
The letter was heavier than usual. And when we opened
it, two yellow tickets fell out from among the two
closely-written sheets.

"What is this?" we all asked at once. "Not money.
And this writing must be English."

We handed the tickets to grandmother who held out
her hand for them. Suddenly her hand began to tremble
and she said, "Perhaps these are steamer tickets. Quickly
read the letter."

After the usual greetings father wrote, "Since Masha
is to come to America she might as well start as soon as
she can get ready. And Rahel had better come with her.
I am sure she can earn at least three dollars a week.
With her help I'll be able to bring the rest of the family
over much sooner, perhaps in a year or so. And besides,
now she can still travel on half a ticket, which I am enclosing with the one for Masha."

Quite bewildered, I looked at mother. Her lips were
opening and closing without making a sound. Suddenly she caught me into her arms and burst into tears.

IX

FOR many days mother could not look at the steamer tickets without tears in her eyes. And even then though she tried to speak cheerfully about my going to America, I noticed that the anxious look which came into her eyes while the letter was being read, never left them. Also I felt her eyes following me about on every step. But once only, she gave way to her feelings openly.

One morning while she was fastening the back of my dress I caught a few disconnected words, which she uttered low as though she were speaking to herself.

"Good Heavens! child twelve years old—care—herself." Then came those inward tearless sobs and I felt her hands tremble on my back.

But grandmother took the news in a manner that astonished us all. When I looked at her over my mother's shoulder, after the letter was read, I saw her sitting at the table in her usual position. Her head was bent low and a little to one side, and her hands were folded in her lap. Very quietly she sat, not a word, not a tear came from her.

Even grandfather, who never took any notice of her except to scold, looked at her in surprise.

"Well, Baila!" he said. "Have you wept yourself dry? Or perhaps you have come to your senses at last and realise how useless tears are. Remember, that you are sending your child away yourself. I can always take care of my needs but you will die in the poorhouse."

Grandfather and grandmother were always quarrelling. Grandfather claimed that she wept her eyes out. And grandmother said that all her troubles came because of his impiety. But when I grew older I learned that there was a deeper reason for their quarrels.

As a rule when grandfather scolded, grandmother would retort with great spirit. But this time it was as if she did not hear him.

She called me and dictated a letter to Aunt Masha, to come home at once. Then she went to her trunk and took out the ball of fine linen thread which she had been saving for years. And while starting a pair of stockings for Aunt Masha I heard her figuring quietly, what we would need for the journey, how long it would take us to get ready, and what day we would start.

As for me, I became suddenly a very important person. At home I was looked upon as a guest. Now mother never pressed me to do any work. On the contrary, as soon as I would start to do something, she would say,

"Run out and play, you will work hard enough pretty soon." Neither did I find it necessary to feign illness as I had often done before that I might be fondled and caressed. No, indeed; now mother would often put baby down to take me on her lap.

And the young women of the village, who never took any notice of me before, would stop to speak to me.

One day, at sundown, I sat on our gate munching a bit of carrot, and watching the red sun disappearing gradually behind the treetops, when I became aware of some one standing in back of me. I turned around and saw Miriam. She was a pretty, gipsy-like young woman whose dark eyes always looked moist and a little red as though she had just been crying.

"So you are going to America," she said, looking at me wistfully, "you are very fortunate. Of course you are too young to realise it now but you will, later, when

you grow older and think of this." She pointed to
Siomka's half-tumbled hut, and the little pig who stood
at the door and squealed to be let in.

"No," she continued, almost in a whisper, "your life
won't be wasted like———." Here Siomka's little pig
squealed louder than ever and Miriam turned suddenly
and went away. .I sat for a long while wondering what
the last word might have been. Then I jumped down
from the gate and ran into the house to look at the
steamer tickets, perhaps for the tenth time that day.

I do not know whether I considered myself fortunate
in going to America or not. But I do remember that
when I convinced myself, by looking at the tickets often,
that it was not a dream like many others I had had, that
I would really start for America in a month or six
weeks, I felt a great joy. Of course I was a little
ashamed of this joy. I saw that mother was unhappy.
And grandmother's sorrow, very awful, in its calmness,
was double now. For I felt that I was almost as dear to
her as Aunt Masha.

When a week passed we cleaned the house as thor-
oughly as if it were for Easter, in honour of Aunt
Masha's coming.

During the five years that she had been away she visited us twice. The last time had been three years before.
And so we were all excited and eager to see her.

As the days passed and the time drew near for her
coming, grandmother became so impatient and nervous
that she would jump at the least outdoor sound, asking
excitedly,

"What is that? I think I hear the rumbling of wheels.
Isn't that some one coming?" Then we would all rush
to the door and windows and find that it was only a cart

passing on the road, or a pig scratching his back against the sharp corner of the house.

One day we really heard a cart drive up to the door. When we ran out we saw a small, plump, pretty young woman in a brown dress jump lightly to the ground.

"Oh, grandmother, quickly come, it is Aunt Masha."

In a moment grandmother tumbled out of bed, but before she could reach the door she was in Aunt Masha's arms. And for a while there was sobbing in every corner of the room.

X

We children scarcely knew Aunt Masha. All I remembered of her two visits, was that both times she had
come to stay a month, but went away at the end of a
week, and that we felt depressed afterwards, and grandmother cried for days and days.

And so it was only now that we began to know her.
When she had been home a short time we found that
she was affectionate, but also severe, and hot-tempered.
If we did not obey her promptly she scolded severely, or
worse still, stopped speaking to us. Aunt Masha was
also a painfully clean person and spent a great deal of
time in washing us. Brother, whose skin was dark, often
appeared, after she was through with him, with his neck
red and tears in his eyes.

But the greatest trouble was caused by Aunt Masha's
personal belongings. Nothing of hers must be touched.
And as we were very curious about things that came
from the city there was a world of trouble.

One morning I arose earlier than usual. All were
asleep except mother and grandfather, who were out.
As I passed Aunt Masha's bed I was attracted by her
little shoes which stood close together on the floor beside her bed, looking like two soldiers keeping watch.
They were the smallest things with high tops, pointed
toes and elastic sides. Often I had longed to try them
on. And once I even asked Aunt Masha if I might. But
she said, "No, you would burst them." Now as I stood
looking at them and at my own clumsy lace shoes, made
by our village shoemaker, I thought, "Yes, they would

fit. Oh, how I should like to try them on, just for a
moment."

I glanced at Aunt Masha's face. The wrinkle between
her eyebrows was there even now, and it was saying to
me, "No!" But the lips which were partly open showing the white strong teeth, seemed to smile, "Yes."

Very quietly I tiptoed over to the bed, took the shoes
and hastened to the bench near the oven. My fingers
trembled so, that I could not open my laces. They became knotted and it took me a long time to break them
open. But at last my shoes were off.

I remember how rapidly my heart beat when I began
to draw one of hers on. I thought, "If it does not go
on easily, I won't force it." But it did, and felt comfortable. And the elastic fitted snugly around the ankles.
With a feeling of pleasure I stepped down on the floor to
see how much taller I looked with high heels. As I
stood up I glanced anxiously toward Aunt Masha's bed.
What I saw sent the blood rushing to my face.

She was sitting up in bed looking as though she saw
a ghost.

"I suppose you have burst them. I told you not to
put them on," she said and frowned. This frown brought
back my earliest recollections of her. I remembered how
I feared it. Now as I stood looking at her it deepened
and deepened until it seemed to darken her whole face,
and reminded me of an angry cloud.

Quickly I took off her shoes, put them near her bed
and ran from her as from an approaching storm.

Outside I met mother, who saw that something had
happened, the minute she looked at me. When I told
her she scolded.

"You should not have tried on the shoes when you

were told not to do it. Now I think you had better go and apologise."

I had never apologised in my life. In the days when I was given the choice between apologising and a spanking, I always chose the spanking. Now when I knew that no spanking was coming I certainly refused to do it. But mother coaxed and begged, and reasoned,

"You are going out into the wide world alone, among strangers. Don't harden your heart against your only friend. Oh, how I wish you had more sense!" She turned away and cried like a little child.

I was miserable. The very thought of apologising made my face burn. But here stood mother crying.

"I won't have many more chances of pleasing her," I thought.

"Mother, I'll apologise, but—not now," I begged. She turned to me. "That is a dear child," she said, looking brighter, "but if you do it at all, do it now."

"What shall I say?" I asked.

"Oh, just say you are sorry you disobeyed."

We went into the house. Aunt Masha was dressed and stood at the window, combing out her beautiful brown hair. It fell all about her, covering almost half of her small body. When she heard the door close she parted her hair in front, as if it were a curtain, and looked. She dropped it quickly when she saw me and went on combing carefully. Slowly I went over to her. "Aunt Masha," I said. My voice sounded strange to me. Again she parted her hair and looked at me. I thought I saw an expression of triumph in her steel grey eyes. This hurt me. And almost before I could think I blurted out, angrily,

"Aunt Masha, I'll never, never, touch anything of yours again, as if it were—swine!"

Aunt Masha fairly gasped. And mother looked horrified. Indeed, I was horrified myself at what I had done. I turned to mother and tried to explain. But I could not make her understand me. I was not good at explanations when I myself was concerned. Quite miserable, I ran out of the house and wandered about in the fields for the rest of the morning.

Aunt Masha did not speak to me for three days. During that time when our eyes happened to meet, I tried to tell her, in a dumb way, that I was sorry. But she always turned her face away quickly. Once when we met near the door, our shoulders almost touching, I saw a smile come quivering to her lips. And so I waited, hoping she would speak to me. But the next moment she frowned it down and passed on as if she did not know me. On the fourth day, at twilight, I came up on her so suddenly, while she was outside, that she gave a little scream of fright. I, too, was frightened, and caught hold of her hand. And she let it stay in mine.

XI

ALL through the Spring, while mother, grandmother and Aunt Masha were sewing and knitting stockings for Aunt Masha and me to take along to America, I wandered about in the fields, restless and unable to play at anything.

Early, while the flowers were still heavy with the morning dew, I would take baby, who was a little over a year old, on my back, tie him on to me with a shawl, so that I could rest my arms when they grew tired, and start out followed by the rest of the children. For hours we would wander about like gipsies.

More often than anywhere we went to the lake, where it was very lively at that time of the year, as the peasant women were bleaching their linens. There, sister and brother would go off digging for flagroot. And I would put the two little ones on the flat rock near the edge and climbing up beside them, we would all sit quietly for the longest while, watching, listening.

It was a pleasant spot. The clear blue water lay quietly rippling and sparkling in the sun. On the edge were the women with red kerchiefs on their heads and beads of many colours around their necks, swinging their wooden mallets in unison. And the neighbourhood rang with the echoes which seemed to come from the dense, mysterious looking forest across the lake. While through the air floated the sweet odour of new wet linen.

But the time I loved this spot best was late in the afternoon, when the light grew soft and the women went away to their homes. Then came a peculiar hush, and yet there seemed to be a thousand voices in the air whispering softly. They came from everywhere, from the tall stately forest trees across the lake, the hazelnut bushes, the flags as the wind passed over them. And the lake, a deeper blue now in the soft light, rippled gently as if with laughter. Sometimes these fairy-like voices would be lost for a moment in the louder sound of a dry twig breaking and falling to the ground, the cuckoo of a bird or the splash of a fish.

I do not know what effect this had on the children. It made me unspeakably happy and sad at the same time. I remember that I used to want to laugh and cry and sing and dance, and very often I did. To dance I would clasp hands with the children, and we would spin around, and around, until we fell down breathless and dizzy.

At twilight we would start for home, walking very slowly and feeling very sad at the thought of bed time.

So the Spring passed.

As the second of June, the day for our departure to America, drew near, I stayed more in the house and followed mother about more closely. Gradually I became conscious of two things. One was the fear of going out into the world. Just what I feared I did not know. And the other was regret. I had not realised how dear to me were my people and home until I was about to leave them. But the one whom I regretted to leave most was grandmother.

Grandfather was not fond of me and so he cared little about my going away. And mother and the children I should see again. But that grandmother cared I knew. And I also knew and she knew that her I should never see again.

One day grandmother and I were alone in the house, at least, I think we were alone. For as I look back now I can see no one but the two of us. I am standing at the

window, and she is walking across the room, with her
slow, hesitating step, and her hands stretched in front
of her for protection. Coming upon a bench in the middle of the room she sat down heavily, saying, with a
sigh,

"It is strange, but the room seems to have grown
larger."

"What is that shadow at the window, Rahel? Come,
child, let me lean on you. There, your shoulder just
fits under my arm. Do you remember when you first
began to lead me about? That was when you still called
yourself by name."

When we reached the window she raised her hand,
shaded her eyes from the strong light and stood quietly
for a while, looking out. Then she said,

"This must be a beautiful day. For my eyelids are
not as heavy when it is clear."

"Oh, grandmother, it is glorious! There is not a
cloud in the sky. And, that thing waving in front of
the window, can you make out what it is?"

"I see a black, shapeless mass. What is it?"

"It is the wild apple tree, white with blossoms."

"H-m-m— yes," she said, meditatively, "it was a day
just like this."

"When, grandmother?"

She did not answer for a long while and when she
spoke at last her voice was low and passionate.

"When God took my sight from me. My eyes had
never been strong. One day in the Spring, it was beautiful like to-day, I was digging in the garden, but a little
while it seemed to me, when I was startled by a crash
of thunder so that the very earth under my feet seemed
to tremble. I looked up. The sun was gone and a black
angry cloud hung over our house. Quickly I gathered

up the tools and hastened toward home. I was but a few steps away when a wind-storm came. It rocked the trees, blew the loosened shingles from the roof, and swept the dry sand in a whirl before me. At the same moment I felt a stinging pain in my eyes so that I could not see the door. In darkness I groped about for long time, till I found it. For twenty-four hours I was beside myself with pain. At the end of that time it went away as suddenly as it came. When your father, who was a little boy then, untied the kerchief from my eyes I asked him if it were night.

" 'Why, mother,' I heard his frightened voice, 'it is daylight. Don't you see the sun across your bed?' Then I knew."

She stood silent and motionless for a while. Then she said more calmly,

"But I must not sin. For if God has taken my sight, He has given me dear little grandchildren who have been everything I wanted. Ah, if I had only been worthy enough to keep them with me!" Here she turned to me suddenly and taking my face between her cold soft hands she said entreatingly,

"Rahel, promise me that you won't cry when you are starting. You hear? It is bad luck to cry when one is starting on a journey. And—I want you to write me whether there are any synagogues in America."

"I promise!"

Still holding my face between her hands she bent over it and looked at it intently. I saw a strained expression come into her face and the eyes move about restlessly under the heavy red lids, as though she were trying to see. Then came a pitiful moan, and tears rolled down her cheeks and fell on mine.

What happened after this I do not remember until the

very minute of starting on the second of June. And
even then, as I look back I can see nothing at first, but
a thick grey mist. But the sounds I recall very distinctly.

There was Aunt Masha's voice crying, a crack of a
whip, horses' hoofs striking against stones. Then there
was a sudden jolt and I felt myself falling backwards.
And now I remember what I saw, too.

When I rose I found myself sitting in a straw-lined
wagon, with my back to the horse. Besides me were
mother and the baby, who were coming to the city with
us, and Aunt Masha who was lying with her face hidden
in the straw, crying aloud.

I remembered grandmother's warning, "Nothing but
bad luck could come to one who is crying while starting
on a journey," and felt sorry for Aunt Masha. But as
we were pulling out through the gate and I saw grandmother looking so lonely and forsaken, as she stood
leaning against the house, and when I saw grandfather
and the children who stood at the gate, looking after us
and crying, I could not keep my own tears back, though
I opened my eyes wide and blinked hard.

We were still but a short distance from the house
when I saw grandmother go in through the open door,
and close it behind her with unusual quickness. As she
was passing the window I caught a last glimpse of her
white kerchief tied about her head.

When we turned the corner I could not see grandfather's and the children's faces any more but I still
heard their voices carried over by the wind.

One by one we passed the dear familiar places. Each
one brought back sad and happy recollections. As I
looked at my favourite bush while we were passing it,
I saw my little make-believe companions spring up in it
one after another. And among them I saw the swarthy

face of my imaginary brother Ephraim. I waved my
hand to him, and then hid my face on mother's shoulder.

When I looked up again the road was unknown to
me.

The drosky is at the door.

XII

WE were bound for Mintck. This was a large city about a day and a half hard travelling from our village. There mother was to see an agent about smuggling us across the border and buy a few necessary things for our journey.

As I had been unable to see mother's people before going, we went a little out of our way to stop with them for a few hours. Shortly before sunset we arrived at their home which stood on the outskirt of a small town.

Mother's father had been dead for some years and the mother was living with her four sons who were blacksmiths by trade.

As we had to pass the shop which was a short distance from the house we stopped there first. All four were busy at the forge, at the bellows one was swinging the heavy sledge and Uncle Hayim, who was the oldest, was shaping a piece of iron on the anvil. Seeing us he stopped and came to meet us. He kissed mother with more than usual tenderness, shook hands with Aunt Masha, and looked at me in surprise. "Well, well," he said, "how tall you have grown. But you are only a feather-weight after all." He laughed as he raised me lightly on a level with himself.

He locked up the shop and we all went to the house. At the door we met grandmother coming from the barn with a pail of foaming milk which she almost spilt in her surprise at seeing us.

She was as different from my other grandmother as a person could be. She was a strong, stocky little woman, so industrious and quick that at times it was hard to believe that there was just one of her. In telling stories, however, she was like my other grandmother. Everything she saw and heard reminded her of a story.

We started to continue on our journey soon after supper. At parting we all cried a good deal and laughed, too, when I refused to kiss my two younger uncles on the ground that they were boys.

"But," said the younger and mischievous one, "you kissed me two weeks ago when I was at your home."

"Then it was different," I said. I could not explain but perhaps I felt that in parting from my childhood surroundings I parted from childhood, too.

Uncle Hayim lit the way to the wagon with a lantern. He held it up high while mother tucked baby and me into the straw, between Aunt Masha and herself.

I was very fond of this uncle and as I lay looking at his face, with the light shining on it, I thought, "Another minute, and I won't see him any more. Perhaps I'll never see him again." Indistinctly, through my tears, I saw the driver climb into the wagon and uncle jump on the axle of the wheel. He bent over me. "Farewell!" he said. At that moment his voice and face were so much like my mother's that I was struck with terror and could not breathe until I found her hand.

As we jogged off I heard uncle calling after us, "Don't forget God." And it seemed to me that the frogs from the neighbouring swamps took up the words and croaked, "Don't forget God! Don't forget God!"

The road was very uneven, and every time the wheels passed over a stone I heard Aunt Masha's head bump against the wagon. Mother gave her some more straw to put there, but she refused.

"What," she said, peevishly, "is this pain or any other pain that I have ever had, compared with what my

mother suffers to-night." And so she let her head bump
as if that would give her mother relief. For a long time
I felt Aunt Masha's body shaking with sobs. But by
degrees it grew quieter, the breathing became regular,
and she slept. Then I saw mother, who I thought was
also asleep, sit up. She took some straw from her side
of the wagon and bending over me towards Aunt Masha
she raised her head gently and spread the straw under it.

Long after mother fell asleep I still lay awake. Every
nerve in my body quivered and my eyes burned. As I
lay looking up into the starlit sky I lived the day over
again. The parting from home! "Could there be anything more painful than parting from those dear to
you?" I wondered. "Will this ache in my heart always
be there? And yet, how strange! It is but a few hours
since I have left grandmother and the children and their
faces have already become indistinct, as though I had
left them a long time ago. And so it will be when I
part from mother. Oh, I can't bear to think of it! Suppose something happens now and I could not go to
America but had to return home. Would I be glad?
Glad to go back to four smoke-covered walls? No! I
would be disappointed, more than that,—life would
hardly be worth living."

To what other conclusions I came that night I do not
remember distinctly. But I recall that gradually I became conscious of the sweet moist night air passing over
my face and the splendour of the stars and was soothed
by their quiet light.

I slept until baby poked his little nose under my chin to
wake me at broad daylight. My first thought was, "I
am in Mintck." I had looked forward with pleasure to
being there. And yet all I saw of it was a dingy courtyard, a sunless room, a drosky and a railroad station.

The dingy courtyard we passed through when we got out of the wagon, and the sunless room was the home of our cousins with whom we stayed as long as we remained in the city. These cousins were the children of father's and Aunt Masha's half-brother, who had died several years before. Aunt Masha knew them as well as she knew us, and mother knew them too, but to me they were strangers.

When we came into the room I saw a small, dark young man with a pale, delicate face, a square-shouldered boy of about seventeen and a girl of my own age with beautiful brown hair like Aunt Masha's.

I remember that I kept in back of mother. The thought of being looked at made me feel quite ill.

During the three days that followed I stayed in the house and took care of baby while mother and Aunt Masha were doing their errands. There was quite some trouble with the agents. They found out that we had no local passport and could not get one. And so they demanded an unreasonable sum of money which mother finally had to pay. And even then, it was just as likely as not that we would be caught crossing the boundary and sent back.

"Your children had better take along plenty of money," the agent said with a smile, while he was pocketing the roll of bills, "for you never can tell how long they might have to wait in Hamburg for a steamer." Mother wept, hearing this. There was so little left to take along.

I think it was on the second day that the boy asked Aunt Masha, "Why don't you take Rahel along and show her the City?"

"In these shoes?" Aunt Masha asked, looking at him severely.

"Well," he said, "you are going to buy her shoes,

are you not? Why not buy them now and let her go along?"

"Look here," Aunt Masha said with terrible calmness, "when I ask for your advice you will give it to me. Until then——." The boy dropped into a chair as if he were shot. Then came a peal of laughter. He laughed and laughed until his whole body rocked and his small twinkling blue eyes disappeared. We all laughed with him. And even Aunt Masha had to frown hard and purse her pretty lips in order not to smile.

On the third morning Aunt Masha bought me a very pretty pair of black patent-leather slippers with two buttons. I remember that after I put them on, I sat most of the time. I wanted to keep the soles clean. And it was only to give baby the pleasure and myself, too, of hearing them squeak, that I walked across the room.

In the afternoon mother sewed the money that was left into the side lining of my little underwaist. "No one will suspect it there," she said. When she was through she spread the waist out on her knee and smoothed out the creases with great tenderness. While putting on the waist I noticed that there were many damp spots on it.

After that there was nothing more to do. Our new wicker basket was ready and stood corded at the door. And there was a small bag of zwieback and two new bright tin drinking cups. I remember how silently we all sat waiting for five o'clock, how white mother's face looked, how unnaturally cheerful Aunt Masha seemed, how attentive the boy was to all of us, how rapidly my heart beat as if I had been running a long distance.

A little before the hour my pale-faced cousin came in. And it seemed to me that he grew still paler when he looked at us and said, "The drosky is at the door."

I don't remember how we left the house. But when we were in the drosky I saw that I had my tin cup in my hand and Aunt Masha had the bag of zwieback and the other cup. We were driven to the station at a speed that made baby's breath come and go in gasps.

The platform was crowded. "Here is the train," my cousin said. "Hurry!" Mother caught me into her arms with a cry that made me forget everything. Half unconscious now of what was going on, I held her around the neck with all my strength.

"A crowded train," I heard. "Hurry!" And again, "You will never get a seat now," and still later, "Oh, I thought you were such a brave girl"—"You will miss the train, Rahel!"

Some one pulled my hands apart. I was lifted from the back and carried into the train. I looked through the window into the crowd for mother. Just as I caught sight of her face the train began to move. I saw her fling out her arms wildly and run alongside of the train for a few steps. Then her arms dropped limply at her sides and she disappeared in the crowd.

I stood for a moment swaying back and forth. Then it grew dark as if night had suddenly come. The tin cup fell out of my hand. I saw it lying on the floor but indistinctly and the distance between it and me seemed immeasurable and grew with every instant. "My cup," I tried to call and took a step toward it. Then it disappeared altogether.

XIII

AUNT MASHA'S tear-stained face, bending over me anxiously, was the first thing I saw when I regained consciousness. Then I found that I was sitting in some one's lap and in my own there were two small, white-gloved hands clasped together. Surprised, I looked over my shoulder and saw under a large, black hat a charming, girlish face. I felt very much embarrassed and tried to stand up at once. But she spoke to me in a quiet, sooth-ing voice and at the same time she drew me toward her so gently and so gradually that I was scarcely conscious of it until I felt my back resting against her, and my head on her shoulder.

We travelled for about an hour when she stood up. She put me on her seat, nodded to Aunt Masha, who was also sitting by that time, and went to the door. When the train stopped she looked at me with a smile, blew a kiss from her finger tips, and was gone.

In wonder and regret I sat staring at the door until I heard Aunt Masha whisper half severely, half entreat-ingly, "Rahel, do stop staring so. You seem to think you are still in the woods."

We were in the train two or three days. When we made long stops Aunt Masha used to leave me in the train and go to get food and drink. I remember the first time she went out I was trembling with fear lest the train should go off before she returned. Each time she went out I would get as near a window as possible and stand ready to jump out in case the train started.

I do not remember how or when we left the train, or how about twenty-five of us, two young men and the rest women and very small children, came to be travelling in a large, canvas-covered wagon, on a country road white with the heat and dust. The first thing I recall seeing was one of the young men bent almost double, so as not to strike his head against the roof, coming toward Aunt Masha and me, who sat in the back. He sat down in front of Aunt Masha and looked at her with a grin which made the tip of his long, thin-hooked nose and red, bristling moustache touch.

"You are a pretty girl," he said, beginning to twirl his moustache and looking at her, through half-closed, blood-shot eyes. Aunt Masha blushed painfully and turned her head away.

"Oh, come, look this way," he coaxed, catching hold of her hands. Aunt Masha grew angry. At the same time I saw that she was trying to control herself and take the whole thing as a joke while struggling to free her hands.

I was furious. To see this stranger touch her, and look at her which seemed to hurt her more than if she were struck, was so awful to me that I could not stand it. "Let go her hand."

"I won't," he laughed and made a vulgar remark at which some of the women tittered. But others called out, "Oh, shame, to speak so to a child."

"Will you let go her hand?" I was hardly able to speak now in my anger. He glanced at me and I saw that he was amused and, as if to carry the fun still further, he drew Aunt Masha's face to his own. Then I lost my head. I jumped up and began to strike at him blindly with both fists.

He was so taken by surprise that he did not seem to realise at first what was happening to him. Finally he let her go and jumping up he caught hold of me. Aunt

Masha screamed and the women interfered. He flung me down into the bottom of the wagon and looked around at the women.

"The little fury," he gasped, "who would have expected it of her? She looked as quiet as a mouse."

I was surprised myself at my daring, but I was not sorry.

From that hour there was no peace. Like a shadow he followed us about on every step. He tried to be on friendly terms with Aunt Masha. I saw this and so seldom left her alone. He read my mind and hated me.

Toward evening of that day we came to an empty little log house so much like ours at home that I could not restrain a cry of joy at the sight of it. The roof, however, was of shingles instead of straw.

When it grew quite dark a few wagons drove up to the door of the hut. There was a good deal of whispering and disputing about which Aunt Masha tried to keep me in ignorance. Her idea was to keep me from knowing everything that was unpleasant. But her way of doing it was as unpleasant as anything could have been. For it was always, "Rahel, go away, don't listen!"

"But why, Aunt Masha?"

"Why? Because I say so!" So I would walk away and watch intently from a distance. I noticed that Aunt Masha did not want to go into a wagon with small children. Nor did the other women who had none of their own. At last, after much talking and swearing on the part of the drivers, which I could not help overhearing, in spite of Masha's precaution, we were all placed. I was put flat on my face between Aunt Masha and her friend, into one of the wagons spread with ill-smelling hay. We were covered up with more of it, heads and all, then drove off, it seemed to me, each wagon in a different direction.

We might have been driving for an hour, though it seemed much longer for I could hardly breathe, when I heard the driver's hoarse whisper, "Remember, people, you are not to make a sound, nor move a limb for the next half hour."

Soon after this I heard a rough voice in Russian, "Who is there?"

"It is Mushka," our driver answered.

"What have you in the wagon?" the Russian demanded.

"Oh, just some bags of flour," Mushka answered.

I felt a heavy hand laid on my back. At that moment it dawned on me that we were stealing across the border. My heart began to thump so that I was sure he heard it. And in my fear I began to pray. But I stopped at once, at a pinch from Aunt Masha and a nudge from her friend. Then I heard the clink of money. At last the rough voice called out loudly, "Flour? Go ahead."

As we started off again I heard the crying of children in the distance, and shooting.

XIV

ONE day, I don't remember how soon after we crossed the border, we arrived in Hamburg. We stopped in a large, red building run in connection with the steamship company. We were all shown (really driven) into a large room where many dirty, narrow cots stood along the walls. Aunt Masha shivered as she looked at the one in which we two were to sleep.

"The less we stay in these beds the better," she said. So, although we were dead tired we went to bed quite late. But before we were on our cot very long we saw that sleep was out of the question.

The air in the room was so foul and thick that it felt as if it could be touched. From every corner came sounds of groaning and snoring. But worst of all were the insects in the cot. After battling with these for some time Aunt Masha sat up.

"I feel I'll go mad," she gasped, clutching her hair. After sitting up a while she remembered seeing a wagon with some hay in it under the shed in the yard, and we decided to go there. We took our shoes in our hands and slipped out noiselessly.

It was a dark night and Aunt Masha was almost as much afraid in the dark as I was. With one arm clasped about each other's waists we groped about an endless time, until we crossed the yard and found the wagon. Fortunately, no one had thought of sleeping in it. Aunt Masha gave a sigh of relief and satisfaction as she nestled comfortably into the hay. Soon she was asleep.

To me sleep did not come so readily. My mind always seemed more active when I lay down at night than at any other time. And since we had been on the journey I could not sleep because of the new and strange things about me.

As I lay thinking, listening, I suddenly caught a whiff of cigarette smoke. I sat up quickly and peered into the darkness. In the direction where I knew the door was I saw a tiny light. My first thought was to wake Aunt Masha. Then it occurred to me that it must be some one like ourselves who could not sleep and so came to stay outside. But as I sat watching the light I saw that it was coming toward the shed, though very slowly.

Nearer and nearer it came and soon I discerned a tall, dark form coming along stealthily. I recognised the slow cat-like tread. It was he with the red eyes and grinning mouth.

I was almost beside myself with fear now that I knew who it was and I pressed closer to Aunt Masha. As he stopped a short distance from the shed and stood listening, I coughed to let him know that some one was in the wagon.

Then only, it seemed as if he realised that the light from his cigarette could be seen and he put his hand behind him. For a minute or so he stood still, listening. Then he went away as stealthily as he came and I saw him crouch down in a corner of the yard.

I sat wondering whether he knew that it was Aunt Masha and I that were in the wagon, and whether he would come again. He did, after a good while passed. Again I coughed to warn him. But this time he came right into the shed and craning his neck he tried to see.

"Why don't you lie down and go to sleep," he whispered, feigning friendly concern. Now I saw that he knew us.

"I am not sleepy," I said, loudly.

"But you will fall asleep if you lie down," he insisted. I noticed that he looked around as if he were uneasy when I spoke loud. So I answered still louder:

"I am not going to lie down. I am going to sit up all night, and if you don't go away at once I'll shout and wake the whole house." Then he turned quickly and tiptoed away, cursing under his breath.

At first I thought I would let Aunt Masha sleep a while and then wake her. But when some time passed it occurred to me that if I could stay up all night without waking Aunt Masha, no one could ever again call me that hated name, " 'Fraid-cat." So I clasped my hands tightly in my lap and sat watching, listening. At the least sound in the yard I felt my hair rise on my head. Several times Aunt Masha moved restlessly in her sleep. Then I too, moved, half hoping that she would hear me and wake up. But she slept on. At one time it grew so dark and so cold that I could not keep my teeth still and it seemed as if the night would never end.

"Oh, now I must wake her." But at the very thought of it I seemed to hear, "Ah, you are a 'Fraid-cat after all." And so I pressed my hand over my mouth and waited.

At last a faint grey light came creeping slowly into the yard. With unspeakable joy I watched the house loom out of the darkness, but it was only when the smaller objects in the yard took on their natural forms, and people began to come and go, that I lay down.

My head scarcely seemed to have touched the hay when I heard Aunt Masha say, teasingly, "Oh, you sleepy head, the night is never long enough for you. Why, your eyes are actually swollen from too much sleep. Get up."

I sat up, not knowing at first where I was or what

had happened. Then recollecting my experience of the
night I wondered whether I should tell Aunt Masha or
not. She had never invited any confidence from me.
And this particularly seemed hard to tell. As I sat,
hesitating, I half saw, half felt the red eyes glaring at
me from the doorway. And so I jumped out of the wagon and ran to get washed.

Our breakfast, which was boiled potatoes and slices
of white bread, was served on long bare tables in a room
like the sleeping room. No sooner was the food put on
the tables than it was gone, and some of us were left
with empty plates. Aunt Masha and I looked at each
other and burst out laughing. To see the bread grabbed
up and the fingers scorched on the boiled potatoes was
ugly and pathetic but also funny.

"To-morrow," Aunt Masha said, "we too shall have
to grab. For the money sewed in your waist won't last
if we have to buy more than one meal a day for a week."
But the next day it was almost the same thing. Going
hungry seemed easy in comparison wth the shame we felt
to put out our hands for the bread while there was such
a struggle.

Aunt Masha managed to get one slice which she held
out to me. "Here, eat it." When I refused she gave
me a look that was as bad as a blow. "Take it at once,"
she said angrily. I took it. I found it hard to swallow
the bread, knowing that she was hungry.

We stayed in Hamburg a week. Every day from ten
in the morning until four in the afternoon we stayed in
a large, bare hall waiting for our names to be called. On
the left side of the hall there was a heavy door leading
into the office, where the emigrants were called in one
by one.

I used to sit down on the floor opposite the door and

watch the people's faces as they came and went into the office. Some looked excited and worried when they came out, and others looked relieved.

When our names were called I rose quickly and followed Aunt Masha. The clerk who always came to the door, which he opened only a little, looked at us and asked our names. Then he let Aunt Masha go in and pushing me away roughly without a word he shut the heavy door in my face.

I stood nearby waiting, until my feet ached. When Aunt Masha came out at last her face was flushed and there were tears in her eyes. Immediately she went over to her friends (she had many friends by that time) and began to talk to them excitedly. I followed her but she stopped talking when she saw me. I understood that I was not to listen. And so I went away.

This went on for almost a week. Each day her face looked more worried and perplexed.

One afternoon the door of the office opened wider than usual and a different clerk came out holding a paper in his hand. He told us that the English steamer for which we had been waiting was in. And then he read the names of those who were to go on it.

I'll never forget Aunt Masha's joy when she heard that we were to sail the next day. She ran from one to the other of her friends, crying and laughing at once.

"The scoundrel," she kept on saying, "he threatened to send us home. He said he had the power to send us home!" Then she ran over to me and in her joy almost smothered me in her embrace.

I don't remember whether it was on this same day or when we were already on the steamer that our clothes were taken away to be "steamed." As my little underwaist, which still had some money in it, was also taken, we spent some anxious hours. The money was not touched. But when I looked at my pretty little slippers I wept bitter tears. They looked old, and wrinkled, and two of the buttons were off.

On the following evening we sailed off in a small white boat. We all sat on the floor of the deck. I dreaded crossing the ocean for I had heard that the water was rough. The boat rocked fearfully, and there was sickness and even death. But when some time passed and I saw how smoothly and steadily the boat went along over quiet water, I felt relieved. Then came something of gladness. I sat quietly in back of Aunt Masha, watching the full moon appearing and disappearing behind the clouds, and listening to our fellow travellers. Their faces, so worried and excited for weeks, looked peaceful and contented as they sat gazing at the moon and talking quietly and hopefully of the future in the new world.

"How beautiful," I thought. "This is the way the rest of our journey will be." For in my ignorance I thought that we would sail all the way across in this little white boat and that the water would always be calm, and the wind gentle. When I whispered my thought to Aunt Masha she smiled at me over her shoulder, a queer, meaning little smile, which puzzled me. In the morning when we came to an enormous black and white steamer I remembered Aunt Masha's smile and understood its meaning.

We were deathly seasick the first three days. During that period I was conscious, it seems to me, only part of the time. I remember that once when I opened my eyes I seemed to see the steamer turn to one side and then disappear under water. Then I heard voices screaming, entreating, praying. I thought we were drowning, but I did not care. Nothing mattered now. On the

fourth day, I became again interested in life. I heard
Aunt Masha moaning. A long time seemed to have
passed since I saw her face. I tried to lift my head.
Finding it impossible, I lay quietly listening, but it hurt
me to hear her moaning. At last it became so pitiful
that I could not stand it.

"I'll die if I don't get a drop of water," she moaned,
"just one drop to wet my throat."

And so as I lay flat on my face I felt about for my
tin cup till I found it. Then I began to slip downward
feet first until I reached the berth underneath. From
there I swung down to the floor. As I stood up the boat
lunged to one side and I went flying to the door and fell
in a heap, striking my head against the door post. I
don't know how long I had been lying there, when I
heard the cabin door open and a man's strong voice call
out, "Up on deck." I opened my eyes and saw an
enormous pair of black boots and the lower part of white
trousers.

The man stooped down, looked at me and gently
brushed the hair away from my eyes. As I was used
now to being pushed about and yelled at, the kind touch
brought tears to my eyes. For the first time since I
left home I covered my face with my hands and wept
heartily.

For a minute or so he stood looking down at me. Then
he picked up my cup, which I had dropped in falling,
and brought me water. I drank some, and pointed to
Aunt Masha. He handed the cup to a woman who came
tumbling out of her berth to go up on deck. Then picking me up as if I were a little infant, he again shouted,
"Up on deck!" and carried me off.

I had heard that those who were very sick on the

steamer and those who died were thrown into the ocean. There was no doubt in my mind, therefore, that that was where I was being carried. I clasped my arms tightly about the man's neck. I felt sick with fear. He climbed up a white staircase and propped me up in a corner on the floor. Then he went away, to fetch a rope, I thought. He returned in a few minutes. But instead of a rope there was half an orange in his hand. He kneeled down in front of me, raised my chin, showed me how to open my mouth and squeezed a few drops of juice into it. A good-natured smile played about his lips as he watched me swallow. Three times between his work he went and came with the half orange, until it was dry.

After a while Aunt Masha came creeping up the steps on all fours, hugging our little bag of zwieback.

From that hour we improved quickly. All day we sat or walked about in the sun. Soon Aunt Masha's little round nose was covered with freckles and my hair was bleached a half dozen shades.

Sometimes while walking about on deck we passed the man who had fed me with orange juice. He always touched his cap and smiled to us.

A week passed.

One day, it was the first of July, Aunt Masha and I stood in Castle Garden. With fluttering hearts yet patiently we stood scanning the faces of a group of Americans divided from us by iron gates.

"My father could never be among those wonderfully dressed people," I thought. Suddenly it seemed to me as if I must shout. I caught sight of a familiar smile.

"Aunt Masha, do you see that man in the light tan suit? The one who is smiling and waving his hand?"

"Why, you little goose," she cried, "don't you see?

It's father!" She gave a laugh and a sob, and hid her face in her hands.

A little while later the three of us stood clinging to one another.

All day we sat or walked about in the sun.

PART TWO

PART TWO

XV

FROM Castle Garden we drove to our new home in a market wagon filled with immigrants' bedding. Father tucked us in among the bundles, climbed up beside the driver himself and we rattled off over the cobbled stone pavement, with the noon sun beating down on our heads.

As we drove along I looked about in bewilderment. My thoughts were chasing each other. I felt a thrill: "Am I really in America at last?" But the next moment it would be checked and I felt a little disappointed, a little homesick. Father was so changed. I hardly expected to find him in his black long tailed coat in which he left home. But of course yet with his same full grown beard and earlocks. Now instead I saw a young man with a closely cut beard and no sign of earlocks. As I looked at him I could scarcely believe my eyes. Father had been the most pious Jew in our neighbourhood. I wondered was it true then as Mindle said that "in America one at once became a libertine"?

Father's face was radiantly happy. Every now and then he would look over his shoulder and smile. But he soon guessed what troubled me for after a while he began to talk in a quiet, reassuring manner. He told me he would take me to his own shop and teach me part of his own trade. He was a men's coat finisher. He made me understand that if we worked steadily and lived economically we should soon have money to send for those at home. "Next year at this time," he smiled, "you yourself may be on the way to Castle Garden to fetch mother and the children." So I too smiled at the happy prospect, wiped some tears away and resolved to work hard.

XVI

WHAT I recall after this is an early morning when we were already established in a tiny room with peacock blue walls and a window looking into a grey courtyard. There was also a small table, a chair and a cot spread with a red comforter. We were having breakfast. But only Aunt Masha and I ate. Father sat opposite us, watched us dip our buttered roll into the hot coffee and asked many times, "Is it good?" His voice was soft with pity and tenderness.

"It is delicious," we assured him. This was the first time in my life that I tasted coffee and the first time Aunt Masha and I had had enough to eat in a month.

Before leaving for the shop that morning father told me that I should have to stay at home at least a week and "feed up." He said laughingly that I looked green in more than one sense.

So we stayed home. And though we feared to venture out of the building we did not lack amusement. Everything was new and interesting. To me it was pure pleasure just to stay in our own room and look and examine our new American furniture, and try to imagine how mother and the children would be impressed.

A great part of the time we stayed out on the stoop. I was dazed by all there was to see. I looked with wonder at the tall houses, the paved streets, the street lamps. As I had never seen a large city and only had had a glimpse of a small one, I thought these things true only of America.

One day while Aunt Masha and I stood out on the stoop we saw a dark little man with a red bandana around his neck and a silver earring in his ear, wheeling what appeared to be a queer looking box. And when I saw him stop and make music come out of it, and the little girls that followed and others that joined begin swaying to the rhythm, their little pigtails flying, the little faces alive with enjoyment, I stood dumb with wonder. At this even Aunt Masha looked astonished. But the next moment she explained knowingly, "Don't you see, he goes about playing in the streets that the children may dance." That seemed very probable. I expected all sorts of wonderful things of America, though at home I had also heard things that were sad.

I had heard one day the mistress of the Inn and Post Office talking of her two sons in America. I heard her say that they were machine operators and they had lost their feet at the sewing machine. I took it literally, as indeed I took everything else. So one day when I saw a rather tall boy of about fifteen pass our door on queer little wheels (roller skates) I could not keep tears out of my eyes. I thought that this must be a machine operator who lost his feet at the machine. That a boy of that age could go about in open daylight on a plain week day, amusing himself, would have never occurred to me.

One night father came home from work a little earlier than usual and took us to Grand Street. I was dazzled by the lights, the display in the jewelry shops and dry goods store windows. But nothing surprised me so much as the figures in the hair dresser's window. One was a blonde, the other a brunette. One was in pink, the other in blue. Their hair was beautifully curled and dressed, each one with a mirror in one hand and the other held daintily on the back of the hair, went slowly turning around and around and smiling into the mirror.

At first I could not believe that they were not alive until father and Aunt Masha laughed at me. It seemed to me nothing short of a miracle to see how perfect the features were, the smile. And I thought, "Oh, America is truly wonderful! People are not shovelling gold in the streets, as I had heard, but still it is wonderful." When I told it to father he laughed. "Wait," he said. And then he took us to "Silver Smith Charlie's saloon" and I saw the floor studded with half dollars!

From Mrs. Felesberg we learned at once the more serious side of life in America. Mrs. Felesberg was the woman with whom we were rooming. A door from our room opened into her tiny bedroom and then led into the only other room where she sat a great part of the day finishing pants which she brought in big bundles from a shop, and rocking the cradle with one foot. She always made us draw our chairs quite close to her and she spoke in a whisper scarcely ever lifting her weak peering eyes from her work. When she asked us how we liked America, and we spoke of it with praise, she smiled a queer smile. "Life here is not all that it appears to the 'green horn,'" she said. She told us that her husband was a presser on coats and earned twelve dollars when he worked a full week. Aunt Masha thought twelve dollars a good deal. Again Mrs. Felesberg smiled. "No doubt it would be," she said, "where you used to live. You had your own house, and most of the food came from the garden. Here you will have to pay for everything; the rent!" she sighed, "for the light, for every potato, every grain of barley. You see these three rooms, including yours? Would they be too much for my family of five?" We had to admit they would not. "And even from these," she said, "I have to rent one out."

Perhaps it was due to these talks that I soon noticed how late my father worked. When he went away in the morning it was still dark, and when he came home at night the lights in the halls were out. It was after ten o'clock. I thought that if mother and the children were here they would scarcely see him.

One night when he came home and as he sat at the table eating his rice soup, which he and Aunt Masha had taught me to cook, I sat down on the cot and asked timidly, knowing that he was impatient of questions, "Father, does everybody in America live like this? Go to work early, come home late, eat and go to sleep? And the next day again work, eat, and sleep? Will I have to do that too? Always?"

Father looked thoughtful and ate two or three mouthfuls before he answered. "No," he said smiling. "You will get married."

So, almost a week passed and though life was so interesting, still no matter where I went, what I saw, mother and home were always present in my mind. Often in the happiest moments a pain would rise in my throat and my eyes burned with the tears held back. At these moments I would manage to be near Aunt Masha so that I could lean against her, touch her dress.

How Aunt Masha felt I never knew but once. Father brought each of us a black patent leather belt. One day she put hers on and came over to me. "Close your eyes, Rahel," she said, "and feel the belt on me." I did. And as I passed my hand around her waist, I said, "This is how grandmother used to see when we put on something new." When I opened my eyes I saw that Aunt Masha's face was wet with tears.

XVII

I THINK it was at the end of a week that Aunt Masha received an offer at her old occupation as children's nurse. As it seemed to her a desirable place and as she wished to begin at once to pay off father for her steamer ticket, she accepted it. So one morning after father left for work a large good-looking woman, owner of a delicatessen store, came for her.

All that morning as she went about the room gathering her things and packing them into a bundle, she was flushed and excited and avoided meeting my eyes.

When the bundle was tied and she was ready to leave she came and drew me towards her almost roughly. "Good-bye, Rahel." I felt her whole body shaking with sobs. "Remember," she commanded, "not to go alone any further than the stoop." And then she added a little sulkily, "No doubt you are glad to see me go."

She took the bundle under her arm and followed the woman, and I went out and stood watching her until she disappeared through the long, dark, narrow hall. Soon I could hear only the click, click of her high slender heels on the wooden floor and on the stone steps. From the hall below the click still came up but faintly and I had to bend forward to catch it. Then I heard the street door slam, resound through the building, and all was silent.

XVIII

During the first two days that followed I missed Aunt Masha dreadfully and felt ill with homesickness, loneliness and even fear. While in my room I tried to find the pleasure and interest of the first days. But now the table, the cot, the chair were merely strange things which seemed to stare at me coldly. Neither could I stay out on the stoop. I tried to do so the first day but felt too timid to go any further than the door. There, as I stood for a few minutes, looking at the people passing back and forth, at the houses across the street, the feeling came to me suddenly that I was utterly alone. "There is not a face that I know," I thought. "Not a spot that is familiar to me. Where are father and Aunt Masha?" I tried to picture them. I saw many streets, rows and rows of brick houses, crowds of people but I could not see their faces anywhere. With a sick feeling of fear I shrank back into the hall.

Father never knew how I was troubled. By the time he came home at night I was asleep or pretended to be.

One day, while wandering about through the tenement, trying to amuse myself by walking up and down the steps, so as not to think of home, I reached the top floor and found that there were no more steps to climb. But instead I saw an open door which seemed to lead into an open space. I stepped over the threshold and stood still. I was not sure that this place was safe to walk upon. Then seeing that it was large, square and solid, I thought "It is a floor, built on top of a house."

I walked to the centre and looked about. I saw roofs and sky on all sides. On some of the roofs I was surprised to see clothes on ropes fluttering in the wind. Here and there from buildings standing out among the rest, I saw flags waving. But what I looked at with joy after a momentary glance at these, was the sky! It was like finding unexpectedly some one dear from home. I sat down on the door step in the shade and looked at the sky and thought:

"The sky is the same everywhere. There is only one. Perhaps mother, too, sister or some one at home is looking at it at this very moment."

This thought made home seem a little nearer. Then I remembered grandmother saying:

"When it is day in America it is night in Russia."

"Oh," I thought, "so they are asleep now!"

In a moment I was far away from Cherry Street. I was in our log house. I stopped at mother's bed. I looked at the children sleeping at the foot of it. I peeped into the cradle. I passed close to grandfather's bench near the stove. I stopped at grandmother's bed and looked at the empty place which was mine.

Suddenly I became aware of some one standing back of me. I looked over my shoulder and saw Mrs. Felesberg with baby in her arms. I felt ashamed of my tears and hid my face in my hands. She did not say anything but sat down on the step close to me, put her arm around me and gently drew me towards her until my face rested in her lap beside baby's small cheek.

From that day the baby became a great comfort to me. I amused him, rocked him and carried him about in my arms when he cried. Often as I walked up and down the floor with him, singing him to sleep, he sent his little hand out, and caressed my face. The touch of the tiny fingers on my eyes would make me feel less lonely.

When Saturday came I felt happy because father

stayed at home. After dinner we went out into the street.
I walked beside father, clasping his hand tightly. I
looked about and wondered how people could find their
way without seeming to think about it. All the streets,
all the houses, seemed so very much alike.

Father stopped at a fruitstand and told me to choose
what I wanted. There was nothing strange to me in
that. At home when we sold fruit, as we did sometimes
during the summer, Jewish people came on Saturday to
eat apples or pears for which they paid the following
week. So I thought it was the same here.

I looked and looked at the fruit: "What shall I take?"
Apples, oranges, plums, pears—all were arranged in neat
pyramids, all looked good and very tempting, surrounded
by fresh green leaves, glistening with drops of water. I
looked at the strange fruits also. I saw long finger like
things with smooth yellow skins, and grapes which I knew
by name only. In a glass case on a square of ice there
were some slices of watermelon.

"What shall I take?" I asked, turning to father. "Anything you like," he smiled encouragingly. I decided on a
slice of melon. I looked up into father's face. I felt
proud of him that he had credit at so beautiful a fruitstand.

As I received the melon in my fingers I saw father
take his hand out of his pocket and hold out a coin. I
felt the blood rush to my face. I stood staring at him
for a moment. Then I dropped the melon on the pavement and ran. Before I had taken many steps I realised
that I was running away from home and turned back.
In passing the stand I did not look to see if father was
still there but ran on.

"My father has touched coin on the Sabbath!"

These words rang in my ears. I was almost knocked

over by people into whom I ran but I paid no attention.
Others stopped to watch me curiously as I ran by. It
seemed to me that it was because they knew what I had
just seen and I ran on with my cheeks flaming.

Suddenly it seemed to me that I had been running a
long while and I felt that I should be near home. I
stopped and looked about, but I could not see the house
anywhere. I ran further, looking about wildly and trying to remember things so as to locate myself. Suddenly
I came upon a dressmaker's sign which I recognised. I
hurried into my room, closed the door carefully, and
threw myself down on the cot, burying my face into the
pillow.

"Father carries money about with him on the Sabbath.
Oh, the sin! Oh, poor grandmother," I thought, "how
would she feel if she knew. Brother is only seven years
old and already he is so pious that he wishes to remain
with a learned Jew in Russia, after mother goes to America, that he may become a great Rabbi. How would he
feel? How would they all feel?"

Then I remembered Yanna, who, on hearing that father was in America, and feeling that perhaps we were too
happy over it, came one day to torment grandmother.

"The first thing men do in America," she had said, "is
cut their beards and the first thing the women do is to
leave off their wigs. And you," she had said, turning
to me venomously, "you who will not break a thread on
the Sabbath now, will eat swine in America."

"Oh, God," I thought, "will it really come to that?
shall I eat swine?"

After what I had just seen nothing seemed impossible.
In utter misery I turned and felt about with my burning
cheek for a cooler place on the pillow. As I did so I re-

membered that the pillow was one which mother gave me from home. I slipped my arms under it and pressing my lips to it I wept. "No, I shall not eat swine, indeed I shall not!"

XIX

ON the following day father came home at noon and took me along to the shop where he worked. We climbed the dark, narrow stairs of a tenement house on Monroe Street and came into a bright room filled with noise. I saw about five or six men and a girl. The men turned and looked at us when we passed. I felt scared and stumbled. One man asked in surprise:

"Avrom, is this your daughter? Why, she is only a little girl!"

My father smiled. "Yes," he said, "but wait till you see her sew."

He placed me on a high stool opposite the girl, laid a pile of pocket flaps on the little narrow table between us, and showed me how to baste.

All afternoon I sat on my high stool, a little away from the table, my knees crossed tailor fashion, basting flaps. As I worked I watched the things which I could see by just raising my eyes a little. I saw that the girl, who was called Atta, was very pretty.

A big man stood at a big table, examining, brushing and folding coats. There was a window over his table through which the sun came streaming in, showing millions of specks of dust dancing over the table and circling over his head. He often puffed out his cheeks and blew the dust from him with a great gust so that I could feel his breath at our table.

The machines going at full speed drowned everything in their noise. But when they stopped for a moment I caught the clink of a scissors laid hastily on a table, a short question and answer exchanged, and the pounding of a heavy iron from the back of the room. Sometimes the machines stopped for a whole minute. Then the men looked about and talked. I was always glad when the machines started off again. I felt safer in their noise.

Late in the afternoon a woman came into the shop. She sat down next to Atta and began to sew on buttons. Father, who sat next to me, whispered, "This is Mrs. Nelson, the wife of the big man, our boss. She is a real American."

She, too, was pretty. Her complexion was fair and delicate like a child's. Her upper lip was always covered with shining drops of perspiration. I could not help looking at it all the time.

When she had worked a few minutes she asked father in very imperfect Yiddish: "Well, Mr. ——, have you given your daughter an American name?"

"Not yet," father answered. "What would you call her? Her Yiddish name is Rahel."

"Rahel, Rahel," Mrs. Nelson repeated to herself, thoughtfully, winding the thread around a button; "let me see." The machines were going slowly and the men looked interested.

The presser called out from the back of the room: "What is there to think about? Rahel is Rachel."

I was surprised at the interest every one showed. Later I understood the reason. The slightest cause for interruption was welcome, it broke the monotony of the long day.

Mrs. Nelson turned to me: "Don't let them call you Rachel. Every loafer who sees a Jewish girl shouts 'Rachel' after her. And on Cherry Street where you live there are many saloons and many loafers. How would you like Ruth for a name?"

I said I should like to be called Ruth.

XX

FATHER made the life for me as easy as he could. But there were many hardships he could not prevent.

We began the day at six in the morning. I would stand dressing with my eyes closed and feel about for my buttons. But once I was out on the street and felt the moist early morning air I was wide awake at once.

When we had been in the shop about an hour a grey-bearded little old man used to come in lugging a big basket of food covered with black oil cloth. He was the shop pedlar. He always stopped near the door, rested his basket against it and groaned: "Oh, the stairs, the stairs in America!" The men looked at him with pity and Atta at the sight of him would sometimes begin to sing "The Song of the Pedlar." If the boss was not in the shop or the men were not very busy, one of them would take the basket from the pedlar and place it on a chair in the middle of the room. Then each shop hand picked out a roll and the little old man poured him out a tiny glass of brandy for two cents. Father used to buy me an apple and a sweetened roll. We ate while we worked. I used to think two cents a good deal to spend for my breakfast. But often I was almost sick with hunger. At noon we had our big meal. Then father would send me out for half a pound of steak or a slice of beef liver and a pint of beer which he sometimes bought in partnership with two or three other men. He used to broil the steak in the open coal fireplace where the presser heated his irons, and cut it into tiny squares. He always picked out the juiciest bits and pushed them to my side of the plate, and while there was still quite some meat he would lay down his fork and push his chair away from the table with an air as if he had had more than enough. He also got me to drink beer. Before long I could drink a full glass. But I did not like it. One day it made me quite sick. After that I refused to drink it.

I liked my work and learned it easily, and father was pleased with me. As soon as I knew how to baste pocket-flaps he began to teach me how to baste the coat edges. This was hard work. The double ply of overcoat cloth stitched in with canvas and tape made a very stiff edge. My fingers often stiffened with pain as I rolled and basted the edges. Sometimes a needle or two would break before I could do one coat. Then father would offer to finish the edge for me. But if he gave me my choice I never let him. At these moments I wanted so to master the thing myself that I felt my whole body trembling with the desire. And with my habit of personifying things, I used to bend over the coat on my lap, force the obstinate and squeaking needle, wet with perspiration, in and out of the cloth and whisper with determination: "No, you shall not get the best of me!" When I succeeded I was so happy that father, who often watched me with a smile, would say, "Rahel, your face is shining. Now rest a while." He always told me to rest after I did well. I loved these moments. I would push my stool closer to the wall near which I sat, lean my back against it, and look about the shop.

Sitting so, I could see Atta and all the six men at work. The baster sat, Turk-like, on his table. He was small and slight. His skin was almost as dark as a negro's and his features resembled a bull dog's. But his was an unusually bright face. His black eyes flashed with intelligence. And when he laughed, showing his white, even teeth, I liked to look at him. Sometimes he would raise his eyes suddenly from his work, assume an earnest expression, open his eyes wide and look at me intently. Then I would know that I had been staring.

The boss moved about heavily at his big table. I could not help looking at him when he spoke or laughed,—his nostrils always dilated and whitened. He often came over to our table to borrow Atta's wax or small scissors. Almost every time he came he tried to pinch her cheek or take hold of her hand. She always dodged, threatened him with the point of her needle, and said half seriously, half jestingly, "Keep your hands off, please." This was the first sentence I learned in English.

The man in the shop who interested me most was the presser. He was almost black and he had a small black beard. His features were regular and good but there was no life in his face and his voice had a tired ring in it. His back was enormous, his chest narrow and he lifted his twenty-five pound iron with difficulty. I often felt sad when I looked at him without knowing why and was glad when he sent me on an errand.

He was the jest in the shop. He had been six years in this country and had not yet decided whether he should send for his wife or, as he often said, "Take a souvenir of America and go home to Russia." The men teased him about his wife and little girl who, they said, would be a woman by the time he decided. I, too, often wondered, "Will he go home? And what will he take as a remembrance?"

One day when I was not busy I went over and asked him if he wanted me to go on an errand. He put down his iron on the flat stone which he used as a stand, and looked at me thoughtfully. "No," he said. As I turned away he called me back.

"Rahel," he said, "if you were my little girl in Europe,

what would you like me to bring you from America?"
I thought for a moment and said, "Earrings."

When he came in the next morning he had a massive
gold watch and chain, a marriage ring, and a small pair
of earrings.

A week later there was another presser in the shop,
one with a straight back and a red beard.

XXI

ONE day a jewelry pedlar came into the shop. He showed us a watch. He told the men that the watch was of fourteen karat gold. But he would sell it cheaply, for fifteen dollars, because it was "second hand."

The assistant machine operator bought the watch for ten dollars. He was living on very little in order to save and send for his family in Russia. "But a good watch," he figured, "is as good as cash, lasts a lifetime." The men all congratulated the operator and teased, "Morris, you shall have to treat to-night."

"I certainly will," he said heartily. "I'll treat the whole shop."

I learned to look forward to these little merry makings and love them. How they also shortened the day!

At noon Morris, the operator, went down as usual to his dinner. He returned in a few minutes looking so pale. Even his lips were white. And when he began to talk his voice trembled. He told the men that he had been to a pawn shop and that he was told the watch was worth at most three dollars. The men were shocked. They held a short consultation and finally told Morris that they would raffle the watch off. Each of them paid a dollar and a half. Morris himself won the watch.

That night we stopped work an hour earlier. Morris bought two pints of beer and some bologna and we feasted.

I liked the life in the shop yet there were times when I felt unhappy. The men often told vulgar jokes. The first time this happened father looked at me and groaned.

"Don't listen," he said, "or pretend you don't hear."

But I could never keep my face from turning red.

One day when Atta and I were alone at our table she said:

"It is too bad that you have a 'tell tale face.' You better learn to hide your feelings. What you hear in this shop is nothing compared with what you will hear in other shops. Look at me." But when I would look over at Atta it seemed to me that her needle actually flew in and out of her sleeve lining and her pretty little mouth looked more pursed than usual.

XXII

WHEN I learned to find my way home alone my hours were not so long. For father was a piece worker and as I was only helping him he could do as he pleased with my time. And so now I came into the shop at seven o'clock in the morning and found my roll and apple already waiting for me. And when I went home at seven o'clock in the evening it was still broad daylight.

Our room was a dingy place where the sun never came in. I always felt lonely and a little homesick on coming into it. But I would soon shake off the feeling. I would cook and eat some soup and then go and stand on the stoop and watch the children playing.

One night as I came out of our room into the hall I caught a few strains of music coming from the roof. I went up and found under the sky, blue and bright with the stars and the city lights twinkling all around, a group of Irish-American girls and boys waltzing to the music of a harmonica. I sat down in the shadow near one of the chimneys and watched the stars and the dancing and listened to the song of "My Beautiful Irish Maid."

After this I went up every evening. At first the girls and boys showed that I was not welcome by making ugly grimaces at me. But as I persisted, for I wanted to know the Americans, they became used to seeing me. And soon they paid no more attention to me than to the chimney near which I sat.

On Friday I worked only the first half of the day, then I would go home to do the washing and cleaning in our room. All morning I would count the hours and half hours and my heart beat with joy at the thought that I would soon leave the shop. When at last I heard the noon whistle from the big paper factory on Water Street I used to bend my head low to hide this joy. I felt ashamed at my eagerness to leave off work. When I came out into the street I had to stand still for a while and,look about. I felt dazed by the light and the air and the joy of knowing that I was free. For at these moments I did not remember the work at home. I would start to walk along slowly, linger under the trees, of which there was one here and there on Cherry Street, and watch the children on the way home from school to lunch. In their white summery dresses and with books under their arms, they appeared to me like wonderful little beings of a world entirely different from mine. I watched and envied them. But I often consoled myself with the thought, "When our children come they too will go to school."

On the stoop I lingered too. I watched the children playing jacks and from minute to minute I put off going in. At last with a feeling of guilt I would realise that the afternoon was almost gone and my work not even begun. But it was at such moments that I did my best and quickest work. I would rush upstairs, catch up the bundle of soiled clothes under my arm and run down into the cellar to the wash tubs. Once the washing was done I did not feel so guilty, and by the time I was at the floor, which I scrubbed with great swishes of water, I sang cheerfully, "After the Ball is Over."

On Saturday father and I used to go to see Aunt Masha. The first time we went and asked to see her, her mistress opened a door in the back of the store and called in a shrill voice, "Jen-nie—, Jennie." To my surprise it was Aunt Masha that came out.

XXIII

KATE, Mrs. Felesberg's eldest daughter, and I became friends. She was seventeen, tall, flat looking and stooping. But her face was very pretty. Her blue-grey eyes twinkled with mischief and her manner was shy and bold at the same time. She was also a great tease. She teased me constantly because on a Saturday, the Sabbath, I would not light the gas nor carry my handkerchief in my hand on the street, nor would I sit down to a meal at any time before washing my hands and saying grace.

"You are like an old woman," she used to say laughingly. "You are more fit for Palestine where the aged are spending their last days, than for America."

She also called me "little village maiden." I think this hurt most. And so I kept away from her. But there was one thing about Kate to which I finally succumbed. She had a beautiful voice and when she sang I forgave her everything and longed to go to her and finally I did.

And now of an evening I stayed in my room and listened to Kate singing and talking about boys.

Besides the door which led into the hall of the tenement and the one that opened into the Felesberg flat there was still another door in our room. Against this our cot stood. There were two rooms on the other side, in which lived a plump, wrinkled little old woman who wore a bit of red worsted around her wrist to keep off the "Evil Eye." With her lived her son, who was single because he would not marry "a worn out shop girl," and a boarder. Kate talked constantly about the boarder and often half in fun, half in earnest, threw kisses at the door.

She told me that he was a machine operator "but he looked like a student." It was while sitting on the cot, with her eyes on this door, that she sang her best. Her sweet, clear voice filled our dull room, escaped through the window and filled the grey yard. People always stood at the window in the house opposite when Kate sang. And from the other side of the door came little bursts of applause.

One night, after Kate had sung one of her Russian songs, we heard a body press against the door and a boyish voice call through the keyhole, "More! sing more!" Kate became almost hysterical with ecstasy. She gave me a pinch, a nudge and a slap, which she had a habit of doing, when she was gay and excited, and bending down to the keyhole she said, "Supposing you sing now."

"Not after hearing you," he said. "But I would like to see you sing as well as hear. May I come in?"

Kate lifted her flushed face, told me what he said, and giggled. "He wants to come in!"

I was curious to see the boy and watch the two meet but I did not want him to come in because father would be home soon and would want his supper. But as I did not know how to refuse I said, "Let him come." Kate barely had time to settle herself on the cot and control her giggles and I to place the chair for him at the little table, when there was a knock at the door. I opened it and saw a boy about eighteen with pale, thin cheeks and bright dark eyes. He stood expectant and smiling. But his face sobered and he seemed surprised when he saw me. I opened the door wide and when he saw Kate's pink, shimmering face, his own brightened again.

He sat down on the chair and we two girls sat on the cot. Neither of them spoke for a few minutes and Kate did not know where to look. Finally he began in English. Of course, I did not understand what they were saying. They paid no attention to me and soon I forgot them too, though it was about them that I thought. I saw Kate and the boy engaged and married. They were living in a beautiful house on Grand Street where you had to ring a bell to go in. A little one toddled about in their rooms and they were happy. One day suddenly I felt Kate shaking me and saying, "Ruth, Ruth, what shall we do? I hear your father's steps in the hall!" I stood up a little dazed. I saw her run and lock the door. Then bidding the boy a quick farewell she hurried into her own rooms and closed the door behind her. In the meantime father was at this door turning the knob. Finding it locked he knocked gently. Without clearly knowing why, I suddenly felt dreadfully embarrassed and irritated that Kate locked the door. I went and unlocked it and father came in. He saw the visitor at once and stood looking at him, first with surprise, then with astonishment and finally with anger. He went over to the table, put down the loaf of bread which he always brought when he came, and opening the door wide he pointed and said angrily in Russian "Vone!"

When the boy went out and the door was closed father turned to me. His face looked so angry that I trembled.

"This is very pretty conduct," he said. "And you are not yet thirteen."

I began to cry and explain at once. But father never listened to explanations, and commanded me to be silent at the very first word.

The next day I told Kate what father said and how he

felt about me, thinking that she would go and explain to him. But she just laughed.

I felt deeply hurt and disappointed, and I could not forget the boy's face as he left our room.

And now a different life began for me. Father thinking that he had given me too much freedom and had spoiled me went to the other extreme. He began to treat me so severely that I could scarcely lift my head. He suspected me at every step and found fault and blamed me for everything that happened.

One Saturday while standing out on the stoop I saw one little girl show a cent to another and boasting that she was going to buy candy. Seeing money handled on Sabbath had long lost its horror for me. It occurred to me that I too would like to have a cent with which to do just as I pleased. I went up at once to our room and asked father as he lay resting on the cot. He looked at me silently for a long moment. Then he rose slowly, took out his pocket book, took a cent from it, held it out to me, and said with a frown that reminded me of Aunt Masha, "Here, and see that this never happens again."

I felt as if the coin were burning my fingers. I handed it back quickly, left the room and walked about in the streets. I felt mortally hurt. I felt that I was working from morning till night like a grown up person and yet when I wanted one single cent———. When evening came I went home, cooked the rice and milk, as usual, put it on the table and then sat down away from it at the farthest end of the cot. Father ate a few spoonfuls and then commanded: "Sit down at the table and eat your supper."

"I am not hungry," I answered. And indeed I was not. I could never eat when I was miserable. The food always seemed to stick in my throat. Father commanded, "Eat whether you want to or not. Eat because I say so!" Again I repeated that I was not hungry. He looked at me and said: "Oh, you are sulking? Very well, we shall see." Without haste he laid down his spoon, took down our coarse linen roller towel which I brought from home, twisted it carefully into a rope and came over to me. Poor father, I know now that he hated to hurt me and took long to prepare to give me time to change my mind. "Will you eat?" he asked. I coughed to steady my voice and said "No." He struck me across the back. My only thought now was not to cry out. "On the right is the little old woman and her family, on the left the Felesbergs. They will hear me. I'll never be able to raise my head before any of them again." And I prayed for strength.

Father never did anything by halves. I felt the towel across my back again and again. Finally he threw it down and said, panting for breath, "Girl, I'll break you if you don't change." And I said in my heart, "My father, we shall see!"

He turned out the gas, went out, slamming the door after him so that the windows rattled.

When it was all quiet, a door opened in our room and Mrs. Felesberg came in with a light and a bottle of vaseline.

XXIV

Now I felt lonely still oftener. For I missed father's confidence and tenderness and Kate's friendship and to this unhappiness more was soon added.

Father and I were on our block one day, walking toward home, when a boy in uniform coming toward us walked into me with so much force that I stumbled backward a few steps and for a minute could not catch my breath. Father looked at me and began to scold as usual now: "How often have I told you to keep to the right. There is no room for dreamers here."

It had seemed to me that the boy struck against me intentionally but I was not sure. The next day it happened again and now my peace was gone. The boy lived in the same building and as often as I met him he hurt me. He never passed me without shoving his elbow into my side or giving my braid a tug so that it felt as if the skin on my forehead would burst. He was as tall as I was and as my hair reached below my waist, he could do this by a slight movement of the hand while his arm hung innocently at his side. He always did it so quickly that I could never catch him at it and I don't believe any one else ever saw him do it. But his favourite way of hurting was to assume an absent-minded expression when he saw me coming, look about, and walk into me, striking my chest with his elbow. This lasted for weeks and my life became a nightmare to me. I began to be afraid to be out on the street. I never left the building without looking up and down the block first. Now that father treated me so harshly I did not like to talk to him about it, thinking that he would lay the blame on me. And as for striking the boy, it did not even occur to me to do so. He was a messenger boy but I did not know it. And even if I had it would not have made any difference. For I, as my grandfather, looked upon uniforms with fear and respect. And beside too, he was a Gentile and "this country was his."

One Saturday morning I rose earlier than usual. I felt happier than I had been for a long time. I had won my father's favour the day before by doing a particularly hard piece of work. He was so pleased that he showed it to the boss and smiled at me in the old way. At noon when I left to go and do the work at home, he came out with me, took me to a shoe store and bought me shoes.

And so this morning early, as soon as father went to synagogue, I too rose and tidied the room. Then I combed out my hair carefully and let it loose. I put on my brown clean calico and my new shoes. These were my first American shoes and though they were much too large and my feet looked rather clumsy in them,—father believed that clothes for children should be large enough to grow in,—still they were new and the buttons and patent leather tips shone and so I was pleased. As soon as I was quite ready I went out to stand on the stoop. I scarcely ever went walking now, as I was in constant fear of meeting the messenger boy. I had not been on the stoop long when I saw him coming from the Clinton Street side. My heart began to beat so that it pained and all my happiness was gone in a moment. But immediately I comforted myself with the thought that I was on the far end of the stoop and that he could not possibly hurt me when I stood there because the stoop was so wide and he would have to walk up the end he reached first. I pressed close to the iron railing at my end and watched him coming. He walked

with a swagger this morning. When he came nearer I
saw a new cap in place of the old one in which I had
always seen him. The little brass button on each side of
the peak sparkled as he moved his head.

Suddenly he saw me. Immediately he slackened his
pace, assumed his absent-minded expression and began
looking about. My heart beat more violently. What
should I do? Run upstairs? I felt sure he would find
a way to hurt me. But I always hated to run away.
I stood still, almost holding my breath as he came nearer
and nearer. As he walked along slowly he kept looking
dreamily across the street and passed beyond our even
end of the stoop a step or two. Then, as if he suddenly
realised it he stopped, looked about and came back. And
now he must pass close to me. The next moment I felt
my toes crushed under his heel. I caught hold of the iron
railing and closed my eyes for a moment. Then I looked
down at my new shoes. One tip was broken and my toes
inside felt moist. I looked at the boy for he had stopped
right opposite me. He was so sure of me and stood
gazing far away and whistling softly. All at once a
feeling of hatred came into my heart, my temples began
to throb and now I did not see his uniform nor did I
remember, as I had often told myself, that this country of
America was his. With one step I reached him, snatched
off his cap and ran and threw it into the gutter and began
to stamp on it. I broke the brim. I crushed the little brass
buttons under my heels, I stamped it into the dirt and
in a moment it did not look like a cap. But I was not
yet satisfied. A few feet away I saw a little puddle
of water. I kicked the cap into it and began stamping
on it all over again. At last my strength began to give
out and I became aware that a number of people had
gathered and that the boy stood among them, gaping at

me. I stopped stamping, tossed back my hair which had fallen all about my face, and passed close to him. I thought, "If he touches me I'll strike him down." But he did not. The people who stood about were staring at me and talking. When I came upstairs and looked at myself in the glass I thought they must have been saying, "The fury," or "The wild thing." My hair was all tangled and seemed to stand up. My face was dripping wet and covered with pink and white blotches, and my eyes looked wild.

I locked the door and sat all morning laughing and crying hysterically and listening for a policeman's heavy footsteps in the hall. I felt sure that a policeman would come and drag me to prison. But when the day passed and nothing happened I became bolder, and in the evening, when I knew the boy would be coming out of the building, I went out on the street. I was curious now as to what would happen next. The boy came out, saw me and passed me quickly and at a good distance away. I laughed quietly to myself and began to walk toward Montgomery Street, where I saw the light of a street lamp shining on a tree.

XXV

ONE evening in the Fall father came home with two brightly coloured frameless pictures and nailed one on the door leading into the Felesberg's rooms and the other on the door leading into the little old woman's. He explained to me that the pictures were of the two men, nominated for the presidential office. The prospective presidents in these pictures were herdsmen. Each one, dressed in fine black clothes and a high silk hat, stood in the midst of a herd of cattle. In one picture the herdsman was short, stout and clean shaven, the cattle were round and sleek and the pasture green and abundant. In the other it was just the reverse. The herdsman was tall, thin and bearded, the cattle had fallen-in sides, and the ground was brown and bare.

I looked at the pictures and took them literally and seriously. One meant four years of plenty, the other four years of famine. But after a while, noticing that no one else seemed at all worried over it, I merely wondered, "What happens on election day?"

Soon after this I saw the Gentile boys on our block begin to store away, into a cellar, all the barrels, boxes, broken couches, torn mattresses, and every stick of wood they could lay hands on. I understood that the preparations were for election night and I looked on silently with pleasant excitement.

At last election day came. In the shop the men were discussing the candidates and there was a cheerful holiday atmosphere. "I bet you a pint of beer Harrison will be elected." "I bet you two pints it will be Cleveland." In the afternoon I heard the men say they would go home early. When I was leaving father too said he would be home before dark.

After supper I climbed out on Mrs. Felesberg's fire escape and looked down between the bars into the street. I saw the Jewish men hurrying home from work and noticed that very few of the Jewish children were out. The Gentile boys were busy dragging forth the barrels and couches and mattresses and piling them up in a heap in front of the four big tenements inhabited chiefly by Jews.

When it grew dark they lit the heaps of rubbish and in a moment there was a great blaze. The sparks flew, the fire crackled and the reflections of the flames danced merrily on the small red brick houses opposite, where the Gentiles lived. From the windows of these houses groups of people were leaning out talking and laughing merrily. Mrs. Felesberg also stuck her head out of the window for a moment, looked down at the flame and said earnestly: "Thank God, there is no wind. And if it comes I hope it will blow the other way." I was beginning to feel uneasy and wished that father had come home before dark, as he said he would. Scarcely any one passed through the block now. I noticed with fear that not a Jew was to be seen on the street. After a little while I saw some one coming from the Montgomery Street side. Though I expected father to come through Clinton Street it occurred to me that perhaps he had decided this other way was safer, and I strained my eyes and watched. When the person came nearer I saw that it was the son of the little old woman. He walked slowly, hesitatingly and kept to the wall. The men and boys around the fire seemed to pay no attention to his coming, but as soon as he was in front of the fire they suddenly attacked him. There was a short tussle and soon I saw him rushed into the hall.

I was beside myself with fear now. "Why doesn't father come? Why did I leave him?" I could not help blaming myself.

Again Mrs. Felesberg came over and looked out of the window and asked, "Isn't your father here yet, Rahel?"

"No," I shook my head. I could not answer her. I pressed my forehead to the iron bars and looked over to Clinton Street. Every time the fire was poked the whole block was lit up and I could see all the way over to the corner. I thought I saw a figure lurking away over in the shadow. "Could that be father?" I thought. "Perhaps it is some other Jewish man. Oh God, will he ever come!"

At last I saw him turn from Clinton into Cherry Street. The blaze flared suddenly and I recognised his tan suit and hat. I jumped up, leaned over the fire escape and watched him coming nearer and nearer, keeping in the middle of the sidewalk. The boys and men stood about the fire laughing, talking, pushing each other. One was playing on a harmonica and a few were waltzing.

At last I saw father almost opposite the blaze. My heart stood still and my eyes felt stretched so far apart that it seemed as though I could never close them again.

"Will they let him pass? Oh, that is too good to be true." And indeed it was. The next moment I saw a black mass of bodies hurl itself at him.

"Father!" I screamed down. My voice struck terror into my own heart. The next moment I was rushing blindly through Mrs. Felesberg's rooms, lit only by the blaze from the outside, knocking myself against table and chairs. At last I was out in the hall and went fall-

ing and tumbling down stairs.   On the first floor I met
him coming up, pale and hatless.   We stopped and looked
at each other.   I was beside myself with joy to see him
alive but I heard myself say, "Father, your hat!"   And
he smiled and said pantingly, "That is nothing, I needed
a new one."

I saw the Jewish men hurrying home from work.

XXVI

I HAD seen from the first that Jews were treated roughly on Cherry Street. I had seen the men and boys that stood about the saloons at every corner make ugly grimaces at the passing Jews and throw after them stones and shoes pulled out of the ash cans. I had often seen these "loafers," as we called them, attack a Jewish pedlar, dump his push cart of apples into the gutter, fill their pockets and walk away laughing and eating. I had run for the apples in the gutter, rolling in every direction, and helped to pick them up. I myself had often walked two blocks out of my way to reach home through Montgomery Street instead of going through Clinton Street where there were three saloons. And yet as soon as I was safe in the house.I scarcely gave the matter a second thought. Perhaps it was because to see a Jew maltreated was nothing new for me. Here where there were so many new and strange things for me to see and understand this was the one familiar thing. I had grown used to seeing strange Jews mistreated whenever they happened to come to our village in Russia.

But after election night I felt differently. I was haunted by the picture of the little old woman's son struggling with the young Irish-Americans near the bonfire, and of my father coming up the stairs, pale and hatless. I was never easy in my mind now except when I was with father. I always sat up at night until he came home; and if he happened to be a few minutes late I was beside myself with fear. I pictured him murdered and burned alive. I listened to every tale about Cherry and Water Streets. I heard that a policeman had

been found in a dark hallway with his head stuck into a
barrel, smothered to death.   And for a time I could
think about nothing else.

One Friday afternoon, soon after election, I finished
my washing and cleaning early and I went out into
the street.   I was returning about five o'clock through
Clinton Street when I saw a Jewish pedlar with a push
cart standing on the corner of Monroe Street and looking about helplessly.   I saw him watching me as I came
up.   When I was near he asked, "Are you Jewish?"   I
nodded my head and stopped.   I saw that his push cart
held fish, mixed with chunks of ice.   "You can do me a
favour," he said in a pleading tone.   "You see this hand-
ful of fish?   This is all my profit.   If I could get over to
that group of Jewish houses on Cherry Street," he
pointed to our tenements, "I could still sell it though it is
late.   But I dare not pass those loafers hanging around
the saloons."   "But, what can I do?" I asked.   "You can
do much," he said with a smile.   "They have great respect for a lady in America."

"But——" I began.   "That is all right," he said with a
wave of the hand.   "You look like a lady.   And if you
will just walk beside me while I am passing the loafers,
they won't touch me."   I remembered now often having
seen Jewish men escorted past dangerous places.   And
the women would as often be Irish.

I stepped into the gutter, and for greater safety laid
my hand on the push cart and walked along beside him.
When we were passing the saloon the "loafers" made
grimaces and shouted after him, but did not touch him.
We stopped at our group of houses.   He thanked me
and at once became business-like.   He shook up the ice
in the push cart and then placing his hand at one corner
of his mouth, American fashion, and looking up at the

windows he shouted lustily: "Hurry, hurry, women! Fresh pike here, fresh pike for the Sabbath."

I found that father was already at home. As I came into the room I saw him sitting at the table before the little mirror resting against the wall, clipping his beard. I was so surprised and shocked to see him actually do this thing that I could neither speak nor move for some minutes. And I knew that he too felt embarrassed. After the first glance I kept my eyes steadily on the floor in front of me and began to talk to him quietly but with great earnestness.

"You had been so pious at home, father," I said, "more pious than any one else in our whole neighbourhood. And now you are cutting your beard. Grandmother would never have believed it. How she would weep!"

The snipping of the scissors still went on. But I knew by the sound that now he was only making a pretence at cutting. At last he laid it down and said in a tone that was bitter yet quiet:

"They do not like Jews on Cherry Street. And one with a long beard has to take his life into his own hands."

"But, father," I said, looking at him now, "must we live on Cherry Street?"

"Yes, we must," he said, turning to me quickly and speaking in a more passionate tone. "They want the Jews to come and settle here. And because it is so hard to live here they have lowered the rents. I save here at least two dollars a month. You don't understand. For mother's journey we need not only tickets and money for other expenses, but we also need money for at least second-hand furniture. This is not like home. There the house was our own. And for the lot and garden we paid one dollar a year. There, too, we were among friends and relatives. While here, if we haven't rent for one month we are thrown out on the street. Do you understand?"

I said I understood.

XXVII

FATHER began to strain all his energy to save the money to send for mother and the children. In the shop one morning I realised that he had been leaving out of his breakfast the tiny glass of brandy for two cents and was eating just the roll. So I too made my sacrifice. When as usual he gave me the apple and the roll, I took the roll but refused the apple. And he did not urge me. When a cold grey day at the end of November found him in his light tan suit quite worn and me in my thin calico frock, now washed out to a tan colour, we went to a second-hand clothing store on Division Street and he bought me a fuzzy brown coat reaching a little below my waist, for fifty cents, and for himself a thin thread-bare overcoat. And now we were ready for the winter.

About the same time that the bitter cold came father told me one night that he had found work for me in a shop where he knew the presser. I lay awake long that night. I was eager to begin life on my own responsibility but was also afraid. We rose earlier than usual that morning for father had to take me to the shop and not be over late for his own work. I wrapped my thimble and scissors, with a piece of bread for breakfast, in a bit of newspaper, carefully stuck two needles into the lapel of my coat and we started.

The shop was on Pelem Street, a shop district one block long and just wide enough for two ordinary sized wagons to pass each other. We stopped at a door where I noticed at once a brown shining porcelain knob and a half rubbed off number seven. Father looked at his watch and at me.

"Don't look so frightened," he said. "You need not go in until seven. Perhaps if you start in at this hour he will think you have been in the habit of beginning at seven and will not expect you to come in earlier. Remember, be independent. At seven o'clock rise and go home no matter whether the others go or stay."

He began to tell me something else but broke off suddenly, said "good-bye" over his shoulder and went away quickly. I watched him until he turned into Monroe Street.

Now only I felt frightened, and waiting made me nervous, so I tried the knob. The door yielded heavily and closed slowly. I was half way up when it closed entirely, leaving me in darkness. I groped my way to the top of the stairs and hearing a clattering noise of machines, I felt about, found a door, and pushed it open and went in. A tall, dark, beardless man stood folding coats at a table. I went over and asked him for the name (I don't remember what it was). "Yes," he said crossly. "What do you want?"

I said, "I am the new feller hand." He looked at me from head to foot. My face felt so burning hot that I could scarcely see.

"It is more likely," he said, "that you can pull bastings than fell sleeve lining." Then turning from me he shouted over the noise of the machine: "Presser, is this the girl?" The presser put down the iron and looked at me. "I suppose so," he said, "I only know the father."

The cross man looked at me again and said, "Let's see what you can do." He kicked a chair, from which the back had been broken off, to the finisher's table, threw a coat upon it and said raising the corner of his mouth: "Make room for the new feller hand."

One girl tittered, two men glanced at me over their

shoulders and pushed their chairs apart a little. By this time I scarcely knew what I was about. I laid my coat down somewhere and pushed my bread into the sleeve. Then I stumbled into the bit of space made for me at the table, drew in the chair and sat down. The men were so close to me on each side I felt the heat of their bodies and could not prevent myself from shrinking away. The men noticed and probably felt hurt. One made a joke, the other laughed and the girls bent their heads low over their work. All at once the thought came: "If I don't do this coat quickly and well he will send me away at once." I picked up the coat, threaded my needle, and began hastily, repeating the lesson father impressed upon me. "Be careful not to twist the sleeve lining, take small false stitches."

My hands trembled so that I could not hold the needle properly. It took me a long while to do the coat. But at last it was done. I took it over to the boss and stood at the table waiting while he was examining it. He took long, trying every stitch with his needle. Finally he put it down and without looking at me gave me two other coats. I felt very happy! When I sat down at the table I drew my knees close together and stitched as quickly as I could.

When the pedlar came into the shop everybody bought rolls. I felt hungry but I was ashamed and would not eat the plain, heavy rye bread while the others ate rolls.

All day I took my finished work and laid it on the boss's table. He would glance at the clock and give me other work. Before the day was over I knew that this was a "piece work shop," that there were four machines and sixteen people were working. I also knew that I had done almost as much work as "the grown-up girls"

and that they did not like me.   I heard Betsy, the head
feller hand, talking about "a snip of a girl coming and
taking the very bread out of your mouth."   The only one
who could have been my friend was the presser who
knew my father.   But him I did not like.   The worst I
knew about him just now was that he was a soldier because the men called him so.   But a soldier, I had
learned, was capable of anything.   And so, noticing that
he looked at me often, I studiously kept my eyes from his
corner of the room.

Seven o'clock came and every one worked on.   I
wanted to rise as father had told me to do and go home.
But I had not the courage to stand up alone.   I kept putting off going from minute to minute.   My neck felt
stiff and my back ached.   I wished there were a back
to my chair so that I could rest against it a little.   When
the people began to go home it seemed to me that it had
been night a long time.

XXVIII

THE next morning when I came into the shop at seven o'clock, I saw at once that all the people were there and working as steadily as if they had been at work a long while. I had just time to put away my coat and go over to the table, when the boss shouted gruffly, "Look here, girl, if you want to work here you better come in early. No office hours in my shop." It seemed very still in the room, even the machines stopped. And his voice sounded dreadfully distinct. I hastened into the bit of space between the two men and sat down. He brought me two coats and snapped, "Hurry with these!"

From this hour a hard life began for me. He refused to employ me except by the week. He paid me three dollars and for this he hurried me from early until late. He gave me only two coats at a time to do. When I took them over and as he handed me the new work he would say quickly and sharply, "Hurry!" And when he did not say it in words he looked at me and I seemed to hear even more plainly, "Hurry!" I hurried but he was never satisfied. By looks and manner he made me feel that I was not doing enough. Late at night when the people would stand up and begin to fold their work away and I too would rise feeling stiff in every limb and thinking with dread of our cold empty little room and the uncooked rice, he would come over with still another coat.

"I need it the first thing in the morning," he would give as an excuse. I understood that he was taking advantage of me because I was a child. And now that it was dark in the shop except for the low single gas jet over my table and the one over his at the other end of the room, and there was no one to see, more tears fell on the sleeve lining as I bent over it than there were stitches in it.

I did not soon complain to father. I had given him an idea of the people and the work during the first days. But when I had been in the shop a few weeks I told him, "The boss is hurrying the life out of me." I know now that if I had put it less strongly he would have paid more attention to it. Father hated to hear things put strongly. Besides he himself worked very hard. He never came home before eleven and he left at five in the morning.

He said to me now, "Work a little longer until you have more experience; then you can be independent."

"But if I did piece work, father, I would not have to hurry so. And I could go home earlier when the other people go."

Father explained further, "It pays him better to employ you by the week. Don't you see if you did piece work he would have to pay you as much as he pays a woman piece worker? But this way he gets almost as much work out of you for half the amount a woman is paid."

I myself did not want to leave the shop for fear of losing a day or even more perhaps in finding other work. To lose half a dollar meant that it would take so much longer before mother and the children would come. And now I wanted them more than ever before. I longed for my mother and a home where it would be light and warm and she would be waiting when we came from work. Because I longed for them so I lived much in imagination. For so I could have them near me. Often as the hour for going home drew near I would sit stitching and making believe that mother and the children were home waiting. On leaving the shop I would hasten along through the street keeping my eyes on the ground so as to shut out everything but what I wanted to see. I pictured myself walking into the house. There was a delicious warm smell of cooked food. Mother greeted me near the door and the children gathered about me shouting and trying to pull me down. Mother scolded them saying, "Let her take her coat off, see how cold her hands are!" But they paid no attention and pulled me down to them. Their little arms were about my neck, their warm faces against my cold cheeks and we went tumbling all over each other. Soon mother called, "Supper is ready." There was a scampering and a rush to the table, followed by a scraping of chairs and a clattering of dishes. Finally we were all seated. There was browned meat and potatoes for supper.

I used to keep this up until I turned the key in the door and opened it and stood facing the dark, cold, silent room.

XXIX

In proportion as life in the shop became harder, it also became harder at home. I had to do the washing and cleaning at night now. One night a week I cleaned and one I washed. I used to hang my dress on a string over Mrs. Felesberg's stove to dry over night. In the morning I pulled it straight and put it right on. The rest of the night I slept. During these days I could not seem to get enough sleep. Sometimes when I remembered how a few months before mother had to chase me to bed with cries and with scoldings it hardly seemed true. That time seemed so far away, so vague, like a dream.

Now on coming into the room I would light the lamp and the kerosene oil stove and put on the soup to cook. Then I would sit down with my knees close to the soap box on which the stove stood, to keep myself warm. But before long my body relaxed, my head grew heavy with the odour of the burning oil and I longed to lie down. I knew that it was bad to go to sleep without supper. Two or three times father woke me. But it was no use, I could not eat then. And so I tried hard to keep awake. But finally I could not resist it. The cot was so near, just a step away. I could touch it with my hand. I would rise a little from the chair and all bent over as I was, I would tumble right in and roll myself in the red comforter, clothes and all. It was on these nights that I began to forget to pray.

But it was only during the first part of the night that I slept heavily. After that I was half asleep, half awake. I was in constant fear of being late to work. Often in the middle of the night I would wake up with a start, tumble out of bed, scarcely conscious of what I was about, and run to the clock which we put on the table for the night. There I stood peering at it unseeingly for a long while. Gradually I would realise where I was, what I was about and that I must see the time. And only now I could see the hands of the clock distinctly, both on the twelve perhaps. How happy I felt when it was still so early. With what a feeling of joy and relief I lay back on the pillow and closed my eyes. But if I happened to wake near five I would not close them again for fear of oversleeping. That was about the time that father left.

One morning when I started up into a half sitting position I saw at once that the light in the lamp was turned up a little and on the table lay the larger part of the loaf of bread. And so I knew that father had gone. I peered at the clock and it seemed to me that it was a quarter to seven, very late. With my eyes half shut I slid out of bed hastily and began to dress, seeing all the while the boss's eyes glaring at me threateningly. It did not take me long to put on my frock, and the coat I always put on as soon as I had the dress on because it was so bitter cold in the room. I buttoned every other button on my shoes, and just smoothed my hair back, leaving the tangles for Saturday. I broke off a hunk of bread, snatched a piece of newspaper and blew out the light. As I felt my way to the door and through the dark hall it struck me how quiet it was at the Felesbergs and the little old woman's and all through the house. At other times when I started the whole building was full of life. Now as I was passing I just heard a door open and close softly, and a slight noiseless movement here and there. In my hurry I did not stop to think about it but hastened on. I drew the street door open. The next moment a

fierce gust of wind tore it from my hand and closed it
with a bang. I had seen that a heavy snow had fallen
over night. I stood for a moment shivering with cold
and fear. Then I wound my braid around my neck under
the collar, and pulling the hair over my ears a little, I
drew the door open again and stepped out quickly. There
were no steps. It all looked flat and white. The wind
moaned and whistled and here and there a huddled dark
form hurried along over the white. I tucked my bread
under my arm, slipped, muff-wise, each bare hand into
the opposite sleeve and started to run. I seemed to be
running very fast and yet I saw that I was making little
headway. The wind was fearful. It struck against my
chest constantly. At one moment it wound my calico
skirt about my knees and I could not take a step. The
next it blew it way up in the air and I had to put it
down with my hands. I stopped and took some minutes
to unbutton my coat with my stiffened fingers and to
fold the fronts tightly over each other on my chest. The
cold lay on it like an iron weight and I could not breathe.
Then I bent my head before the wind and ran on. Soon
I was exhausted. "Where am I?" I wondered. I stopped
and looked about. It looked so unfamiliar with all the
white under foot and the rows of houses on each side of
me standing so still. They looked like stone walls. "It
is like a prison," I thought. Suddenly it seemed to me
that I was in prison and the dark forms were pursuing
me and I ran in terror. I turned this way and that way,
not knowing nor heeding now where I was going. My
skirt flapped and the wind blew the snow into my face
blinding me as I ran. I tried to run clear of the walls
but I saw that they were on each side of me enclosing
me whichever way I turned. I finally came into a space
where I felt the walls rose higher than ever and the space

between grew narrow. There was something familiar to me in that, though I dared not look about. I ran to a door, stopped and clung to it and pressed my face against it. My eyes closed. My numb fingers groped until they found and closed over something which they recognised at once.

Instinctively I had run to the shop. And now I stood before the door holding on to the brown porcelain knob. I was never so happy before to see the shop door. I leaned against the door and looked at the dark windows of the shops opposite and realised gradually that I had left home too early. "The shop must be closed," I thought. "I must wait here until it opens." I pressed into the corner of the door. The wind kept flapping and fluttering my dress and sweeping the snow back and forth before me. Soon I felt my knees bending of their own accord and so I sat down. I saw my bread slip from under my arm. It made me feel a little uneasy to see it lying there on the snow. And so I watched it for a moment. I put out my hand to tuck my dress about me and I felt my head lean back against the door. I was beginning to feel very comfortable. I seemed to be sitting on something soft and I no longer felt the cold. The wind was growing quieter, and quieter, and the street lights shone so faintly.

I felt a slight pressure on my arm, then it became heavier. And soon I felt myself being shaken quite roughly and a familiar voice saying, "For God's sake, girl, what are you doing here?"

It was the presser from our shop. He helped me up and asked me again what I was doing there. I wanted to explain but could not move my tongue. So I just looked at him.

"Come quickly into the shop," he said. He caught

hold of my arm, pushed the door open and pulled me along with him. Even now I remembered that he was a soldier and tried to draw back. But I doubt whether he even felt my resistance. He drew me along into the hall and up the dark narrow stairs. He unlocked the door, propped me up against a wall and said, "Now stand here until I light the gas." When there was a light he put me on a chair near the fireplace, covered me up with coats and then began hurriedly to shovel the ashes out of the grate into a pail. I kept my teeth closed tightly and sat watching his every movement. He soon had a crackling fire. He lifted my chair close to it and made me hold my hands out. I saw him empty one little bundle of wood after another into the grate. "I won't put any coal on until you are quite warm," he said; "it would take too long to burn up." Then he mumbled to himself, "When he sees how much wood I used this morning he will hang himself and I'll never hear the end of it."

When my tongue had thawed a little I told him how I happened to be out so early. Then he asked me whether I had anything to eat. I remembered that I had dropped my bread near the door on the snow and told him so. He went out and found it. "Good!" he said, "you have bread and I have some slices of smoked salmon." He took it out of his overcoat pocket, wrapped in a paper, drew a chair close to the fire, sat down and held it out to me.

I said, "I don't care for any." He looked offended. "If you won't accept anything," he said, "it means that you would not give anything of yours either." To show him that it was not so, I began at once to break my bread in half. But my fingers were still too numb so I gave it to him. "Good!" he said again, "you will take half of my salmon and I'll take half of your bread."

He cut the bread with his penknife which he never for a moment let go out of his hand.

"It is from home," meaning from Russia, he said, flashing the blades before me.

While we sat eating and holding our hands to the fire he told me about himself. He said that he had escaped from the Russian army a year before and that his wife and two year old little girl were still in Russia. He was trying to save and send for them. As I watched his face while he was talking I wondered that I ever disliked him. I thought now that he had a very kind face and if it were not for his long moustache which he often twirled, he would have been good looking.

I also told him about father and myself and mother and the children in Russia. I told him that we hoped to send for them in the spring. "That is why I am working so hard," I said, looking at him earnestly. He looked at me too and his eyes seemed to be laughing at me. But he said seriously, "Yes, you have to sweat for your slice of bread." He rose and stood for a moment looking at the door and listening. "There he comes, the Vampire," he said. "I hear his footsteps in the hall."

XXX

THAT morning I could not get warm in the shop. The boss gave me three coats to do instead of two, by mistake I thought. I spread two on my lap and the third I hugged close to my chest as I worked on it. I should have also liked to keep my own coat on. But I was afraid that if he knew how cold I was he would think I could not do as much work and would send me home and make me lose half a day's pay. Chills were running up and down my back and I could scarcely bend my fingers to hold the needle and I pricked my thumb. My fingers were so numb that I did not feel it. Indeed I did not know it until I saw a tiny red stain on the white sleeve lining. I looked and looked at it, and could not at once believe my eyes and my heart pounded with fear. I wondered: "Shall I take it to the boss at once? He will make me pay for it. How much is a sleeve lining? Fifty cents, perhaps even a dollar." I determined not to show it to him at once. I finished it, folded it and laid it on the floor under my chair.

When I finished the other two coats I took them over to the boss. I felt sick at the very thought that he might ask me for the third one. But he did not. He looked at me crossly and wanted to know whether I was sleeping over my work.

All morning I sat thinking about the blood stain and wondering what the price of a sleeve lining was. Finally I could not stand it. I had to know. I bent over the table toward Betsy and asked how much a sleeve lining is. "Why?" she wanted to know. "I am just wondering," I said. She looked at me sharply. "Have you damaged one?" she asked.

My face began to burn. I bent my head low over my work and did not answer.

For the noon meal all went out except the presser and Betsy. I pulled the coat out from under my chair and looked at it. I was so miserable that I could not help crying. Betsy looked at me in surprise and the presser came over. I showed them the stain. The presser thought he could take it out with benzine. He took it over to his table and there he rubbed and rubbed it with a tiny cloth, and held it away from him, and looked at it from all sides. Finally he became impatient. "An unusual thing a stain on a coat," he said, and flung it into the pile on the boss's table.

XXXI

ONE day I noticed that there was a good deal of whispering among the men in the shop. At noon when all went out to lunch and I ran out to get a slice of cheese for mine, I saw that the men had gathered on the street before the door. They were eating sandwiches, stamping about over the snow and disputing in anxious earnest whispers.

In the shop the boss looked gloomier than ever.

"I'll not have any one coming into my shop and telling me what to do," he shouted to a strange man who came over to his table to talk to him. "This shop is mine. The machines are mine. If they are willing to work on my conditions, well and good, if not, let them go to the devil! All the tailors are not dead yet."

At our table Betsy whispered: "The men joined the union. The boss is in a hurry for the work." There was a twinkle in Betsy's usually lifeless eyes.

I had no idea what a union meant or what all this trouble was about. But I learned a little the next day. When I came in a little after six in the morning, I found only the three girls who were at my table. Not a man except the boss was in the shop. The men came in about five minutes to seven and then stood or sat at the presser's table talking and joking quietly. The boss stood at his table brushing coats furiously. Every minute or so he glanced at the clock and his face looked black with anger.

At the first stroke of seven the presser blew a whistle and every man went to his place. At the minute of twelve the presser again blew the whistle and the men went out to their noon meal. Those who remained in the shop ate without hurry and read their newspapers. The boss kept his eye on us girls. We began last, ate hurriedly and sat down to work at once. Betsy looked at the men reading their newspapers and grumbled in a whisper, "This is what it means to belong to a union. You get time to straighten out your bones." I knew that Betsy had been a feller hand for many years. Her back was quite bent over and her hands were white and flabby.

The men returned a little before one and sat waiting for the stroke of the clock and the presser's whistle. At seven in the evening when the presser blew his whistle the men rose almost with one movement, put away their work and turned out the lights over their tables and machines. We girls watched them go enviously and the boss turned his back towards the door. He did not answer their "Good-night." In the dark and quiet that followed his great shears clipped loudly and angrily.

One Saturday afternoon father came home and showed me a little book with a red paper cover which he took from his breast pocket. "This," he said, "is my union book. You too must join the union." He told me he had heard that a few of the feller hands had organized, and a mass meeting was to be held in a hall on Clinton Street that evening. He took me to the door of the building at eight o'clock, saw a young woman enter and told me to follow her. As I had no idea what a meeting was like or what to expect I was dazed and dazzled by the great number of lights, the red carpet covering the floor, and the crowd of people already seated on benches along the walls. The middle of the room was not used.

I glanced about from the doorway for a seat nearby. But the only ones I could see were in front. And for

this I finally aimed, looking neither to right nor to left
and feeling painfully conscious of my shabbiness. The
seat I was forced to take was right in front and only
about two yards away from the small square platform.
I was so uneasy at being exposed from all sides that it
was some time before I forgot my bare head, my red
hands with the cracked and bleeding skin and my shoes
with their turned up noses—already worn out and still
too large for me. By that time a young man was standing on the platform speaking. I had seen this young
man two or three times before. He lived on Cherry
Street a few doors away from us, and Kate Felesberg
had told me once that he was a "student." What he was
saying now was something like this:

"Fourteen hours a day you sit on a chair, often without a back, felling coats. Fourteen hours you sit close
to the other feller hand feeling the heat of her body
against yours, her breath on your face. Fourteen hours
with your back bent, your eyes close to your work you
sit stitching in a dull room often by gas light. In the
winter during all these hours as you sit stitching your
body is numb with cold. In the summer, as far as you are
concerned, there might be no sun, no green grass, no
soft breezes. You with your eyes close to the coat on
your lap are sitting and sweating the livelong day. The
black cloth dust eats into your very pores. You are
breathing the air that all the other bent and sweating
bodies in the shop are throwing off, and the air that
comes in from the yard heavy and disgusting with filth
and the odour of the open toilets.

"If any of you know this, and think about it, you say
to yourselves, no doubt, 'What is the use of making a
fuss? Will the boss pay any attention to me if I should
talk to him? And anyway it won't be for long. I won't

stay in the shop all my life. I'll—perhaps this year, or next——.' Girls, I know your thought. You expect to get married! Not so quick! Even the man who works in a shop himself does not want to marry a white-faced dull-eyed girl who for years has been working fourteen hours a day. He realises that you left your strength in the shop, and that to marry you he would take on a bundle of troubles, and doctor's bills on his head. You know what he does most often? He sends to Russia for a girl he once knew, one who has never seen the inside of a shop. Or else he marries the little servant girl with the red cheeks and bright eyes.

"And even if you do marry, are you so secure? Don't forget that your husband himself is working in the shop fourteen hours and more a day, breathing the filthy air and the cloth dust. How long will he last? Who knows! You may have to go back to the shop. And even worse than this may be awaiting you. Your children may have to go to the shop! And unless you, now, change it, they may have to go back to the same dull shops, the filthy air and the fourteen hours. In the winter before daylight your little daughter may have to run through the streets in the rain and the snow in her worn little shoes, and thin coat. She will stand trembling before the boss in the same dull shop, perhaps, where you had once stood. She will sit in the same backless chair, rickety now, with her little back bent, for fourteen hours."

He seemed to be looking right at me. I tucked my feet far under my seat and bent my head to hide my tears. "Who is this man?" I wondered; "how does he know all this?"

He continued: "Each one of you alone can do nothing. Organise! Demand decent wages that you may be able to live in a way fit for human beings, not for

swine. See that your shop has pure air and sun, that
your bodies may be healthy. Demand reasonable hours
that you may have time to know your families, to think,
to enjoy. Organise! Each one of you alone can do nothing. Together you can gain everything."

For a moment the room was perfectly still. Then
there was a storm of applause and the people rose and
began to press close to the platform. I went to a vacant
seat in an out-of-the-way corner and watched the people
going out in groups and talking excitedly. When the
hall was almost empty I went over to the secretary's
desk. "I want to join the union," I said.

Our feller hands had not been at the meeting but they
too had joined the union. And now our shop was a
"strictly union shop." I'll always remember how proud
I felt when the first evening at seven o'clock the presser
blew the whistle and I with the other girls stood up with
the men. But not many girls joined the union. And so,
it was soon broken up. During these weeks I began to
go to night school. I went to the class right from the
shop without supper, for the doors of the school closed
at half past seven. When I came into the class, the
lights, the warmth to which I was not used, and the
girls reading in a slow monotonous tone, one after another, would soon put me to sleep. Before I dropped off
the first night I learned one word, "Sometimes." It was
the longest word on the page and stood out among the
rest.

I left the shop soon after the union broke up. I don't
remember why or how it happened. The boss of the
next shop where father found work for me was kind.
The first morning when I came in to work, seeing the
girls put me at the end of the table where it was dark,
he came over and made them let me sit near the window.

"She is still a little girl," he said. "She must grow."
And at night he told me that I need not stay after half
past seven. He was kind to me in other ways too. I
had an unfortunate habit of losing needles. It always
seemed to me that I put my needle away quite carefully
after I broke off the thread; but when I needed it again
I could seldom find it. And as father never gave me
more than one or two needles at a time I was often in
great distress. One day when I lost my needle and was
looking about on the floor, on the table, and in my dress
and feeling very miserable, he came over and asked me
very seriously, "What's wrong?" I felt that the time I
was wasting was his and I mumbled guiltily: "I lost my
needle." Without a word he went over to the men, borrowed two needles at once and brought them to me.
After this whenever he saw me looking about for my
needle, he would take a whole packet out of his breast
pocket and give me one or two, and say laughingly,
"Here, Ruth, is a needle, and don't look so unhappy." As
he was not a tailor I knew that he kept the packet of
needles to have them to give to me.

I felt happy in this shop. The men sat at a separate
table and I never heard an unkind or obscene word.
Every night I had something to tell father about the
boss's kindness. Father was glad that I was so fortunate
and often told me, "Try your best to keep this place."
And I did. I worked as quickly and as well as I could.

One Friday when the boss was paying his workers he
said to me, "Ruth, I am short of money. Do you mind
coming over to my home to-morrow morning at ten
o'clock for yours?" I said I did not mind. Indeed I
was glad I could do something for him though it was so
little.

Since I had been working in this shop and was not

so hard driven and humiliated, I blossomed out again. My hair was always well combed out and on Saturdays I wore it loose. Now too I was wearing new shoes. And I had a new navy blue cashmere dress, the first dress I had ever had, that was not home-made and too large for me, and it cost me a week's wages and many tears. But it was worth it. It was so pretty and gave me a great deal of joy. With this dress even my yellowish brown coat did not look so bad.

So dressed, and feeling very cheerful, I started out the next morning a little before ten. I ran and skipped over the snow, and clapped my hands together often to keep warm. I found my boss in a room I thought gorgeous with its carpeted floor and upholstered chairs. He was alone. I saw and felt at once that there was not the calm and quietness about him to which I was accustomed. He greeted me in the middle of the room, touched my hair with his fingers, and then went and sat down. I remained standing. "You look very holiday like," he said. I thought he too looked "holiday like." He was wearing a new blue suit, his brown hair lay smoother than ever and his dark reddish moustache was curled. After a moment or so he said quite abruptly, "Come, Ruth, sit down here." He motioned to his knee. I felt my face flush. I backed away towards the door and stood staring at him. He too sat quite still looking at me. Then he rose and with his usual slowness and quietness put his hand into his pocket, took out a roll of bills, counted off three dollars, and brought it over to me at the door. "Tell your father," he said, "to find you a new shop for to-morrow morning."

I walked home weeping bitterly. I did not know what I should tell my father.

In my next shop there was only a single set. The

boss himself was the machine operator and of course there was the baster, a finisher and a presser and I was the feller hand. And at the end of the week the boss would leave his machine and run out to Hester, corner Orchard Street, the tailors' "hangout," and bring a man for a couple of days to put the finishing touches on the coats before they went out to the warehouse. Shops of this kind were called "One horse wagons."

This boss was also single. He was an ill-natured young man. He was tall and so thin that he looked all dried up. He did not trust any one, any further than he could see. Instead of having his machine face the window, like other operators, he sat with his back to it and faced the room so that he could see every one of us. Me he kept at his machine, making me use a corner of it, as my table, so that he could have me constantly under his eye. He scolded and teased and swore from morning until night. He told us every day in the week that we were not earning our money, that we were botchers, that we had nothing to worry us, while his hair was turning grey, that every year he was losing a hundred dollars while we risked nothing and lost nothing. We were only getting money which we were not earning. His voice as he talked sounded through the shop like the drone of a bee—except that it was full of poison. Bits of white foam would soon gather in the corners of his thin mouth. And I used to imagine that the blood in his veins boiled and bubbled as water boils and bubbles in a kettle over a fire.

He employed only the cheapest kind of labor and so he was in constant trouble in the warehouse. He never sent a lot of coats without receiving some back to fix. He always made me do the fixing, as my time was the least valuable. He would stand at the back of my chair

and while showing me what to do he would pour out all
his wrath on me.   On these nights when I rose to go
home I could not straighten my back.   And though it
was often bitter cold when I came out on the street I
walked home slowly, keeping near the wall.

One day, instead of bringing the work home to be
fixed the boss took me along to the warehouse and made
me do it there.   When I told father about it in the evening he got the idea that I was a very valuable hand and
told me to ask for a raise on Friday.   All week I could
not get the thought out of my mind, that I must ask for
a raise.   When Friday came and it was time to go home
I kept putting off talking to the boss until all the other
workers were gone and I was alone.   At last I put on my
coat and went and stood at his machine.

"What do you want?" he snapped.   I could not get
the words out of my mouth at once.   At last I said
weakly, "I want a raise."

He dropped the work on his machine and sat staring
at me.   The light of the gas jet over his machine fell
full on his skeleton-like face.   The expression of hatred
in it frightened me, but I stood still.   Finally he said between his teeth, "Say it again.   Let me hear you say
it again and I'll throw you down the four flights of
stairs."

I went to the door and said, "I want my pay."

He bent his head over his work and said, "I haven't
any now.   You will get it Sunday morning when you
come to work."

When I told it to father he said, "When you get your
pay Sunday you won't go there again."

Sunday morning when I came to the shop I found all
our men gathered on the street before the door.   The
presser looked at me.   "I am afraid, little girl," he said,

"you are going to have a rest now. The shop is closed and the boss is nowhere to be seen. We have just sent a man to his home." Soon the man came back and said that the boss had not been seen in his boarding place since Friday night. The presser looked at each one of us, one after the other, "How long does it take to go to Canada? Twenty-four hours? Well, then, he is probably there now." The baster collapsed on the doorstep. He was a grey little old man. He had been sick and this week's wages were the first he had earned in a long while.

I stood a while, then I walked away from the shop. "Where next," I wondered.

XXXII

AND now I came into Mr. Cohen's shop. I had to work here as hard as in any of the other places. But of this shop I think with pleasure, because here every one, from Mr. Cohen to the little boy in knee pants who came after school hours to pull basting, was good and kind. Here too there was just a single set. Mr. Cohen himself was the baster. All day he sat on his big table with his legs crossed and worked very hard to save the wages he would have had to pay a baster, and do his own part of the work too. The machine operator was his partner. He was a small shy young man with a very pink face, small black moustache and eyes. When he was angry no one ever paid any attention to him because he wasn't really angry. He could not be. His name was Fine, and Gussie, the feller hand, used to say that he was as fine as his name.

One day Mr. Cohen was showing me how to make the little bars in the corners of the coat pockets. Finding that I learned it very quickly, he conceived the idea of teaching me other parts of the trade so that I could help out all the "big" people. And so I helped Gussie, who sat right opposite me at the narrow bench-like table, with the felling, and she taught me how to cross-stitch labels. I helped the finisher who sat next to me. This was the part of the work that father had taught me. And Mr. Cohen taught me how to sew on buttons, which was considered an art in itself. For a properly sewed-on button on a coat has to stand up high and stiff and straight as though on a leg. Mr. Cohen showed frankly that I was a valuable hand and that he was pleased with me and paid me three and a half dollars instead of three which I had been getting.

And so now again I lifted my head a little. My work was more interesting because it had variety. I liked variety, and I liked the people, all except the presser. He was the only one in the shop that used vulgar and obscene language.

In this shop when the time to go home came it used to please me to stay a few minutes longer. It was always Mr. Cohen's partner who reminded me that it was time to go home. He nearly always said the same thing "Ruth, you look so busy! Aren't you going home tonight?" I liked to hear him say it. I liked to feel that some one was concerned about me. I used to sit and wait for it.

Sunday morning no one worked very steadily. The men used to talk over the amusements of the day before. I used to hear them talk about Shakespeare's plays, the Jewish theatre, Jacob Adler in the Jewish King Lear. I listened to them and wondered, "Who is Shakespeare? What are plays? Who is Jacob Adler who makes such a wonderful King Lear?"

About this time my own Saturdays became less dull than they had been. Aunt Masha left her place as nurse girl. In reality she had been a general house maid. She had had to cook, scrub and wash. She had had to eat in a windowless little kitchen at the wash tub and sleep on the floor. She said she was utterly tired of this kind of life and wanted to try the shop. Father soon found her one where the boss was willing to teach her how to fell coats on condition that she would work for three dollars a week for some time after. And so she moved into a tiny bedroom with two other girls and I saw her more often. On a Saturday morning now she would come, supervise the washing of my hair, and tell me quite often that I was as stubborn as ever. And in the afternoon she would take me along with her to visit her friends. Usually the young men and women gathered in some one's home and spent the whole afternoon singing and dancing Russian dances. None of them paid any attention to me or thought of asking me to join them. I used to sit down in an out-of-the-way corner and watch them. When I learned the dance songs I used to sing for them, and soon they began to depend upon me. As I sang I watched them and longed to dance too.

Among the young men there was one who was distantly related to us. He had been ten years in this country and he spoke English well. I thought he was nicer and more polite than any of the others. Often I sat imagining that I too was dancing—I was the tall dark-haired girl with whom this young man usually danced. Sometimes I wondered what I would do if he really came and asked me. One day it occurred to me that perhaps if I wished very hard he would come. And so I sat singing, and wishing, and watching. One day when I saw him stop before me and ask me to dance I was not at all surprised. It seemed quite natural. Hadn't I wished so hard! I never knew how I went through that dance. When he led me back to my chair and I was seated he bowed with a slightly exaggerated politeness as one sometimes does to a child, and said in English, pronouncing each word slowly and distinctly so that I should understand, "You—dance—like—a—little—fairy."

When Aunt Masha and I were alone I asked her, "What is a fairy?" She did not know. I asked many of our acquaintances but no one knew what a fairy was.

XXXIII

So a year almost passed and spring came.

At home in our village with the first warm days the birds would return to our neighbourhood and we could hear the "click, click" of the storks that came back to build in the old stump in the cemetery. In the air there was an agreeable smell of the moist earth warming in the sun. The earth seemed to swell and burst right under our feet so that we could almost feel the plant life pushing its way to the light long before we could see it.

Here with the first warm days I saw the children on the street appearing in lighter clothing with bright new tops and jumping ropes. They seemed more free. Their laughter rang merrily and they responded more reluctantly to their mothers' calls to "come up stairs!"

I too longed to stay out. Many mornings as I hurried to work through the soft air and early sunshine a sick feeling would come over me at the thought of the shop, the dust-covered, nailed-up windows, the weight of the black heavy coats on my lap. In the winter I had been glad enough when the coats were big and heavy. They kept me warmer. But now the coat on my lap seemed to weigh a ton and kept slipping and slipping from my lap all day long as if it would drag me down. I could not make out what was wrong. I felt depressed and tired even when I got up in the morning. Often too I felt a little sick though nothing hurt. One day while standing at Mr. Cohen's table I bent down to pick up something. When I straightened again I felt the blood in my temples beat as though with hammers and everything on the table seemed topsey-turvey. I had to stand still with my eyes closed for some minutes before I could see things in their right position and places.

The next morning when Mrs. Cohen brought her husband's coffee, as she did every morning, she sat down next to me at our little table to pull some bastings, which she always did when she came, and began to talk to me. She asked me some questions about my family and myself. I told her I thought we would soon send for mother and the children and admitted that I had not been well for some time; when I climbed steps my heart beat so that it pained and I could not stoop down without growing dizzy.

Mrs. Cohen was a middle aged, kind woman, and so pious that not a hair of her own could be seen from under her light brown wig. She glanced at me now. "You do look pale," she said, and then advised me to go and see her doctor. I was scared. I had never been treated by a doctor in my life. At home the old women of the village knew a charm prayer for every ailment and grandmother would brew tea out of different blossoms which we gathered in the spring.

In the evening I told father for the first time that I had not been feeling well and that Mrs. Cohen offered to take me to her doctor. Father took a good look at me for the first time in a long while and showed alarm. He told me by all means to go with Mrs. Cohen and gave me a half dollar for the doctor.

A little before three o'clock the next day Mrs. Cohen and I were in the doctor's office. He was a big, blonde, clean-shaven Gentile man. He looked into my eyes and made me shake my hands downward to see if they would grow pink. I shook and shook my hands but they stayed almost white. The doctor smiled cheerfully. "We'll soon fix you up," he said; "stay out in the air, and——."

Mrs. Cohen explained that I worked in the shop and that my mother was not here. "Oh," he said, looking displeased. He drew up and stuck out his lips, put his elbow on the desk, rested his chin in one hand and sat staring out of the window and drumming. He sat so long that I thought he had forgotten all about us. Finally he caught up his pen and quickly, as if to make up for lost time, wrote a prescription. "Here," he said, handing it to me. "It will help some." I held out the half dollar. He looked at it on my palm for a moment, then took my hand in his great big one and put it down playfully and said, "That is all right. But 'feed up.'" This was the first time I heard these two little words. But from now on I was to hear them often and for many years.

I stayed out the rest of the afternoon. It seemed strange to be idle on a week day. I sauntered along through Grand Street toward the ferry, looking into the store windows.

That night I sat up for father. He laid the large brown loaf on the table when he came and sat down on the chair alongside of it. I saw at once that he had something pleasant to tell. He was not smiling but his face looked all lit up. After hearing what the doctor had had to say and cautioning me to take the medicine regularly he began slowly, drawing out his words almost as grandmother had often done, and smiling now quite broadly, "You know, Rahel, I think with this week's wages we have enough money for the steamer tickets, the journey and a little over."

He put his hand deep into his pocket, took out the long baggy purse and laid it on the table. Then he drew the white muslin curtain over the lower part of the window, and told me to lift the lamp from the bracket to the table. He began to count and I breathlessly watched his fingers as they turned back the bills.

"Ten, fifteen, twenty, thirty," and so on he counted. Finally he said slowly, "Yes, we have enough."

I could not realise that it was true, that we could send for them at once. Then the thought came, "In three months they might be here!" I laid my arms on the table, buried my face in them and began to sob. Father laid his hand gently on my head. For once he did not scold me for my tears.

XXXIV

A LITTLE over two months later father and I stood in line before one of the windows in the main post office on Grand Street, waiting for mail. During these two and a half months we had sent the tickets and heard that they had been received and that mother was selling out everything but the pillows, the linens and the candlesticks. Then a letter had come saying that they had started. That night Aunt Masha cried bitterly. For then we knew that grandmother and grandfather were alone, separated even from each other in their old age. For where she went to stay they would not keep him, and where he stayed they would not keep her.

Now we were waiting to hear whether mother and the children had crossed the boundary safely or had been caught and turned back as father had been the first time he started for America. We should have had a letter two days before. Father was very pale as he stood waiting his turn. At last he was at the window and the clerk handed him a post card. It was in sister's handwriting. She and I did all the corresponding. Neither father nor mother could write.

"Read quickly," father said, giving me the card and bending over me. His voice trembled. I spelled out the words; "We crossed the boundary safely—and we are all well, thank God."

"Thank God!" father repeated after me. Then he threw his head back and laughed joyously. "They will soon be here."

One week later, early on Saturday, father, Aunt Masha and I went looking for rooms. All day we

walked about, climbing many stairs. For of most rooms
the rent was too high. At last we found a small three
family rear house on Broome Street where the two rooms
on the middle floor were empty. We reached the rear
house by passing through the long hall of the front tenement, into a yard, and then climbing a high stoop. Both
rooms had windows facing the yard and the rear windows of the front tenement. The water was in the yard
and had to be pumped. But father saw many advantages
and I too saw how I could turn the tiny hall where the
upper tenant had to pass into a kitchen. So we rented
them for seven dollars a month.

One morning a few days later I was not well and
father told me to stay home. (There were often days
now when I was not well.) I thought this a golden opportunity to clean "the new rooms." So I started quite
early from Cherry Street for the house on Broome
Street. I borrowed a pail and a scrubbing brush from
our neighbour in the basement and went to work on the
floors. They were unpainted and thick with dirt. I
scrubbed and rinsed, changing the water often by carrying the pailfuls of dirty water into the yard and pumping up fresh water. At first it seemed impossible that
I could get them clean but soon the grain of the wood
began to show. When I was on the last little piece near
the door I sat back on my heels and surveyed the clean
wet boards with a feeling of pleasure. The clothes on
my back felt damp, and drops of perspiration were rolling from my cheeks down my neck. I looked at my
hands, the palms and fingers were water soaked and
all crinkled up. I remembered mother saying that I
had the hands of a lazy girl, and that I touched soiled
things with my finger tips. "Oh!" I thought, "if she
could only see them now!" And with a feeling of satis-

faction I dipped my hands into the pail of black, muddy water up to the elbows and sang a song made up on the spot.

"Oh, how I'll scrub,—how white our floors will be."

In the evening we parted from Mrs. Felesberg (not without tears) and moved into our new rooms. Then the furniture came. I spread newspapers over the floors, tucked up my dress into the belt and ran about showing the men where to put each piece. The large square table went into the centre of the big room and the six chairs all around it, the two folding cots were put at the further end in the same room, the big bed into the bedroom. And I placed our old kerosene oil stove on a new soap box in the little square hall, taking care to leave at least a foot of space for our neighbours upstairs to pass. I looked on this little corner as "the kitchen" and the large room as the "front room." I longed for a front room!

When the men were gone father and I looked about our rooms and at each other, and we smiled happily.

As the days passed and the time drew near for their coming, I became more and more impatient and nervous and found it more difficult than ever to sit in one place in the shop and think about the work. However, I did not always think about it. Often as I sat sewing on buttons or felling a sleeve lining I pictured them on the steamer and went over their whole journey in my mind, sure that it was very much as my own had been. First I saw them jogging along in Makar's straw-lined wagon from our village to Mintck, then travelling by railroad and finally packed into a wagon of mouldy hay and driven through swampy meadows in the dead of night, stealing across the boundary. Though a year had passed I could still feel the Russian soldier's heavy hand on my back, and hear his thick voice demanding, "What have you here?" The answer a jingle of silver coins and the thick voice call, "Drive on!" I pictured them sleeping in the bare, dirty little cots in Hamburg. I saw mother with the four children standing in the large hall all day for a week and waiting for their names to be called. Then I saw them in the midst of a hundred others bent over to one side or stooping under their bundles, passing through a sort of tunnel. Meekly, and looking neither to right nor to left, they followed a uniformed person. "Tramp, tramp, tramp," I heard the dull sound of many feet and two onlookers calling to each other, "The Emigrants!" and the echo calling back, "The Emigrants!"

"But now," I thought joyfully, "they are on the steamer, very near America. How will mother like America? Will she be much shocked at father's and my impiety?" For I too was not so pious now. I still performed some of the little religious rites assigned to a girl, but mechanically, not with the ever-present consciousness of God. There were moments of deep devotion, but they were rare.

Sometimes when I thought of it I felt sad, I felt as if I had lost something precious.

The steamer was due on a Friday night, so they would have to spend still another night on it. That Friday both father and I came home earlier than usual. While he was washing up and polishing his shoes, and brushing his clothes, I cooked a fish dinner for seven people for the next day, and at the kind invitation of our neighbour over us, put it on her ice into the crowded little ice-box. Then I remembered that mother had no candles to light on the steamer. I would light them here. She usually lit five, one for each child. So I found a red brick on the street, washed it clean under the pump and used it as a candle holder. We had not bought any candle sticks, as we expected our beautiful brass ones from home. I placed the clean brick on the table in the "front room," covered now with a new white oil cloth. Then with a drop of the hot tallow from each candle I stuck them firmly on the brick in a straight row. I placed two white loaves at the other end of the table and covered them with a clean small towel. I lit the candles and embracing them three times, I covered my face with my hands and whispered the consecration prayer for my mother on the steamer. Then as I looked around the room I felt for the first time in this country the joyous Friday night spirit of the old home, in the new one.

I sat out in the yard until father would be ready for supper. I watched the stars appearing one by one. From the open windows father's cheerful voice came chanting the Friday evening prayer. In the basement a rocker creaked and a little boy sang, "Sweet and low, sweet and low."

The next morning at ten o'clock father and I again stood in Castle Garden. I do not know whether Aunt Masha was with us or not. As 1 look back now I can only see father and myself, he talking to an officer and I standing with my face pressed against iron bars. In what an agony of joy and fear I stood there! At first I was neither surprised nor disappointed when I looked about and did not see them at once. Feeling sure that they must be there, I could wait. Then it flashed through my mind, "But perhaps they are not here! Perhaps they missed the steamer, perhaps they fell ill!" Then I saw them. It was as I often pictured them. Mother with baby on one arm, a bundle on the other, and the eight year old boy at her skirt, was following a uniformed American. She walked slowly with her head a little bent and her eyes on the ground. Her face looked so uncertain, as if she were not yet .sure whether her journey was at an end and whether this was the place where she would meet us. After her came sister, quite bent under a bundle on her back and with the little four year old girl holding on to her skirt. Though she was so bent under her bundle her head was raised and her eyes were looking about eagerly. Then they met mine, and as she recognised me she dropped her bundle and ran screaming, "Mamma, there they are! There they are!"

A few minutes later I heard my mother's tearful joyous voice close to me, "Rahel! Rahel!"

With baby on one arm, a bundle on the other.

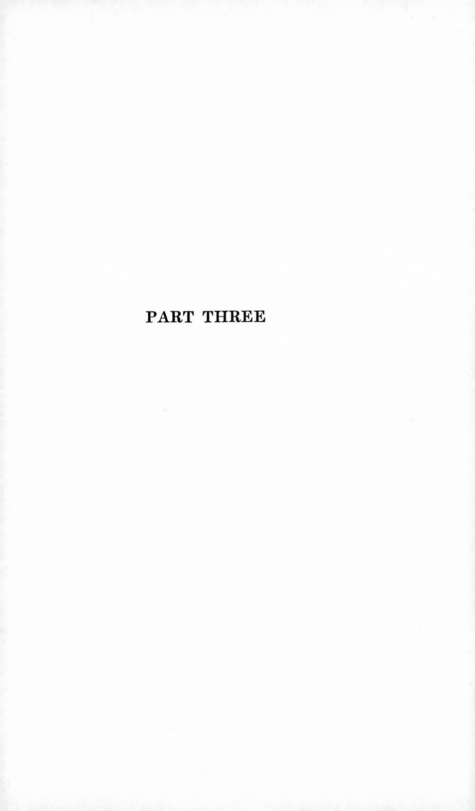

PART THREE

PART THREE

XXXV

For days father kept asking mother to tell him about herself, home, our friends, and relatives. He never seemed to grow tired of hearing it and she repeated the same thing over and over again. And I walked to and from the shop, spent the day there, and what was left of the evening at home, as though I were in a happy dream. Often during these first days I feared that mother's being here was only a dream. Often at such moments I watched her sitting at the window sewing, making a little shirt perhaps, out of a bit of muslin. I would go over to her, lean up against her a little shame-facedly, and ask her, "Mamma, are you really here in America?" She understood. She would laugh a little, press a corner of the little shirt to her eyes and say, "Yes, I am here." One day she said sadly, "Yes, all life is like a dream. To-day we are here, to-morrow God knows." Then she added, as though she were following a thought in her own mind, "Ah, if I had my youth to live over again, and if I had only known that I would have to be in America!"

"What then, mother?"

"Then," she said, as tears rolled down her cheeks and fell on the stitches, "I would have learned how to write even if I had had to go without bread sometimes. Ah, if at least I could write to my mother!"

So even during these happy days there were tears.

Mother, like Aunt Masha and myself, and all others

that I have known, felt bewildered and uncertain about herself and everything she did and said during these first days. It was pathetic to see how she looked up to me because I had already been here a year, and probably showed off a little. She treated me like a grown-up girl and allowed herself in her lovely quiet way to be guided by me in many little things.

The children were a constant care and delight, especially the two little ones. It was amusing to see how they were impressed by the different things. The little girl, four years old, thought it quite wonderful to have water right in the yard and running so easily. So as many times a day as she could steal away she would be found at the pump with her shoes and stockings off pumping water over her two little bare feet and rubbing them industriously. Once on hearing the baby—now two years old—screaming in the yard, we ran out and found him lying flat on his little stomach with his fair, curly head under the pump while the four year old stood at the handle, one little hand pumping with great difficulty and the other rubbing his head.

Often in their play they imitated what they had seen on their journey. Being lately from the steamer they played "crossing the ocean." She was the great ocean steamer. She would stand in the middle of the yard, her feet wide apart, her hands on her little hips, rocking herself slowly from side to side, and roaring with great earnestness in imitation of the waves. Meanwhile the baby would drag the dish pan and a wooden spoon from the closet and strut around and around the yard banging on the pan and crying, "Metach! metach!" in German, announcing the meals on the steamer.

Sister surprised me with her fearlessness in going about everywhere and her quickness in adopting American ways. She found her way quite easily. She would wash and dress the children, curl their hair on her finger, "American fashion," and take them out into the street. She would take them along wherever she went. She never stole away from them as I had often done from her. She and I shared one of the cots in the "front room." We used to lie with our arms about each other, whispering until way into the night.

The boy, eight years old, was serious and sensitive and would not stand for any trifling. He liked to stand out on the street before the door and observe life in America. As no money could be spared for new clothes the children had to wear out what they had. His shoes, made by our village shoemaker, were in excellent condition in spite of the rough treatment of fumigation and the wear-and-tear of the journey. But shoes more than any other article of clothing showed the "greenhorn." And so often he was so tormented by the children in the street that he would come into the house in tears. He begged and cried and demanded "American" shoes but it was no use. So he tried to see what he could do by knocking and rubbing them on stones. But these shoes of the homely strong Russian leather could stand it without showing more than a few scratches.

One day when he went out into the street he did not return until dark, and then he was in his bare feet. On being asked what he had done with his shoes he said, with tears and an expression which said that he was prepared for the worst, that he had thrown them away. "Where?" He did not know, himself. Fearing that under a threat of punishment he might be weak enough to go and look for them, he threw them so that he himself should not be able to find them. He flung them, he said, from a strange roof, one in one direction, one in the other. He told his story and stood before father with his eyes on the ground ready to take the punishment which he knew would follow.

That evening when father went out into the street he brought back a black strap of fringed leather with a wooden handle and hung it up in the big room on the door.

Of father and myself, I was the more Americanised. Under pressure I could converse in English a little while, he could not talk it at all. So he left translating the children's names to me. I was delighted. I longed to call them by names that were not only American but also unusual. So as I sat in the shop I spent many hours thinking and sounding each name in my mind over and over again. But when I finally decided on all the names I felt uneasy at the thought that there was no resemblance between the Hebrew and the English names. So I just translated them into English after all. Sister, whose name was Leah, we called Leah; the little four year old girl changed from Meriam to Miriam; the baby was Asra. But at least one I could not resist calling by an uncommon name. I called the boy Morgan, though his name translated was Ezekiel.

I knew I had a leaning toward things which I heard people call "queer." I felt ashamed and hid it whenever I was aware of it. I felt ashamed of my desire to call my brother Morgan but neither could I bear to give it up. So I called him by that name only when no one was by who was likely to ridicule me.

Mother had been here only a short time when I noticed that she looked older and more old-fashioned than father. I noticed that it was so with most of our women, especially those that wore wigs or kerchiefs on their heads. So I thought that if I could persuade her to leave off her kerchief she would look younger and more up to date. But remembering my own first shock, I decided to go slowly and be careful not to hurt her feelings. So, one day, when I happened to be at home and the children were playing in the yard, and we two were alone in the house, I asked her playfully to take off her kerchief and let me do her hair, just to see how it would look. She consented reluctantly. She had never before in her married life had her hair uncovered before any one. I took off her kerchief and began to fuss with her hair. It was dark and not abundant but it was soft and had a pretty wave in it. When I parted it in front and gathered it up in a small knot in the middle of the back of her head, leaving it soft over the temples, I was surprised how different she looked. I had never before known what a fine broad forehead my mother had, nor how soft were her blue-grey eyes, set rather deep and far apart. I handed her our little mirror from Cherry Street. She glanced at herself, admitted frankly that it looked well and began hastily to put on her kerchief as if she feared being frivolous too long. I caught hold of her hands.

"Mamma," I coaxed, "please don't put the kerchief on again—ever!"

At first she would not even listen to me. But I sat down in her lap and I began to coax and beg and reason. I drew from my year of experience and observation and pointed out that wives so often looked so much older because they were more old-fashioned, that the husbands were often ashamed to go out with them. I told her that it was so with Mrs. Felesberg and Mrs. Cohen. "And this nice woman upstairs," I said "if she would only take off her wig and——."

Mother put her finger on my lips.

"But father trims his beard," I still argued. Her face

looked sad. "Is that why," she said, "I too must sin?"
But I finally succeeded.

When father came home in the evening and caught
sight of her while still at the door, he stopped and looked
at her with astonishment. "What!" he cried, half earnestly, half jestingly, "Already you are becoming an
American lady!" Mother looked abashed for a moment;
in the next, to my surprise and delight, I heard her
brazen it out in her quiet way.

"As you see," she said, "I am not staying far behind."

XXXVI

It was "slack" in our shop. Every week Mr. Cohen made me stay home a day or two. It was slack all over the city at all trades. Writers and lecturers now refer to that time as "the memorable years, 1893-94. Years of extreme economic depression." We felt this depression when one day father came home from the shop at three o'clock in the afternoon. Not to alarm mother, who had been here only two months, he made light of the rumour that people were out of work all over the city. But when a few weeks passed and he began to stay home three and four days a week, he looked openly alarmed and began to talk of moving back to Cherry Street. And when two brothers and a sister, who were from our part of the country, came one night and asked to be taken in as "lodgers," we finally decided to do it. So, with our lodgers, we moved into a "room and two bedrooms," on Cherry Street again, this time between Jefferson and Clinton Streets. The rooms were on the stoop in the rear. The toilets, for the whole building, were in the yard, facing our windows, the water pump in the street hall. The rent was ten dollars a month. We gave the two brothers the little hall bedroom with the window, for the sister a cot was put up for the night in the large room with us children. They paid five dollars a month. So now we felt easier as our rent was only five dollars a month.

But our easy days were not many. One night, soon after we had settled in our new home, Mr. Cohen called me over to his table, just as I was leaving, and told me that he had no work for me for the next day. This would make three days out for that week. Mr. Cohen saw that I was troubled and began to explain.

"You see, Gussie is a woman and needs the money while you——." I felt irritated. I felt that because I was a child I was paid little. And even then they did not seem to think that I needed the money, as though I didn't have to live and help support my people. I burst out: "I too need it. My people have just come and——." I felt miserable. Gussie and I were good friends.

"Oh, very well," Mr. Cohen said, quickly, "take turns then."

A week passed perhaps when again just as we were going home, Mr. Cohen told Gussie that he was sorry but there was so little work that there was no use of her staying on. I dared not look at her face as he talked to her. When we came out into the street she walked away from me without saying "Good night."

One by one I watched the men in our shop laid off. Finally there was just Mr. Cohen and his partner left. Then my turn came.

A short time after I began to stay home father's shop was closed altogether. Every day now all over the city shops were being closed. Nevertheless father went out every morning, always looking bright, and hopeful of finding at least a few hours' work. He would return at noon looking not quite so bright. He was not discouraged, but as week after week passed, his face grew thinner and the smile that had always lit up his whole face became rare. But still he spoke cheerfully. "This can't last much longer," he would say. "There must be an end to it. It is almost two months now."

All this weighed more heavily on mother. Her face was paler, her features stood out sharply and her eyes seemed to have gone deeper into her head. She was always serious and now she looked as if a dreadful calamity were hanging over us. "Among strangers in a strange country." She began counting the potatoes she put into the pot and would ask the children over and over again when they wanted more bread, "Are you sure you want it?"

Two months passed and a great change seemed to have come over the people. The closed shops turned the workers out into the streets and they walked about idly, looking haggard and shabby. Often as I sauntered along through Cherry or Monroe Street I would meet some one with whom I had worked. We avoided each other. We felt ashamed of being seen idle. We felt ashamed of our shabby clothes. We avoided each other's eyes to save each other pain and humiliation. The greeting of those who could not possibly avoid one another was something like this, "What! A holiday in your shop, too?" Nor would they remain talking long. Both would stand looking away gloomily for a few minutes and finally with a short nod they would walk apart dejectedly.

Every day I saw on Cherry and Monroe Streets grocers closing up and women at the pushcarts haggling more and more desperately over a cent.

"How much are these bananas? Five for a cent? They are not any bigger than my finger, and the skin is all black."

"Oh, very well, take six! Take six for God's sake and go. I haven't made a cent to-day."

One day as I was walking on Grand Street toward the Bowery, I saw a tall, slim man, coatless and bare-headed, with a rag bag over his shoulder, bent over a garbage can. There was something familiar to me about him. I was on the opposite side of the street and stood looking at him. And soon I remembered. He was, or he had been, a machine operator. He and his wife had been a merry couple and they had a sweet baby whom they adored. They had lived in our old 338 Cherry Street over the Felesbergs. I had often been in their home and watched them singing and dancing with their baby. Now I hardly recognised him. A ragged grey shirt covered his back. His long thin body was bent. His face looked black and hollow. But what struck me with horror was that he seemed entirely unaware that he was among human beings. He acted as though he felt himself in a lone desert. Feverishly he stood stirring the can with a stick. His eyes looked into it eagerly, and his lips were moving.

As I recognised him I ran toward him a few steps. Then the full meaning of it all struck me. I threw my arms over my head and ran from him in terror.

One day while mother and we children stood out on the stoop a woman we knew came over to us. She lived by doing all sorts of odd things, particularly by match-making and recommending girls to places of domestic service. And as she walked about the street, attending to her business, she knit a stocking. She was a stout, elderly woman, and wore a kerchief tied under her chin and tucked away behind her ears.

She barely glanced at me and as her eyes returned to her quickly moving needles, "Missus," she said, "I have a place for your girl with a very nice family." Mother's lips drew together tightly. Without looking at mother the woman kept on talking in a slow persuasive tone. "There are only six in the family. They live on Clinton Street near Grand. I think they would pay her six dollars a month. Will you let her go?"

My mother's face was white. "No!" she shook her

head. She climbed up the stoop steps and went into the house.

I followed her and asked, "Why don't you let me go, mother? Out of the six dollars we could pay our share of the rent for a whole month and have a dollar over."

She turned away from me, leaned against the wall and cried, "Is this what I have come to America for, that my children should become servants?"

It was three months now since father and I had earned anything. We owed the landlord five dollars for this third month. We gave him just what the lodgers had paid us. What there was left of our own money we kept just for bread and a little milk for the two smaller children. Father used to bring the big round loaf of bread from the bread stand on Hester Street when he came home at night. We were always in bed then and the light in the lamp was turned low but I was often awake. Mother would sit up to wait for him and open the door and he would come in on tip toe, lay the bread on the table and sit down heavily beside it. Then mother would cut some of the bread, sweeten some hot water in a glass and give it to him. Then she would sit down on another chair near the table and sit staring on the floor in front of her while he ate his supper. He used to chew every mouthful a long time and drink the hot water slowly. Sometimes in the stillness I could hear a deep half-stifled sigh.

They seldom spoke. Once I heard father ask, "How are the children?"

"How should they be?" she answered. "Hanging onto life." She covered her face and sobbed.

In the morning father was gone on his daily hunt for work before we were up. He no longer came home at noon now, for when he was away he did not have to eat.

The two older children, Leah and Ezekiel, were going to school and the two little ones we kept in bed as long as we could that they might be warm. For it was winter now and we had not much covering. Mother had not brought her five pillows, linens and candlesticks after all. She had sold everything in Hamburg for a few dollars, hearing a rumour that she would be allowed no luggage except what she could carry. Then she heard that the rumour had been raised that the emigrants might sell out.

When the children came from school they would go out on the street and to the docks and pick up bits of coal, paper and wood and then we would make a fire. We used to put on water to boil and draw our chairs close to the stove, to draw all the warmth we could out of it. When our lodgers came home they often complained of the bitter cold in the house but they were not very well off themselves. They made knee pants and seldom had more than two days' work a week.

The small school which the children attended was, I think, connected with a church or a missionary society. One day when the children came home they told us that any child in the class who would say a prayer received a slice of bread and honey. Mother looked at them and asked them to tell her about it. Sister said, "There is nothing to tell. If you just bow your head as you sit at the desk, and repeat the prayer after the teacher you receive a slice of white bread and honey."

We heard a great deal about the missionaries that winter. On Grand Street, at the corner of Attorney Street, there was a big store with green shades which were always drawn. In this store we knew the missionaries held a meeting every Saturday. We heard that the head of the missionaries was a baptised Jew. I heard my parents express their anger because they came and settled right in the heart of the Jewish neighbourhood. We children used to run past the store with a feeling of fear and then stand at a little distance and look at it. I often went back to look inside through a worn part of the shade, and saw a man standing up and talking and a few people in the back of the room listening. Week after week the man preached almost to an empty room. Still we hated to have them in the neighbourhood to tempt our people.

One Saturday afternoon father came home and said that he had just passed the missionaries' store on Grand Street. "They are doing good business these days," he said. "As I passed, the door opened and I saw the place crowded with people." We heard that any one who went there and listened to the lectures received food and clothing.

A young man, who was a friend of our lodgers, used to come to visit them. When he became well acquainted with us he would come in at any time during the day, even when his friends were out. Of course he was out of work. It was six months now since he had earned anything. He looked like the rest of us, shabby, despondent, half-starved. If he happened to come in when we were having a meal mother always invited him to eat with us. He would take the bread which, like father, he chewed slowly, and often said, "This is very good bread."

He would sit and argue with mother, trying to convince her that it was no sin to accept food from missionaries when one was almost starving.

"But do they give it to you? You have to show that you believe with them, that you accept their religion."

"Even so," he said. "The sin would be theirs for making such demands from starving people."

After he was gone mother said, "That is all talk. He is not religious but after all he is a Jew. Oh, God," she would say, with a touch of pride, "one only has to look into his sunken eyes to see starvation and yet he does not go to them."

Another month passed and all our money was gone. For a week or so we borrowed from our lodgers ten and fifteen cents at a time until we had a dollar. Then we did not know what to do. We would not ask the coal man and the grocer to "trust" us. We had never owed any one, and father and mother shrank from the very thought of owing. Besides, the coal man and the grocer hardly knew us. We had not bought much coal and bread was a cent cheaper at the big stand on Hester Street. On the morning when father took the last few cents he went away earlier than usual. And mother walked about with slow shuffling steps from room to room. As the children were leaving for school she asked them without looking at them, whether bread and honey was still given to the children at school.

"Yes," sister said, "to those who bow their heads and pray."

The boy was already out of the room when mother called after them. "You can bow your heads and pray."

Then she went into her dark bedroom.

XXXVII

MOTHER did not come out of the room that day. In the morning I was awakened by hearing her moaning. I lit the lamp and went in and looked at her. Her face was red and her chest rose and fell rapidly. For the first time this morning father looked really discouraged when he left the house. After the two older children went to school I tucked the little ones into one of the cots to play. Every day they remained in bed more willingly and played more quietly. I gave mother some water and milk and went in to ask our front neighbour what I could do for mother. She said she would see that a doctor came and made me understand that there were doctors who treated without a fee. And then she added: "As long as your mother is ill you need not fear that the landlord will put you out. It is against the law." I ran to mother with the good news. When I told her she looked at me as if she did not understand, so I explained: "It is a law in America that when you are sick——." Mother turned her face to the wall and gave an unpleasant chuckle which ended in a sob.

The doctor came at three o'clock in the afternoon. I lit the lamp and showed him into the sick room. He stopped in the middle of it, looked about at the walls and the ceiling, and shrugged his shoulders. After he examined mother he shrugged his shoulders again. Finally he wrote out a prescription, said crossly that he would come again the next day at ten o'clock and went away.

When father came home in the evening and I told him that the landlord could not put us out, he told me to use the money which the lodgers had just paid us for the medicine and bread and coal.

Mother grew worse. All day I walked from the children's cot to her room, where a little lamp burned steadily now, and then back to the children's cot. I felt as though I were in a nightmare. I never remembered mother ill before. She was the strongest in our family. And now to see her lying so still with her eyes closed and not even moaning, filled me with terror.

The doctor came every morning at ten o'clock. He did not tell me what her illness was and I dared not ask. Every day he would sit down on the bed, make me hold the lamp so that the light fell on her face, and sit looking at her. And I watched his face and hers and tried to understand. Sometimes I saw mother trying to rouse herself from her stupor. She would give her head a shake as if she were trying to shake something off. I could hear her teeth close tightly and her chin seemed to square a little. Then she would open her eyes and I saw for a moment a steady, determined look. I had often seen her so when she had something to overcome. I understood that this was the fight in her. I remembered the same look when she was planning father's escape from the constable in Russia. And I recalled seeing it one snowy, stormy night when one of the children woke up choking with the croup and she could not get any one to go for the doctor. The road lay through a thick wood and wolves had been seen there. So she wrapped herself in a shawl, tucked up her skirt, took a staff and started. At dawn she returned struggling through the snow in front of the man, making a path for him. I noticed that the doctor always looked pleased when he caught this expression. Gradually I began to understand that he depended on the fighting spirit in her. And I too began to look for it.

Beside the doctor two other people came every day, the landlord and the young man, our lodgers' friend. The landlord was a gentle, quiet, prosperous looking old man with a white moustache. He wore fine black clothes, black gloves and a high silk hat. It was strange to see him among us. As long as we had some money to pay he came every week and inquired whether father was working. But now that we had nothing to give he came every day. He would knock gently on the door, come in on tip toes and ask quietly and cheerfully, "And how is your mother this morning?" When I told him, "The same," he would give a short nod and tip toe out with his head bent a little lower. I used to look forward to his coming. He was the only person who came among us that did not show suffering. I used to wish he would stay a little and talk to me.

The young man would come in, ask about mother and then sit down on a chair near the window from where he could see the whole house, and sit watching me as I went from mother to the children and then back to her.

Once Aunt Masha came. She was dressed in an old brown dress which in better days she had discarded. She stayed a little while, gave the children a thorough washing and went away. I believe now that she must have come more than this once, but this time is the only one I can recall during this period.

One day a well dressed strange young man came in. He made sure of our name at the door and then came and sat down at the window, opened a little book and began to question me about my family, my father's name, his trade, how long he had been out of work, how much

he had earned, how long mother had been ill and so on.
As I was answering his questions I was in agony of
fear, wondering whether this had anything to do with
the landlord and whether after all we would be thrown
out into the street. He stopped for a few minutes and
I sat down on the cot closer to the children. The young
man continued:

"Where does your doctor come from?"

"From Essex Street dispensary."

"Do you need anything?"

I stared at him. He looked up and asked over again,
patiently,

"Do you need anything?"

"Do we need anything!" I could not believe I heard
right. It seemed such a strange question and I did not
answer and he repeated the question in Yiddish. I finally
did understand and I heard myself say, "No." Still
thinking that I did not understand he asked:

"Do you need any clothes?"

I shook my head.

"Do you need any shoes?" He looked at mine.

"No," I said.

"Do you need any food?"

"No——"

"Have you everything?"

"Everything," I repeated, but I could not look at him.

He wrote rapidly for a few minutes and then he went
away.

I went in to mother and bent over her, thinking that
perhaps I could tell her about it. The heat beat from
her body and her eyes were closed. I touched her and
she opened them. And when I looked into them I knew
she would not understand.

In the evening when father was home our neighbour

brought in four dollars. "A strange young man left it," she said, and the next day there was a half ton of coal.

Friday came. Even now, as I look back, it seems to me that weeks had passed since mother fell ill. And yet it might have been only days. This morning she lay in deep unconsciousness and the doctor spent a longer time looking at her. After I got the children to play quietly in a corner I began to prepare for the Sabbath. There was little to prepare as there was no cooking to do. I polished our candlesticks which we had bought here, and scrubbed the floor in the large room and then began to wash up the floor in the sick room. The light of the tiny lamp hanging on the wall only seemed to increase the gloom. How I wished, as I crept about on my hands and knees, that mother would wake and see how industrious I was, how I was tormented for ever having hurt her!

Late in the afternoon our lodgers' friend came. When I looked at him I was shocked and I knew that he had been to the missionaries. He was dressed in new clothes from head to foot and his face was clean shaven. He stood still with his back against the door for a moment and his face reddened as I stood staring at him. He asked his usual question about mother, and took his seat at the window. And, as if to try his first sermon he began to upbraid me for my pale face and red eyes, saying that mother would get well much sooner if I were more cheerful. Also, I ought to cheer up for the sake of the children,—a girl almost fourteen years old ought to know better—and so on.

I bought two candles for a cent. I had a cent for candles, for we could go without bread but not without consecrating candles. I cut them in half to make four and placed them into the candlesticks. When it grew dark I lit them, gave one to each of the children, and we all walked and stood beside mother's bed. It took us a long time to rouse her. We had to repeat again and again, "Mother, this is Friday night." At last she opened her eyes and looked at all our faces one after the other. And when she realised what we wanted her to do, she raised her hands but instead of the usual prayer the words came, "God have pity on my children!"

At midnight I tumbled out of the cot thinking that I heard her calling. When father and I bent over her we saw that a change had taken place. Her face was paler and was wet with perspiration.

"Medicine!" She made out the word with her lips. Father gave it to her, and then she told us in that voiceless way of the sick, that she dreamt her father who had been dead a long while came and brought her a bottle of medicine. Father's face lit up with joy. "Thank God!" he said, "that was a good dream."

When the doctor came the next day and when he looked at mother a smile lit up his cross face. Another doctor was with him. "Look at this," our doctor said, pointing to the ceiling and walls. "And she has pulled through in this room. God! but she must have a constitution of iron!"

With his usual gruffness the doctor now ordered chicken soup, milk and wine for mother. And only now father went and told our neighbour openly of our difficulties. She advised him hesitatingly to go and apply at "Eighth Street." Eighth Street was how we referred to the United Hebrew Charities.

Monday morning after eating some bread father started for "Eighth Street." He returned in the evening empty handed and sick with humiliation. When he reached the building there was already a long line of people. He stood all day waiting for his turn. He was nowhere near the "window" when the place closed. Next morning, he left at dawn. The day passed and it was dark when we heard his footsteps in the hall. When he opened the door, we saw a pair of chicken feet sticking out of the bag. Father sat down at the table and wept like a child.

He flung them from a strange roof.

XXXVIII

Now it was sister who was supporting the family.
She ran errands for the women on the block and
"minded" the babies. She was eleven years old and
small for her age, but no one who looked at her face
hesitated to trust her. Sometimes a mother would leave
her children with her and go out to work. And sister
would tidy up the house, dress and feed the children and
keep them out. Often when I ran out for something, I
met her in the street, wrapped in a woman's coat and
carrying one little one on her back while two or three
others were at her side. Her freckled small nose looked
pinched, but she would look up so bravely with her soft
grey eyes as she stood slightly bent under her burden.
And in the evening she would bring home a few nickels.

One night she was taken to a wedding to take care of
two children. The next day we two stood at the window
and she was telling me about it. That hour impressed
itself on my memory. It was cold and raining but there
was a good fire in our stove. Father, as usual now,
was out "looking for work"; the boy was in school;
mother, still a convalescent, was lying on a cot napping;
the two little ones were playing quietly in a corner, and
we two were at the window. What she had seen would
have seemed wonderful to her at any time. In her present half-fed state, and in the same worn little plaid dress
in which she had come from Russia, she had been almost
overcome by the sight of the splendours. Her eyes were
big and in her voice there was still expression of awe
as she described the immense hall, the lights, the bride
in her white lace veil and train, the bridegroom with a

white flower in his buttonhole.   As the children in her
care were only two and four years they soon grew
tired of running up and down the slippery floor.   So
she had to go early to the little retiring room at the back
of the hall.   This room was almost dark.   There was
a little table and a couch.   On the couch a few children
were already sleeping so she sat down on the floor opposite the door with one child in her lap, pillowed the other
against her side and sat and rocked them.   She sat
rocking them all through the night.   The children
weighed heavily against her.   But sometimes when she
could raise her head a little, she watched the dancers
passing the door.

"The women looked so beautiful," she said, "in pink
or blue, or white silk; and their hair shone as they danced
by.   When the music was low I could hear them laughing, they looked so happy!"

She looked thoughtfully for a moment into the yard.
The rain was splashing down on the red roofs of the
toilets.   From a line a few pieces of clothes were flapping.

"I wonder," she said, "how it feels to be happy!"

Soon after this the agent came again and told mother
that she had a place for me.   This time mother had to
let me go.   I did not mind going.   It was not only that
we were in dire need, I wanted to know how it felt to
be a servant; also how the rich people lived.   There was
no doubt in my mind that the family where I was going
would be rich.   How else could they keep a servant?

I packed a few things into a newspaper and mother
went with me to the door.   She neither cried nor spoke
but when I looked at her I knew what she was suffering.
We all felt as if I were going a great distance away.   I

kissed the children, and sister ran out and watched me from the stoop as I walked away with the agent.

This family also lived on Clinton Street, near Broome. Their name was Corlove. Mrs. Corlove was a tall, angular woman with a yellowish complexion and sharp grey eyes. She engaged me for two months and I was to receive six dollars for the first month and seven for the second.

When the agent was gone she told me that the baby whom she was rocking was two weeks old and that the floors were dirty because there had been a party the day before. Then she gave me an old skirt and told me where to find a pail and brush. There were three rooms. The kitchen and bedroom had windows looking into a courtyard but it was as dark in there as in our windowless bedroom at home. And I had to scrub them by gas light.

When I was through Mrs. Corlove looked under the bed and into the dark corners of the kitchen, and I saw that she was pleased.

There were six people in the family. Besides Mr. and Mrs. Corlove and their three children, Mrs. Corlove's brother lived with them. I sat down to supper with them at the table. There was soup, meat, potatoes and a heaping plate-ful of bread. I felt almost overcome at the smell and abundance of the food. But I clasped my hands in my lap and waited for the others to begin. At the first mouthful I remembered that there was nothing but bread at home, and I could not swallow.

Directly after the dishes were put away Mrs. Corlove gave me two old quilts and a pillow and showed me how to make a bed of chairs in the kitchen. This room connected the bedroom and the "front room" where a flaring gas light burned and the family sat up talking.

I heard the clock strike eleven when they went to bed. This was Wednesday night. I fell asleep thinking that I would ask Mrs. Corlove for half of my wages the first thing in the morning and take it home so that mother could use some of it for the Sabbath.

The next day I rose early and worked all day. I swept and dusted, polished the stove and the candlesticks. I washed some of the clothes and prepared the vegetables for supper. And all the time I kept thinking about the money and could not get up courage to ask. So I kept putting it off from minute to minute. Each new piece of work I began I told myself: "When I get through with this, I'll surely ask."

So the day passed and again it was after supper. I felt disgusted with myself. I realised that I was capable of putting it off forever. It occurred to me that I must do it suddenly without giving myself time to think. As this thought came I fairly ran into the kitchen where Mrs. Corlove was and asked her breathlessly:

"Will you please give half of my wages in advance?"

She looked at me hard and said she would talk it over with her husband. Soon I was called into the front room. I stood before them and they both looked at me. Mrs. Corlove said:

"You may take the money to your people Saturday."

My heart sank and I stood without being able to say a word. Then I heard Mr. Corlove ask: "Do you want it sooner?" His voice was kind. I nodded my head. He took a roll of bills from his pocket, counted off six dollars and gave it to me. I crammed it into my hand and hastened into the kitchen where my little shawl hung on a nail. I wrapped it around my head and shoulders and ran out.

I could have sung for joy as I went, half running,

half walking. I held my hand with the money against my breast under the shawl. I had never had so much money in my possession.

"What will mother buy?" I wondered. "Perhaps meat and a Sabbath loaf and candles."

I could see them all sitting around the table covered with a white cloth and bright with the candlesticks and the lights, and I could hear father saying grace over the white loaf.

I went into the house without knocking. Everything looked so strange to me, as though I had been away a long time. The lamp in the bracket burned dimly and was smoking a little and there seemed so little life. I could not help comparing this home with that other brightly lit cheerful home.

The children came running to meet me at the door. I felt their loving arms about me, and mother, both frightened and glad, asked: "What is the matter! You are all out of breath!" Then I opened my hand and showed them what I had.

XXXIX

LIVING with the Corloves was a great change for me. At home I had been spared all the hard work for my health had continued to be poor. But now I was suddenly treated not only as if my strength were normal but unlimited. I rose when the men rose to go to work, and as they had to come into the kitchen to wash at the sink, I would creep into the niche behind the stove to dress. On Monday morning, as I crouched there, I listened for Mrs. Corlove's footsteps and the thud of the big bundle of clothes on the floor. When I heard it I crept out quickly, whether completely dressed or not, and my work began. I carried up the coal from the cellar and made the fire, I lifted the boiler half filled with clothes, I washed and scrubbed all day long. When night came I crept gladly in between the two soiled quilts on my chairs. And though the house was full of life, for the gas lights flared, the people talked and the children ran races from room to room, I slept. Tuesday and Wednesday I ironed. On Thursday I scaled the fish and plucked and cleaned the fowl. Soon my hands grew red and coarse and I was no longer repelled at touching soiled or mushy things. I would run out to the store with my hands covered with flour or black with the scrubbing water, for Mrs. Corlove could never wait for me to wash them.

One Thursday, while I was cleaning out the fowl, she called: "Run to the store quickly and never mind your hands." As I was running down the stoop steps I thought I caught sight for a moment of my mother's face. It looked so pale in the light of the street lamp. I had been thinking of her and in my present haste and usual absent-mindedness, I thought that I was still seeing her in imagination and did not stop to look but ran across to the grocer's. But a few minutes later, as I was coming back, I was more alive to things, and the thought of that moment took more concrete form. I thought that I must have really seen her and that it would be just like my mother to come and stand there hoping to see me. I ran to the shadowy spot near the street lamp, but no one was there. The next moment I caught her hiding in the hall of the next building.

Mother managed it so that I should see some one or other from home often. Usually it was my sister and brother. They would knock timidly on the door and come in holding each other tightly by the hand and remain standing near the door. I felt timid and humble myself in this house. But to see them hurt me so that I often wished mother did not send them. Mrs. Corlove would usually call to them: "Come, sit down, children." Then she would pick out an apple from the glass bowl, which usually stood on the table, cut it into four parts, give us each a quarter and put the fourth quarter back.

Little by little I began to know Mrs. Corlove and the rest of the family too. I thought her an excellent housewife but exacting and in other ways too not over-generous to me. She always doled out the food on my plate. It was usually the tail of the fish, the feet and the gizzard of the chicken, the bun to which some mishap had occurred. And she would look through the whole bowl of apples to find for me a spotted one. She rarely failed to remark at meals: "What an enormous appetite you have!" She always said it with a smile of surprise as if she were merely interested. So she covered every act with a coating of kindness. Sunday was wash day so she would send me to bed early on Saturday night and without supper. For that night no regular meal was prepared because we had "a good dinner." The first two or three times she exclaimed: "Surely you cannot be hungry after such a meal!" After that she did not need to say it. I used to lie awake and try to make believe there was no food in the house. I had never found making believe so hard as in those days, for all the time I kept seeing the sweetened bread in the bread box. Late that night I would see the family sit down to tea and cake.

It was hard to see sweetmeats and food about and not take them. Perhaps if I had had enough even of coarse food the temptation would not have been so great. But I could never eat enough even of bread with Mrs. Corlove's eyes watching me. And if you were only fourteen, and perhaps even if you were older, you too would be likely to begin thinking of a way to take it. You would say perhaps, "After all, she never told me not to take it." And if you did remember her forbidding eyes you would say to yourself: "Perhaps I only imagined it." At any rate that was the way I reasoned one day, when Mrs. Corlove went to the butcher and there was a cold cracker dust pan cake in the pan on the stove. For weeks I had watched Mrs. Corlove bake these pan cakes. I had often had to carry plateful after plateful to some one or other in the family, and I could see the steam rising from them and the tiny drops of hot butter breaking up like bubbles. At these moments the desire to taste them was so strong that it was a pain. And this time there was one such cake left over as if to tempt me. It was morning. I went about sweeping and dusting and all the time I could see the cake on the pan. Finally I went to the

stove and stood looking at the cake and tried to imagine
how it would taste cold.   My mouth watered and I could
think of nothing else.   Then, as if of its own accord, I
saw my hand go out and take it.

No sooner was the act done than I felt like Eve, perhaps, after she ate the apple.   I took the two steps into
the dark corner near the stove and pressed my face
against the wall.

Mrs. Corlove missed the pancake immediately on her
return.   She said nothing but she gave me a look and
a smile that hurt more than blows could have done.

Mrs. Corlove's brother was a big ill-natured fellow.
His sister put up with all his whims and she seemed fond
and proud of him.   I used to hear her boasting to her
friends that he was musical.   He was a machine operator
and when he was not working he would sit for hours
in the rocker in the front room playing "After the Ball
is Over" on the accordion.

Mr. Corlove was quite different from his family.   He
was gentle and kind to everybody.   When he was in the
house I did not feel so timid and liked to come out of
the dark kitchen into the front room.   He was a foreman
in a large clothing shop and when he found that I knew
of the shop he spoke to me as to a fellow worker
of the same trade.   He often took my part against his
brother-in-law who enjoyed making me get up from the
table and wait on him.   He even defended me against
his wife.

I had learned during the first days that being Mrs.
Corlove's servant meant that I was everybody's servant.
When Mrs. Corlove's relatives came to the house they
ordered me about as freely as Mrs. Corlove herself.   But
I never gave this a thought.   This was her home and
they were her guests.

One day a sister-in-law of hers was moving. A few days before Mrs. Corlove told me to take the pail and brush and go scrub the floors in the new rooms. I seldom fully realised things until they had happened and were past. And now too, not until I was in the empty rooms and saw the filthy, hard trodden floors, did I fully perceive the injustice of Mrs. Corlove's order. Then I sat down on the floor and cried passionately. I cried not only for this but for many other things which I could not understand or understood but vaguely. I cried until I was again patient and meek. Then I went on my knees, scrubbed the floors and went home.

The gas was already lit in the kitchen and Mrs. Corlove was preparing supper. She looked at my face with surprise when I came in but said nothing. I went about helping with the supper and keeping out of sight as much as I could. But Mr. Corlove had not been in the house two minutes when he asked his wife: "What is the matter with her?"

"Oh, nothing," she said lightly, "Fannie, you know, is going to move to-morrow."

"Well?"

"So I sent her to scrub her floors."

He stopped in the middle of the kitchen and looked at her as if he did not understand.

"Do you mean to say," he asked, drawing out his words, "that you sent her to scrub Fannie's floors?"

"Oh, three little floors!"

I never imagined that a man so quiet and gentle could look so angry. His dark eyes flashed fire and he said hard things. Late that night from my chairs I heard them talking this thing over, as I had often heard them talk other things over.

"Every one's comfort is more to you than mine," she sobbed.

"You know it is not so." His voice was very tender. "You don't seem to realise how unjust it was to the girl. You hired her to do your work, not Fannie's, and she is still but a child. Supposing it was our little Tynke!" His voice dropped so low that I barely caught the words: "Who knows," he said, "to-day, it is this man's daughter; to-morrow, it might be ours."

In the silence that followed I heard the little girl's crib moved and I knew that the mother moved it closer to her bed.

Near the end of my second month I remember a beautiful day in March. Mrs. Corlove rarely left the house but on this bright warm day she took all the children and went out and I was left there for the first time quite alone. It was Wednesday afternoon and I was sitting at the window making barley noodles. It seemed so quiet after the hustle and bustle of preparation to go out. I chopped and listened to the rhythmical sound of my two knives and watched the streak of sunlight on the window sill which came slanting in between the two tenements.

Gradually I began chopping more and more slowly. Finally I laid down the knives and rested my hands on the edge of the bowl. I saw that my hands were coarse and red, and here and there where the skin was cracked they were raw. I remembered how I had wanted to know how it felt to be a servant and I laughed at myself.

"I should not like to be a servant all the time," I thought. I looked out of the window and gradually I began to reason it out. I realised that though in the shop too I had been driven, at least there I had not been alone. I had been a worker among other workers who looked upon me as an equal and a companion. The only

inequality I had ever felt was that of age. The evening
was mine and I was at home with my own people. Often
I could forget the shop altogether for a time, while as
a servant my home was a few hard chairs and two soiled
quilts. My every hour was sold, night and day. I had
to be constantly in the presence of people who looked
down upon me as an inferior. I felt, though in a child's
way, that being constantly with people who looked upon
me as an inferior, I was, or soon would be an inferior.
I was looked upon as dull, nothing was expected from
me and I would have nothing to give. The pancake in-
cident had made a deep impression and had been tor-
menting me. I understood that under these conditions
and in this atmosphere what had happened once was
bound to happen again. Little by little I would become
used to it and not mind it. My whole being shrank from
this and similar things to which it might lead. I realised
that I could not boast many qualities. But to what I had,
even if it were only not to be sly, I clung with all my
strength. "No," I concluded, taking up the knives, and
beginning to chop quickly to make up for the time lost,
"I would rather work in a shop."

XL

A FEW days later I left the Corloves. My belongings were wrapped in a newspaper and tucked under my arm, and I had seven dollars in my hand. I stopped on the stoop. The sun shone and the April breeze felt like a caress. It seemed strange not to have to hurry. Only now did I realise how tired I was. I felt my hands burn and my whole body tremble a little.

I stood looking about, feeling both joy and regret. For I left the Corloves not with indifference. I had grown fond of the children, and even Mrs. Corlove herself, as I grew to know and understand her, I did not dislike her. But what a joy it was to know that I was free! Father would find work for me at once, for there was now a sprinkling of work over the city and he himself was working at last. But this day at any rate was before me. How I loved the sun! I walked home slowly, basking in it.

Before many days passed I was working in a shop on Canal Street. Father had not yet been working a full week. But after the hardship we had suffered eight dollars every week seemed a fortune. Mother began paying off what we owed the landlord and she even managed to save a few cents every week for a piece of material to make up a little dress for whichever one of us needed it most. The children were going to school and things were running smoothly.

But it was not for long. Soon again mother went about her work looking worried and perplexed and we children were again aware of the darkness in the bedroom and that the sun never came into the big room. "Perhaps," mother sighed, "a human being must not have it comfortable long or he would forget God."

This was the trouble: with the coming of the warm days my health became so poor that I had to stay away from work quite often. Mother was the more alarmed because she could not understand what was wrong. There seemed nothing wrong. But the slightest exertion made my temples throb. and my head go around. The shop where I was working now was on the top floor. I would stand long and look up the stairs before beginning to climb. It seemed like a dream that I ever ran up and down stairs for pure amusement. Then came a morning when I could not get up at all. I stayed in bed two days and mother made inquiries and found that Gouverneur Street Dispensary was not far away and "quite free." So on the third morning, which was Monday, she helped me dress and we started. Many times on the way we had to stop to rest on door steps. At last we came to a small ground floor building near Gouverneur Street dock. A policeman stood at the door and a few people were in line. We took our places and the policeman told us the door would open at nine o'clock.

I stepped a little out of the line to lean against the wall. The sun was beating down strongly on our heads, but from the water a refreshing breeze came up and we could hear the boats, while from a reddish, smoke covered building came the cry of geese.

Mother, too, was looking around. She was easily interested in everything about her. She remarked now: "That must be a slaughter house," and then, partly perhaps to take my attention away from myself, she motioned sadly to the line. This was our first experience with a Dispensary.

There were three people in the line ahead of us. Next

to me was a man with his arm in a sling who looked like an Irish dock laborer. Next to him another, with sawdust clinging to his clothes, wavered unsteadily. The first was a woman whose home I knew was the dark hallway and the park bench.

As we were going in the policeman handed us each a red cardboard ticket with a black number on it. I saw the woman, as she passed him, raise her chin and steady her step. We all sat down on the first bench. I leaned against my mother, closed my eyes, and sat waiting for my turn.

This doctor, like the first I had seen, raised my eyelids and asked how long I had been so pale. He advised mother to feed me up and keep me outdoors. I translated what he said and mother asked timidly, "Ask him what is the matter." He understood and answered in German "Anemia."

And now I became mother's first care. She saved on food that the others needed and bought milk and meat for me, and that I might be able to eat it in peace she would take the children out of the house. Often the little girl would refuse to go out. She would raise herself on tiptoe to look into my plate and lisp wistfully: "I wish I were sick."

In a few weeks I was strong enough to go to the shop again. But what took weeks to build up I lost in a few days and soon again I was staying home, this time going to the Dispensary regularly. As I stood there in line or sat on the bench in the waiting room, waiting for my turn, I grew to know many of the people who, like myself, came often, and to be familiar with every nook and corner in the room. I came every week and one week was exactly like another. There was the same room, many of the same people, and each time the same thing happened. First, on coming into the waiting room, we would all sit down, heavily. After this it became very still in the room. I would close my eyes for a moment with a feeling of relief at having my feet off the floor. Then, rested a moment, I would look about at the others. I knew at once from their faces, and even from their unconscious backs, I could gather who was better, who was worse, and who was the same. Then I would look about the room. There was the same unpainted, cleanly scrubbed floor, the shining brass knobs of the two doors on the right, and the one on the left, and the tiny staircase leading up. Then again I would study the men and women, more slowly this time, and aware now of every sound and motion, a hand unsteadily raised to the forehead, a half suppressed cough sounding loud in the stillness, a patient sigh, a feverish look. Next as the time of waiting lengthened, I became aware of the air in the room, the hot breath of sick people mixed with the odour of medicines, the breath of tobacco and stale whiskey. At this period of waiting I lost my interest in everything, my spirit had sunk with a heavy depression. Of the rest of the people some dozed heavily, some moved about restlessly in their seats and others, like myself, were given over to dull apathy.

Then one of the doors on the right would open quickly and cause a stir on the benches, and a wave of new life passed through the room. I loved to watch the patients coming out of the doctor's office. Every face looked brighter, more hopeful.

XLI

When we finished paying what we owed the land-lord, our lodgers moved away, and we moved again into three rooms on the same block but nearer to Clinton Street. We were glad to find rooms so near, for we could save the moving expenses. Late one night when father came home from work he and mother carted over the furniture on a push cart, the children carried the clothes and pots and pans in their arms and I stayed in the new rooms and put things in their places as they came in.

We liked moving from one place to another. Every one on Cherry, Monroe and other streets moved often. It meant some hard work but we did not mind that because it meant change in scenery and surroundings. None of the places were pretty and most of them were dingy. But moving even from one dingy place to another is a change. And then, too, some were less dingy than others. Here, for instance, the living room, instead of being painted an ugly green that had made everything look dark, and that had depressed our spirits, was a bright pink. Also there were two windows facing the street through which the sun came in. And if there was less privacy, for the rooms were on the stoop, just a few steps above the sidewalk, it was pleasant to sit down near the window and watch the people passing by. Across the street there was a blacksmith shop. I liked to listen to the ding, ding of the hammers beating in unison and we could see the sparks flying. Sometimes a bright, healthy, young face, all covered with grime, was pressed against the heavy grating of the blacksmith shop window. One day the young man saw me looking over and he grinned. Cherry Street is not a wide street and he probably saw my embarrassment for he threw his head back and laughed heartily. All these things were important when I was fifteen years old and we lived on Cherry Street.

The first neighbour with whom we became acquainted in this house was the dressmaker who lived across the hall. Her husband was a carpenter. Whenever he was not working I would see him sitting at the window reading a book. One day when I went in to see the Raisens I found that the husband was out and the book was lying on the table. I had long been curious about it and now I took it up and sat down at the window. Of course it was in Yiddish. I began to spell out the words. I had not read since I came to this country and had almost forgotten how. But as I read line after line it became easier and easier and soon I forgot all about everything and did not hear Mrs. Raisen working at the machine, her three little ones romping about the room, the clattering of the heavy trucks passing the window and the ding, ding from the blacksmith shop. I became aware of these things again only when I heard Mrs. Raisen saying, "Girl, you are blinding your eyes." Then I looked up and saw that night had come.

I found from Mr. Raisen that these books could be borrowed from soda water stand keepers, if one left fifteen cents security and paid five cents for the reading of the book. I listened to all the details with discouragement. For when could I hope to have twenty cents saved! Nevertheless I began to save, or rather, I determined to put away the very first cent I had. But in the meanwhile I watched out for Mr. Raisen's book. He rarely forgot to put it out of sight for he had three mischievous little children. But whenever I saw it on the table I would go in and read it.

At last one night I brought home my first volume. I took the lamp out of the bracket, placed it on the table, and opened the book. I had told the stand keeper to give me anything as long as it was with vowels. For I had only learned to read the Hebrew print that had the vowels. These consisted in dots and lines printed under each letter.

In the meantime the children gathered around me and mother came over with her sewing and looked at me disapprovingly, sadly, "What a child you are," her eyes seemed to say. "How little sense you have. If you had spent this money on nourishing food——" And again, "True, you did not ask for the money, you saved it. But where did it come from?"

I understood this as plainly as if she had uttered the words. Poor mother, she was often worried over how to live and save on our six or seven dollars and over my health. And so, partly with the hope of cheering her up a little and partly to draw her attention away from myself and a possible scolding, I began to read aloud. In a few minutes I looked up and saw her stitching quickly on the little dress she was mending. I could see she was listening but the sad look had not left her eyes. But when again I looked up the little dress lay forgotten in her lap and on her face there was a healthy look of interest and curiosity. The only stories she had ever heard before were from the Bible.

From that time many happy evenings were ours. Mother always listened reluctantly, as if she felt it were a weakness to be so interested. Sometimes she would rise suddenly during the most interesting part and go away into the dark kitchen. But soon I would catch her listening from the doorway.

And I lived now in a wonderful world. One time I was a beautiful countess living unhappily in a palace, another time I was a beggar's daughter singing in the street. Of course we never drew more than one little book a week, about two hundred and fifty pages for five cents. But I got all I could out of it. I read it aloud, I reread it to myself and I lived it when I was not reading. Almost every book had a song or a poem. These I learned by heart, found appropriate melodies for them out of the great stock of Russian peasant songs that I knew, and when Aunt Masha and her friends came on a Saturday I would sing to them. Mother always seemed uneasy when she heard these songs, and sister would look at me with astonishment and her truthful eyes seemed to say, "Oh, how can you!"

I did feel guilty but the next time they came I had a new song for them.

One day when I went to change my book the stand-keeper looked over his three shelves of books, high over his stand, and said finally, "I don't believe I have another book with vowels."

"No more books!" I pictured an impossible existence in our house without the joy of reading. "Look well," I begged him.

He stood up on a high stool and began rummaging about on the top shelf. "Here," he said, "is the last one, and I don't think you will like it. It is a thick, clumsy volume."

A thick volume! Could a book be too thick? And what did the clumsiness matter!

"Let me see it," I said, controlling my eagerness. For I had learned that people were often charged according to the desire they showed for the article. I turned to the first page of the story and read the heading of the chapter: "I am born."

Something in these three little words appealed to me more than anything I had yet read. I could not have told why, but perhaps it was the simplicity and the intimate tone of the first person. I had not yet read anything written in the first person.

My eager fingers turned to the title page and I uttered the words half aloud, "David Copperfield. By Charles Dickens."

"I'll take it," I said. I laid the five pennies on the zinc covered soda counter and walked away slowly, expecting and fearing to hear the standkeeper's voice calling after me and demanding an extra five cents because the book was so thick. But when the danger of that was passed I fairly ran home with my prize.

What a happy two weeks we spent! We lived little David's life over with him. Mother cried when he and Peggotty bade each other farewell through the keyhole, and then she laughed, at her tears, remembering that it was "only a story." And as I sat in the shop, felling sleeve lining, I would go over in my mind what I had read the night before. With what joy I looked forward to the evening when after supper we would all gather around the lamp on the table and sister or I would read aloud while mother sewed and the little ones sat with their chins very near the table. For if there was any joy to be gotten out of anything they must have their share. And so they would sit blinking sleepily and trying hard to understand but finally they would fall asleep with their heads on the table. Then mother, sister and I would move closer to each other and I would read in a lower voice.

When we were through with David Copperfield we felt as if we had parted from a dear friend. We could not bear to read anything else for a whole week.

The next book we drew was without vowels. Sister and I had never dreamed it would be so easy to learn to read it. In a week we read it as fluently as the other. And now reading material was not so limited. A flying newspaper in the street, a crumpled advertisement sheet, I would smooth out tenderly and carry off home, happy in the expectation of what was awaiting me. I tried to understand everything I read but if I could not, I read it anyway. For just to read became a necessity and a joy. There were so few joys.

Women at the push-carts haggled more and more desperately over a cent.

XLII

ONE night about this time when I came into the house
I was shocked at what I saw. Father was sitting on a
low box in the middle of the room. He was in his stocking feet, his elbows resting on his knees, his head bent
between his hands. Sister stood near the lamp in the
bracket, reading a letter and crying bitterly. My thought
was of grandmother at once. I went over to sister and
looked over her shoulder. After a lengthy and cere-
monious greeting, it read:

"Your mother is dead. But you should not grieve.
You should be glad. For she suffered much in these
two years." It was an old woman that wrote the letter
and what she told of grandmother's suffering is too horrible to repeat. The letter closed with: "I only hope and
pray that he who breaks every home, he to whom no bond
is sacred, the Czar of Russia, may know at least for one
year in his life the sorrow and loneliness she has known."

It was also about this time that a man came from
our part of the country and gave us news of grandfather.
He was in Mintsk in a Home for the Aged. The man
had seen him, and said that he was well but at times his
mind was like that of a child. He spoke of his children
in America and his eyes were full of tears. But soon
he chuckled gleefully. "Brother," he said to the man,
"come, I will show you something." He took him by the
hand and led him to a cot standing in a corner. He
looked around cautiously like a shy little squirrel and
then took a tiny bundle in a red bandana from under the
pillow. He patted the little bundle and smiled brightly
at the man. "You see, brother," he whispered, "as long

as I have this I have no fear of want." He untied the knot with his poor old trembling fingers and the man saw a few little lumps of sugar and a few crusts of bread covered with green mould. All his life the thought of want in his old age had been his one fear.

XLIII

THE warm days passed but my health did not improve. On the contrary, it grew worse and I worked less and less—a day in one shop, a half day in another, for I had no steady place now. Often after I had worked a morning in a shop the boss would pay me for the half day, and tell me he had no more work. I understood that I was not doing enough and it did not pay him to keep me. When I had the strength and the courage I would go to other shops and ask if they needed a feller hand. It did require courage to enter a shop for the people stared, my face was so pale. When I did not have the courage I went home and was glad to lie quite still on the couch.

In the autumn I had to stay at home altogether. What little I had earned was badly missed. Winter was coming and none of us had even half warm enough clothing. So father decided that sister should leave school and take my place.

She had just learned to read and write a little, and of course she could speak English. It was thought that she had made good progress in the short time, considering the drawback she had had, in not knowing the language. We all felt sad, mother particularly, that her education should end here. Sister herself took it in a way characteristic of her. Her days in school had been happy ones. She had been known and loved by teacher and pupils throughout the little Henry Street school. And like the rest of us she did not look upon "free schooling in America" in a matter-of-fact way. She, a little Jewish girl from an out-of-the-way Russian village of which no one

ever heard, was receiving an education! It seemed a
wonderful privilege. But when she saw that this was not
to be after all, she did not utter a single word of protest
or complaint.

On the first morning of going to the shop, for she was
starting in as a finisher on buttonholes, she rose very
early, as I had once done. I lay on the couch in the front
room, which was my place now, and watched her. This
morning reminded me of that first one when I left for
the strange shop. Sister was about the same age, there
were the same preparations, the same grey light in the
room. The only difference was that now mother was
here to put the thimble and scissors into her little coat
pocket, and tuck the little bundle of lunch under her arm,
and close the door after her, and then stand so still with
her face pressed against it.

I stayed in the house all day. I felt despondent. I
often felt in the way. When night came or it was time
for father to be home from work, I went out. I had
begun to feel in the way when father was in the house.
As the illness or semi-illness continued mother became
even more tender and devoted. But father's sympathy
waned. This illness was such a long, drawn-out affair.
It had had no definite beginning and promised to have no
end. And besides, he saw that I suffered no pain, I was
merely pale and not over strong. What of that? He
himself was not strong. He found sitting in the shop
harder and harder as the years were passing. He had
been working as a tailor since he had been twelve years
old. And just now his eyes were troubling him. For
he had inherited grandmother's weak eyes. And so he
felt, no doubt, that just when I should have been a greater
help to him I became a care and expense.

Besides this there were other unpleasant features. For

people in my parents' circumstances it was not a usual thing to keep a daughter at home. And so, inquisitive relatives and neighbours began to ask why? Why was I staying at home? What was the matter with me? Why was I so pale? My parents felt they must hide the truth even at the cost of lying, for I was growing up—and what man would marry a sick girl! But it must not be thought that now we lived only in trouble. We had our joys too. They seem very trivial but they helped to make up our life.

Father belonged to a society in which he was an active member. The men often came to our house to talk things over with him and he felt important and often offered our front room for committee meetings. Before they opened the meeting they always assured mother that they would not keep us up any later than ten o'clock. But when the time came they were so deep in discussion that they never even heard the clock strike the hour. I used to sit down in the doorway of the kitchen and front room from where I could see all their faces and listen to their heated arguments. Always it was a piece of burial ground that was the subject of discussion and when a member, or any one belonging to his family, died, whether the rest of the members should contribute an extra dollar to cover burial expenses, and whether as a society they should or should not employ a doctor and pay him out of the society fund. At twelve o'clock or even later they would at last break up with the question of the burial ground and the extra dollar and the doctor still unsettled.

Then mother and I would go into the front room coughing and choking from the cigarette smoke, and open up the folding cots, and carry the sleeping children to bed. The two little ones often cried at being awakened to undress. But father, if he had succeeded in carrying a point and in the knowledge that he had served the society in giving the room, went to bed smiling.

Sister was happy in a friendship she had formed. The little girl was the oldest in a family of boys. The mother was always sick. And this little woman of eleven went to school, where we heard she was remarkably bright. And between times she took care of the mother and the boys and the house. She went patiently, with her back a little bent, from task to task and was always sweet and bright. Sister made friends with her one Friday night when she sat with her little brothers on the iron steps of the tenement, telling them stories. And my mother, after visiting the sick woman, would often tell herself and us too, "Children, we must not sin. Indeed we have a great deal for which to be grateful."

While I, having more time now, dreamed more, I rarely had a book to read, now that I was not working. But, as I lay on the couch with my eyes closed, I made up stories for myself. They were of the life I saw about me, with little variations to suit myself. Some of the stories were short, some were long and I continued them from day to day. Once or twice I tried to write the things. But the moment I had the pencil in my hand my mind became a blank. I did not know where to begin, what to say. And when I finally succeeded in writing a few sentences it seemed to have no meaning. "And yet," I wondered, "in my mind a few minutes before, they did have meaning."

Often too I thought over religious questions that I heard or which came up in my mind. I was still religious but I could no longer accept my religion without question. And these questions perplexed me and I felt guilty that they should come up at all and tried to put them away from my mind.

Now also that I had time I began to go to night school and sister came too. I only knew how to read a word here and there. I sat in the class and followed each girl that read, with my finger on the page. If I happened to lift my finger I could not find the place. Sister would have sat near me and helped me but I felt ashamed to let her help me because I was the longest in this country. She read well and made good progress. But I sat trembling with nervousness all evening. I could never learn to forget that there were people all about me. And the time I spent in waiting for the teacher to call on me to read I can only count among the greatest sufferings I ever had. I would sit with my hands lying cold in my lap and my face turning hot and cold by turns. Most of the time I was unable to follow, I was so upset. And when the teacher called on me at last and I stood up with my book in my hand I seemed to see nothing but a blank page. Then I would hear a queer sound like of some one sick. The next moment I was sitting down. And yet I could not bear to stay away. I had a feeling that the world was going on and I was being left behind. This feeling drove me on and I went to the class and learned painfully a word or two at a time.

XLIV

ONE day when I was sixteen years old a neighbour
came into our house. She glanced at me on the couch
and at mother sewing at the window.

"What!" she said, "is your daughter still ill?" Mother
bent her head lower over her work but answered lightly,
"Yes, but it is nothing."

"You know," the neighbour smiled after a few moments, "I think I know of a remedy."

Mother looked up for the first time. "Yes?" she asked.

"Yes," the neighbour smiled again. She would not
say what it was and went out with a mysterious nod and
smile for each of us.

In the evening after supper, two days later, while I
was preparing to go out for a walk, mother said she had
no sugar for the morning. She laid the money on the
table and said with unusual quietness, "Sugar is fifteen
cents a paper nearly everywhere but there is one store
where you can get it for fourteen."

"Where?" I asked. I was at the mirror combing out
my hair and stood with my back toward the room.

"It is on Broome Street near Market."

I turned quickly but mother was already walking into
the kitchen. I thought it very queer, but did not say
anything. I braided my hair, put on my hat and coat,
and ran out. I began to run at once, for I was always
afraid of the cold. As I ran I thought again of my
errand and wondered at it. True, we never stopped at
any distance to get a thing a cent cheaper, but to go as
far as this for a paper of sugar seemed extreme even

for us. And mother's manner surprised me even more as I recalled it now.

When I reached Broome Street I looked up at the numbers and found that I still had a distance to go. I walked leisurely now for I was no longer cold. An agreeably warm sensation was tingling through my whole body and the air seemed sweet. I was also conscious of a vague happiness and wondered. There seemed so little cause. One hour before I had been so miserable. The cause seemed that father was irritable, mother sorrowful, and the light in the room was dim, and I knew that the next day it would be the same, and the day after, and the day after that.

I found the grocery a one-window store. A bell tinkled over the door as I entered. No one was in so I went and leaned on the wooden counter to wait. Presently a fair young man with a ruddy face and stooping shoulders came in from a door at the back. He asked mechanically what I wanted and pushed the paper of sugar across the counter with scarcely a glance at me. I saw a corner of a lump of sugar sticking out through the bag so I asked, "Will you please put this into another bag? I have quite a distance to go."

He looked up quickly and stared at me for a moment. Then he took a bag and began slipping the sugar into it. The bag broke so he crumpled it up, threw it under the counter and took another one.

"Where do you live?" he asked, working with marked slowness and tearing this bag too. "On Cherry Street," I said. He was silent but I noticed that his face looked more animated than it had been. At last my sugar was safe in two bags, and he handed it to me instead of pushing it across the counter as before.

"How is it out?" he asked, glancing at me shyly for

the second time and then looking toward the door. With people that were shy I felt at ease, almost bold. So I answered pleasantly, "Fine! It is cold, but there is no wind." And now, since I had spoken to him I thought it would be rude not to say good night. As I was walking toward the door I was aware that he stood still looking after me. It was only later when I recalled these details that I realised I had noticed them.

Again, about two days later my mother asked me hesitatingly and without looking at me, "Well, what do you think of that young man?"

I looked at her in surprise. "What young man?" I asked.

"The young man from the grocery store on Broome Street," she said.

"I did not think of him. Why?"

Then with great earnestness mother explained to me that the young man was a possible suitor and a very desirable one, that he was getting an excellent living out of the store and that he very much wished to become "further acquainted," and, a meeting had already been arranged for Saturday.

I was bewildered by what had been happening. I was grown up, a young man was coming to see me! I would soon be married perhaps! The thought "I am grown up!" came again and again. It seemed incredible. I remember late one night, perhaps it was that very first night, when it was still all through the house, I rose from the couch, took the tiny night lamp from the nail and tiptoed to the half length mirror hanging between the two windows. I held it up and looked at myself earnestly for a long minute. "So I am grown up," I thought.

During the few days that followed there was a great hustle and bustle in our house. Our first furniture had long ago been broken up, and a second-hand couch for two dollars that had been added since, now stood on three legs. So mother brought forth the homespun linen sheet, which she had as a relic from home, and spread it over the couch. "When will there be a better time to use it than now?" she said and smiled at me. And father went out and bought two straight back chairs and a rocker, and we were ready to receive the young man.

He came Saturday about three o'clock accompanied by a middle-aged man who introduced himself as "the oldest uncle." I shrank behind my mother and a cousin who had been invited to be present to give her opinion of the young man. At last the first few minutes, the worst part, was over. We were all seated. Father and the uncle sat at the table opposite each other and at once began a lively conversation to which the rest of us sat and listened respectfully.

When I felt more at ease I observed the young man. I felt as if I had known him a long time. It seemed quite natural that he should sit with his neck shrunk into his collar and keep his hat on like the two older men and be quite as old-fashioned as they were. Then in my mind arose the image of another young man. He was the imaginary companion of my childhood grown older. He was tall and dark and not at all shy.

I sat thinking so until I noticed the uncle observing me from time to time and I became uneasy again. But I too observed him. I liked him. He reminded me of Mr. Peggotty from David Copperfield. He was a large, strong, ruddy-faced man with a hearty, frank manner. He was leaning on the table with his hands clasped in front of him and he looked right into my father's face as he talked. He was relating his experiences as a news-

dealer. At last he sat back in his chair. My heart began to beat uncomfortably.

"Now," he said, "supposing we talk of things nearer
our hearts." I was aware that even the children avoided
looking at me.

"Tell me," the uncle asked in his frank blunt way,
glancing at me and then looking at my father, "why do
you want to marry off that girl? She is so young, and
not at all homely. What is the haste?" There was a
tone of suspicion in his voice as if he feared a bad
bargain.

There was a buzzing in my ears and I wanted to run
away. Indistinctly I heard my parents answer something
and at the same time I suddenly saw the young man
standing before me and asking: "Will you come for a
walk with me?" I rose quickly, went into the bedroom
and stood with my face pressed against the clothes hanging on the wall. Then I came out dressed in my childish
hat and coat and we went out. And now I heard him
talk for the first time since I bought the sugar in his
store. His tone was earnest, and a little eager, his ex-
pressions,—we spoke Yiddish, of course,—were almost
Biblically old-fashioned, as if he had just come from
some pious Russian village instead of having been in
America five years. He told me that he had three uncles.
I recall these words spoken confidently but piously.
"My uncles are all espoused and with the help of God
they are making a living." I gathered that he wanted
me to know, that as a member of this family he too felt
confident of being able to make a living. He talked the
whole while to the same effect. His tone became more
eager and persuasive. From this and his looks and
manner his thought of myself was very clear to me.
I felt a little pleased, but that was all.

When we came home we had cake and tea and then they went away.

That evening and the next day my parents looked quietly excited and expectant. The next night, while we were at supper, a message came from the matchmaker saying that the young man and his family were "pleased" and would be happy at an "alliance."

Father was so pleased at the news that his face became quite radiant. He sat back in his chair and laughed joyously. It appeared that he had not expected it. "A girl without a cent to her name," he said, quite lost in wonder. Mother too looked pleased, but she was not so humble.

"Not every girl needs a dowry," she said.

I could not understand why father was so happy. He looked at me. "And what do you say, Rahel?" he asked.

The question troubled me suddenly. Somehow I had never quite realised that this question would really be put to me and that I would have to answer it. I rose from the table but could find nothing to say. "Well," father said in an easy tone, as if he were quite sure of the outcome, "there is plenty of time. Think it over. Take until to-morrow night and decide." My mind was in a tumult.

In the meantime the matchmaker practically lived in our house. He came in during the morning, he came in the afternoon and again at night when father was home. He would sit for hours singing the young man's praise,—his wealth, his business abilities and his character. And soon he succeeded in making my parents feel that this was one chance in a lifetime.

When next father asked me, "Well, what do you say?" I trembled. "I have not decided yet," I told him quietly.

He was patient but he did not look so at ease as the night before, nor so sure.

"Do you want to see him again?" he asked.

I said: "No."

He thought for a moment. "I don't see what you want," he said. "He is a nice quiet young man and the main thing, he is not a wage earner. The smallest business man is worth ten workingmen. Tell me definitely to-morrow night. We cannot keep the people waiting for an answer any longer. This is not child's play, you know." When father was out of hearing mother added sadly, by way of help perhaps, "It is true that you are young, but you see, father is poor and you are not strong!"

I went into the bedroom and wept with my face buried in the pillows. "Why did I have to decide this? I had never been allowed to decide the smallest thing before— the shape of my shoes, the length of my dress."

The next evening I could not bear to face father. I saw that I must answer him definitely and I did not know what to answer. When it grew dark it occurred to me to go out into the street. I could always think more clearly in the air and while walking.

It was a mild, clear night and there was a half moon. I walked so I could see it ahead of me. It calmed me to watch it and soon my brain did clear a little and I was able to realise something of my situation.

"Father is poor and I am not strong." These words had impressed themselves on my mind and now I caught at them.

"It is clear then," I thought, "that I must marry. And if I did not marry this young man whom could I marry? A tailor?" At the thought of a tailor the young man rose in my estimation. I also saw an advantage in that he was a grocer. "My people could live near and get things at cost price, bread, butter, sugar, potatoes. It will be a great help." But on the other hand I could not picture myself living with the strange young man and his mother. I knew now that he had a mother; she was blind. He was her only son and she would live with him then as now.

It struck me how similar my fate was to my mother's. She too had married an only son, and his mother had been blind. And now I recalled many tragic incidents in my mother's early life. Grandmother had loved her son passionately and was often so jealous that though she had been a kind and extremely pious woman she did not scruple to talk to her son against his wife and influence him to unkind actions and speech. Mother would weep and rebel. "I'll never talk to her again," I would hear her say. But soon she would remember grandmother's affliction and she would forgive her.

Would this mother too talk to her son against me? I realised that I was neither so good nor so patient as my mother. "I would not stand it," I thought, "I would run away. But, if I did not marry this young man, what then?"

Again I saw our dimly lit home, father cross and irritable, mother sorrowful, always the same with no change and no hope. And now it would be worse. For father would feel that I had had a chance to better things and did not do so. But is that all there is in looking forward to marriage? An uneasy fear—and what is love!

When I reached home supper was already half over. I sat down at the foot of the table and mother gave me my soup. The children seemed to be sitting at the table more mannerly than usual and father spoke quietly of trivial things in the shop. He scarcely seemed to notice me. He was always afraid of making us children feel too important. But I knew that there was one thought only in every mind. My heart beat as if it would burst. I leaned against the table and sat looking into my plate and stirring and stirring my soup for I knew I could not lift my hand.

At last I heard father lay down his spoon and push his chair away from the table a little.

"Well," he asked in a "by the way" tone, "what have you decided?" It grew so still, even the breathing seemed to have stopped. And in this stillness I heard myself say, "Yes."

I did not look up. I knew that every face had grown brighter. It was pleasant to know that I was the cause. I had been nothing but a sorrow so long.

He stood stirring the can with a stick.

PART FOUR

PART FOUR

XLV

AND now a new life began for us, and for the second time I became an important person. The children fairly strutted about and boasted about their "oldest sister." And father talked to the members of his society of the coming engagement. How happy his face looked and how cheerfully he spoke! To him this was the beginning of a new life. He had scarcely ever known what it meant to be free from anxiety. First, from early childhood it was the fear of the army where he would be compelled to violate the laws against God: "Thou shalt not kill" and the fear for the blind and helpless mother he would have to leave behind. In this fear he grew up to manhood. And then with blood money, borrowed and saved on bread and his mother's tears, he bought a false name. Then his life was in constant fear of human beings, often in fear of his own shadow. Then being found out, and all seeming lost, his escape to America, then the struggle of a stranger in a strange land, which led to only a hand-to-mouth existence, without any change, without hope of change. But now, he felt, at last things began to look bright. One child was already grown up. He was branching out, he was to be allied with a fine respectable family, with men of business. Now on a Saturday afternoon after his nap, he would not have to walk in the street aimlessly, he would go to visit his son-in-law. He would sit at a comfortable table, drink tea and talk business. His opinion of business men was high. It was his dream some day to lay down his needle and thread and perhaps open a little candy store or a soda water stand. But up to this time it had been no more than a dream. For when could he hope to put away fifty or seventy-five dollars! Now, however, with the prospect of having a son-in-law in business the dream looked nearer reality.

And so he beamed at mother and teased her. "Hanah, you are going to have a son-in-law soon." Mother too looked happy but I did not find it so easy to understand her. Her manner to me reminded me of the time, four years before, when the ticket came for me to go to America. Her eyes followed me about as they did then. Often while she sat in a corner over some work I saw from the expression of her face and the occasional motions of her head and lips that she was arguing something out with herself, as was her habit, looking at it from every possible point of view. Often too her eyes were on my face in dumb inquiry.

And I, at present, I found it easier to understand every one in my family than myself. My people were happy, home was cheerful, I received some new clothes. The choice was left entirely to me for the first time in my life. And I chose what I liked, pretty material for a dress and it was given away to a dressmaker to be made. I chose a pretty pair of shoes and saw that they were the right size. And when I put them on they looked so small and dainty after the others, and fitted so snugly, that when I walked I felt as if my feet scarcely touched the ground. And yet deep down in my heart I felt so troubled. Why? I could not have told. So passed the first week after I had said that little word, "Yes."

Saturday the young man came. I still thought of

him as the young man, and we went out to buy an engagement ring. We went to a jeweller he knew.

I stood at the glass case and watched him try one little diamond ring after another on my finger. To my surprise the pleasure I felt in receiving the diamond ring was not as great as I had expected. He asked me to choose and I chose a very small stone in a simple setting. The ring was bought and left to be made smaller. And now I would have been glad to go home alone. But when we came outside he asked me to come and visit some of his relatives. I realised suddenly that I had duties now, new duties. In the meantime he entreated, "Please come! I have promised my youngest uncle. They expect us." So I went.

This uncle had recently married. I found him a very agreeable man and his wife charming. She took me at once under her protection. Soon more relatives arrived and she introduced me as "Israel's bride." Some of the women exclaimed openly at my youthful appearance and the men slapped Israel on the back and winked at him. His face was flushed with pleasure. Soon we sat down at a feast of fruit, cake and tea. And as the relatives sat peeling their apples or oranges they became curious to know whether Israel's bride had any accomplishments. "Can you sing?" they asked me. I said, "A little," and I sang.

When it grew dark and I went to get my hat and coat the young aunt followed me into the bedroom. She took my face between her hands and looked into my eyes. "It is so strange," she said, "to hear a little thing like you singing these sad songs."

Directly the next day my parents began to prepare for the engagement which was to be on the coming Saturday night. A great "crowd" was expected. Aunt

Masha managed to procure the use of an empty loft in
the new shops on Jefferson Street through the janitor
whose daughter was her friend. And to this loft with
parcels and bundles many excursions were made during
the week by mother and the children or father, when he
came home from work at night. No one looked so happy
and excited as father. He invited all the members of the
society, and their wives and children, and mother invited
half of Cherry Street. Every one must come and par-
ticipate in their happiness, no one must be overlooked or
offended. Aunt Masha invited all her friends. Aunt
Masha was not the rosy-cheeked girl she had been. But
she looked contented. She listened and advised girls in
their love affairs, and took part at engagements and
weddings with an "elderly aunt" air. We all felt that
she had settled herself down to a single life. But there
were times when she would not talk to us and she looked
morbid and cried for days and days.

Her friends were four mature girls. They often
came to our house for me to dress their hair, for which
I seemed to have a knack. They praised me for it but
otherwise they never took any notice of me. Now, however, they looked at me curiously, and as I had once been
envied for going to America I was envied now because
I was going to be married. Not one of the girls had
their families in this country, or a comfortable home.
One spoke to me openly. She had been a pretty blonde
girl when I came to this country, but now her face had
no colour and she stooped as she walked. "You are
very fortunate, Rahel," she said. "I am tired of the
shop, I want something more than a folding cot for my
home." And she sighed and walked away from me
with her shoulders drooping more than ever.

When Saturday came there was a great deal of excitement in our house. All the children had their heads washed and sister curled their hair and helped mother get dressed. The smallest boy, six years old now, sat crying with a swollen cheek and had to be comforted with sweets. And I walked about from room to room and was of no help to any one. As soon as it grew dark Aunt Masha and the girls came, and carried me off to a hairdresser, and as usual now I who had always been last everywhere was first. I sat down in the chair and my friends stood about me. My hair was carefully brushed, braided and wound all about my head and sprinkled with gold tinsel. When I came home and put on my first long dress, and looked into the mirror I saw that I looked at least eighteen years old. And then it occurred to me that this was my day! That perhaps I'd never have another such day, and the desire came to be happy this one night.

I went to the hall early, for indeed the loft looked like a hall now. It was bright with lights and there were two long tables laden with fruits and candies prettily arranged in glass bowls and decorated with fringed red, white and blue papers and fancy paper napkins. Folding chairs stood along the walls and the floor was sprinkled with candle scraping for the dancing. And when the people began to arrive I saw that this was indeed my day. No one looked upon me as a child, every one was kind and attentive. Even the elderly people came up to shake hands with me. The blood began to beat rapidly in my veins and my heart throbbed with excitement. After the formal ceremony, when the plate was broken, and Israel slipped the little diamond ring on my finger, I refused to sit down next to him at the head of the table. I felt as if intoxicated. Instead I walked about, talked to the girls and flirted with the young men. Then I danced. I danced with the men, I danced with the girls, I danced until both families were alarmed and begged me to stop. I assured my mother in a whisper that I never felt in better health in my life and continued to dance. I saw that Israel was not looking very happy. He was sitting in a corner, looking neglected. It meant nothing to me. Once when I stopped for a few moments he came over and begged me to sit down. At the same time two young men came sliding up and asked me to dance. The two stood disputing and jesting. Each one claimed that he had been first. In the meantime a waltz began, a third young man was passing and I took his arm and went off laughing.

But as the evening advanced I grew more and more tired and at last I felt quite limp. The guests were gone, Israel and his family were also gone, and the janitor turned out the lights on a room hazy with cigarette smoke and tables covered with fruit skins and crumpled paper napkins. We went out into the still, cold morning. I fell a little behind my people who were discussing the success of the party, and walked wearily, listening to the sound of my own footsteps and wondering, "And what will be to-morrow?"

XLVI

ABOUT the middle of the week a message came from Israel's mother inviting me to come and spend a day and a night with them. I looked at mother, I had not yet gotten over the effects of the engagement night. I felt worn and looked paler than usual. But she asked me, "Will you wear your new dress?" So I knew that I was to go. The minute it was decided I was stirred with curiosity about Israel's home and his mother, whom I had not yet seen, for she had not been to the engagement. Because she was blind I expected to find her looking like grandmother, tall and frail, and with sweet pale face and hands. But soon I found that she was not at all like that.

I found Israel in the store. He looked so pleased to see me and at once led me to the door in the back of the store and as he pushed it open I saw in the middle of the kitchen and right under the gas which was lit, a large strong looking woman in a brown dress and wig. "Mother, here is Ruth!" he said. His voice was full of excitement and she put out her hands and took mine. So we stood for a long minute. The light was on her face and I could see it working with emotion, and there was a look in it that I had often seen in grandmother's face when she wanted very much to see. After a little while Israel took my hat and coat and the mother walked straight to the table and drew out a chair for me. It was a surprise to me to watch her quick sure step. She sat near me and talked all afternoon. Her voice was strong, deep and monotonous; and as she talked almost without a stop it was like listening to a machine grinding steadily. She told me all about her brothers, Israel's uncles, their honesty and ability in business, and of their happy lives at home. She seemed to talk with a view to entertaining me. But I felt also that she wanted me to know the kind of a family I was coming into. Then she talked about Israel. She said that he was a good, dutiful son. I believed it. I could see from his manner, from the way he looked at her and from the way he listened to her,—for when there were no customers in the store he too came and listened,—that he was good to his mother.

I gave her all my attention but when I grew tired I looked about. So this is where I am going to live, I thought. This room which was a kitchen, dining room and bedroom in one, was all I could see. But I also noticed a closed door right opposite the one leading into the store and a little dark window with iron bars high up near the ceiling in the wall on the right. This was the only window in the room, and it looked into the dark hall of the tenement. On the little window sill I noticed two books, and I promised myself to see soon what they were.

Gradually, from talking about the uncles and her son, the mother led to the marriage. "You see," she said, with a wave of her large, brown strong hands, "I have everything that is necessary in a household. There will be no need to buy a thing." My heart sank when I heard this. I had dreamed of a new bright home. "And this is not all," the mother continued, "there is another room. Come, I'll show you." She rose and opened the door I had noticed. There was a current of chill, stale air and I followed her into a room where there was dim daylight. "When we moved in here," the mother kept on talking, "we did not bother fixing up." I could see that. All the furniture stood in the middle of the room. There was a couch, a bureau, some chairs and an ice box, and against one wall the pieces of a white iron bed. Everything was grey with dust and cobwebs hung from the ceiling. The two windows were long, narrow and barred with iron. It looked to me like a prison. I shivered and went to the door. "Are you going in?" the mother asked. I said, "Yes, I am so cold." I could not keep my teeth from chattering. I could not picture the room except with the dust, the cobwebs and the iron barred windows, and the mother's deep monotonous voice as an accompaniment.

During the evening business was at a lull in the store so Israel was more in the house. He stood near the stove with his hands spread out for the warmth, and with a smile watched his mother moving about the room performing little duties here and there and still relating the merits of her relatives. He often glanced at me. He looked as if he too had something that he wanted to say. But he also looked as if it could wait, there was no need for hurry. We had not yet spoken since I had come. But I noticed, or, more correctly, felt that his manner toward me was different from what it had been before the engagement. It was more intimate though we had not seen each other since nor did we know each other any better. I felt uncomfortable.

At last, when there was a pause in the mother's talk I asked Israel, "Do you read sometimes?"

"Yes," he said slowly, "when I have nothing better to do."

"What are those two books? May I see them?"

He stood up on a chair to reach them, blew the dust from them and gave them to me. Then he too sat down at the table and watched me turn the pages. I felt hap-

pier now and having the books to which to give my
attention I also felt more at ease.

The first book turned out to be one I had already read.
I was delighted. It was like meeting a friend. And
the thought that Israel had read the same book was a
sort of link and made me feel more friendly toward him.
So far we seemed to have had nothing in common, nothing to talk about. But now there was the book. I glanced
at the pages here and there and asked enthusiastically
what he thought of this or that part, and how he liked
this or that character. He was still smiling but he merely
answered "yes" or "no" to my questions.

The second book was a translation from the Russian
into Yiddish, partly letters, partly diary. I looked it
through and was at once filled with a burning desire to
read it. The intimate tone of the first person in which
it was written made me feel as if that some one were
actually talking to me. I could feel his presence. "Shall
I read it aloud?" I asked Israel. "No," he said, without
any interest. "What is the use?" He even looked as if
he would have liked me to put the book away. But the
only time I put a book away at home was when I was
forced to. And here I knew no one would even hint that
I put it away so I took my advantage and read. But
the thought that I was rude and that the boy felt hurt
perhaps, made me feel uncomfortable. So every now and
then I would look up, say a word, or smile at him. I
could smile now, I felt so happy when I read.

In this way the evening and the next morning passed.
Late in the afternoon Israel hastened in from the store
looking excited. "Ruth," he said eagerly, "will you come
into the store for a minute? I want to introduce you
to a customer of ours." I rose from the table, scarcely
knowing what I did; I was miserable in a moment. Meet-

ing strangers was a great hardship. And this seemed so unnecessary, merely a customer of Israel's. I could say I did not want to go. But that seemed like a child. And to say that I did not like to meet strangers was also impossible. A person of that kind was thought a boor. Israel looked at me but only saw my unwillingness to go. He looked slightly annoyed and explained as if he were sorry that explanations should be necessary. "But she is our best and oldest customer, and she asked to meet you." This explanation made it still worse, though why I could not have told at the moment. His mother too joined him in explaining and urging. So I rose and followed him into the store. My cheeks were burning and I dreaded the light and the stranger's eyes. At that moment Israel was more of a stranger to me than he had been a little while before. I stopped at the counter right near the door in the back. Further than that I would not go and Israel had to call his customer to the back part. I saw a tall, dried out looking woman in black with sharp, dark eyes that looked me over at once. Israel introduced us. She smiled, I nodded. And now my only thought was to go back into the kitchen, when I saw Israel push a slip of paper and a pencil toward me and lift a basket of bags and bundles to the counter. "Will you put down these figures while I call them off?" he said. What was my trouble of a few minutes before compared to what I felt now? I never could add a row of figures correctly. And since I had come to this country I had scarcely even written any numbers.

A sick feeling came over me with the shame that was awaiting me. I took the pencil and bent over the slip of paper and heard Israel call "10." Ten, I repeated to myself, looking at the paper blindly, and wondering, "Which comes first, the one or the nought?" Ages seemed to pass since I had heard the number called. I put down something. "17" I heard Israel's voice again. And again I wondered which came first. How the blood beat in my temples! I decided to keep all the ones on one side, to the left. "23" Israel called. And now it seemed as if I must break down. In Yiddish many people read numbers like the script, from right to left, which would read three twenty although written (23). When I had been learning as a child it had been a great puzzle to me and now it bewildered me altogether. Suddenly it occurred to me that if Israel called the numbers in English it would be easier for me for at least some of them I could write as they sounded. He did and it was easier. So I stumbled on from number to number. Often I felt as if I must give up but still went on. At last I saw Israel put the last package into the basket. "Now, add it," he said. This was the hardest yet. Again I did not know from which side to begin, the right or left. But I added it somehow, and then I straightened up. "It is ninety-six cents," I said and stood holding the little piece of paper in my hand and looking at it. I would have given anything not to have to give it up. But Israel was holding his hand out for it and the woman's eyes were upon me. So I laid it in his hand and stood waiting. I thought he would go over it at once and show me the mistakes right before the woman. But he did not. He just folded it and put it into the basket. I felt grateful for that.

The woman said good-bye, Israel took the basket on his arm and they went out. When the door closed behind them I leaned across the counter. Nearly all the strength of my body had gone in the effort. And as I waited I thought, "If Israel had known me a long, long time could he, would he have done this? Why did he do it

at all? Was it to show the woman that he was not
marrying an illiterate or was it to keep me a little longer
in the store and give his customer a chance to see me?
Had he been talking to her about me, or did he wish at
once to begin breaking me into the business?

The bell over the door rang and I straightened up.
Israel came up smiling and said in his inoffensive way
and yet with great earnestness, "There was a mistake."
I opened my eyes wide in pretended surprise.

"Really?"

"Yes," he said mildly but with still greater earnestness. "It was even four cents more!"

For a moment I could scarcely believe that I heard
right. "Is that all I made a mistake in?" I thought,
"four cents!" Then I looked at Israel, his earnestness
struck me funny and I mimicked him a little. "Four
cents more!" Then I laughed while he looked on puzzled. I laughed and laughed and tears were running
down my cheeks. "Oh, there is hope for me," I thought.
"In time I can learn to add even with two people looking
on."

XLVII

THE next day was Friday and Israel kept his store closed in the evening. He came to our house about seven o'clock and showed us two little tickets which were still unfamiliar to my family and myself. "These are for the theatre," he said, "for to-night." The children looked at me with bright eyes. "You will tell us all about it," they said, and mother looked quite excited as she helped me dress. I remembered Mr. Cohen's shop, and recalled what I had heard the men say about plays and actors. I thought, "Perhaps I'll see Jacob Adler in King Lear!" We walked to the theatre in silence. Indeed we were never anything else but silent. This was the second time I was out alone with him. The first time had been when we went to get the ring. Then, I merely felt awkward while walking with him. But now I felt nervous and miserable. The silence oppressed me and as we walked along, his sleeve, as if by design, kept coming in contact with mine, and I kept edging away, but very slowly so as not to hurt his feelings. For I was not sure it was by design that he brushed against my sleeve. In our seats in the balcony it was the same way. He was very attentive but chiefly with looks, and his elbow was on the arm of my seat. I pressed into the farthest corner and the edge of the arm cut into my back. I sat and could think of nothing but how to keep clear. Of the play I have a blurred picture of an angry king, dressed in scarlet and white, on a throne, and a throng of people. I knew the play was not King Lear.

The walk home was again a silent one through the streets now almost deserted. I remember how glad

I was when I caught sight of our tenement. I never remembered it looking so nice as it did now in the pale
light of the street lamp which stood right in front of it.
The hall door as usual stood open and the light shone
through the hall all the way to our door. I stopped in
the doorway and Israel stopped on the stoop. I felt under obligation to him. I felt that I ought to say something but could not think what. So I said good night and
turned to go when he called "Ruth!" His voice sounded
so muffled. I faced about and he came and stood near
me. "I want one kiss," he said. I felt panic-stricken.

"Oh, I couldn't!" I said, "I couldn't possibly. Indeed
I couldn't!"

"But, we are engaged now," he said in a hurt tone as if
he felt he were within his rights. Then it was, or had
I been realising it little by little all along, that it flashed
through my mind what married life may mean with a
person for whom one does not care. I stepped backward
toward the door repeating again and again, "I couldn't
possibly. I am sorry but I couldn't," and then I knocked.
Israel said good night and walked down the steps, and
mother let me into the front room lit by the tiny night
lamp. "How was it?" she whispered. I whined, "I am
tired!" She tiptoed away meekly and I sat down on
the couch and wondered how I was to live through the
night.

In the morning when mother came into the front room
and looked at me she cried out, "My God, how you look!
Do you feel so sick? Why did you not call me?"

"I am not sick," I said. Then I broke down. I told
her that I could not marry Israel. I clung to her and
begged her not to blame me. She spoke tenderly and
tried to quiet me. The children gathered around the
couch and father came in. I expected he would upbraid

me. But he was as tender as mother who stood with her arms tight about me. "Hush! hush!" he said, "if you feel so unhappy you need not marry him."

"And won't I be forced?" I asked.

"You won't be forced."

"Can no one force me?"

There were tears in his eyes. "No one can force you."

Still I kept asking it over and over again and laughed and cried hysterically.

My mother helped me over to her own bed in the bedroom and I tried to rest. I lay facing the door and could see all the way through the kitchen into the front room where mother and father talked in whispers and the children walked about on tiptoes. I lay wondering what father would tell Israel. He would come to-day for this was Saturday and he kept his store closed.

He came about one o'clock. I saw him stop for a moment with his back against the door and stand there almost smiling. My parents greeted him about as usual but more quietly. Soon I heard mother say still more quietly, "Ruth does not feel well." He was not at the door now and I could not see his face. But I heard him ask anxiously, "Did you have a doctor? Shall I call one?" Mother answered something. All this seemed to me unnecessary conversation. "Why doesn't father tell him?" I wondered. Suddenly a fear came over me. Perhaps father would not tell him after all. I remembered now that he had such a way of putting off doing a thing when we children wanted it done. And the more we wanted it the more reason he saw why it should be put off. "Wouldn't next day do or next week, what is the hurry? We must learn to be patient and wait." So I thought that now too he might put off telling Israel. He might even think that if he let it go for a while this little storm about my not wanting to marry would soon blow over and things would be as usual. I was in despair again. "What shall I do?" I wondered. Then it occurred to me to take the thing into my own hands. I was sorry I was not dressed but I could not stop to do it now. Not ten minutes longer could I bear to be engaged. I called to mother and asked her to tell Israel that I wanted to talk to him. Mother went slowly back to the front room. As he was coming in I could not see his face very distinctly for the light was at his back. But I could see that it looked anxious and was sorry, knowing that I would soon hurt him. He came and leaned up against the door post. He asked me too whether he should call a doctor. I answered something and then I was silent. I did not know where to begin or what to say. Suddenly I burst out that I did not want to get married and wept bitterly with my head in the pillow. I said I was sorry for the unpleasantness and the trouble but I would not get married. I would never marry at all. "But why?" he asked finally. His voice sounded as if he did not take me seriously. A moment before I had decided not to tell him, to spare him the hurt. Now when I saw he did not take me seriously there was only one thought in my mind, to be free of the engagement. So I said, "Because I do not love you." "Oh," he said, in a matter of course tone, "you will love me after we are married." And then he gave me many instances of his uncles and his aunts and his mother. I was in despair. How could I impress it upon him that for me this thing was impossible? And then it flashed through my mind how I could make him see it in a moment. I sat up and in my eagerness I stretched out my hand and laid it on his sleeve and he came a step nearer.

"Listen," I said, "you wanted to kiss me last night."

I could see that he felt a little guilty. "That was all right," I said. "I can imagine that if I loved you it would have made me happy. But as it is, the very thought of it drives me mad."

Even in that light I could see that his face changed colour and he stepped back and leaned heavily against the door. As I saw him weaken I quickly followed up my advantage. I took the little ring from under the pillow and pressed it into his hand. "Now go," I begged him. "I am so sorry, but please go, go!" And he went, and I sat and watched him; his step was unsteady and his back more bent than usual, he looked like an old man.

XLVIII

THAT night a message came from Israel's mother. She said, "I pray that you may have a thousand bridegrooms but not one shall you marry. I wish you no other ill but this!" Mother cried bitterly and father, who had been so quiet, so silent all afternoon, went out into the street still without saying a word. Only now I really believed that the engagement was off. And now all my troubles seemed small. I rose and dressed in my old clothes. I did not think they looked so shabby and faded, nor were the shoes so clumsy and large. I was not sorry for what had happened. I was never sorry for any experience I had had. At the time when it was hard, I could not help grumbling but later I was even glad. This thing I knew! I went to mother and tried to comfort her. I crept up to her mouse-fashion. We all loved fondling but we were not used to showing it. Mother looked at me sideways and said, "Go away, mouse!" But I saw the shadow of a smile in one corner of her mouth, so I pressed closer to her. "Don't cry," I said, "when you and father are old and the children are all married, you will be glad to have some one left at home."

Later that night, when the children gathered around the lamp on the table to do their lessons for Monday I too sat down among them and as I watched them write I suddenly remembered the diary I had read in Israel's home. I took a sheet of paper and a pencil and wrote a few words, in Yiddish of course. Then I crossed them out and wrote again trying to improve them. So I kept rubbing and crossing out. But finally when I was at the bottom of the page a sentence stood clear which I translate now. "I feel new joy in life and in freedom." I often attempted to write about what I felt or thought or saw. Most of the time after I wrote a sentence and the meaning was not clear at once I grew despondent and tore it up. But sometimes I was patient and determined like to-night, and when I succeeded I felt extremely happy and kept the bit of paper. I kept what I wrote that night and a few days later I copied it into a little penny note book. I was determined that I too would write a diary though I did not clearly know what a diary was.

When next I wrote in the little book I had already been working two weeks. The shop in which I found myself now was a piece work shop, not of the better kind. The work was cheap, the prices low and the men scarcely lifted their heads except to crack jokes. Oh, those jokes! I was older now and it was harder to sit among the men and listen. I translate what follows, the first sentence in the little book. "I hate the shop, I feel sick, I feel tired, I cannot see any meaning in life." This time I made a great effort to keep at work and I kept up as long as I was able to walk to the shop. Then again I lay on my back on the couch, and now it was as usual in our house. But now I did not care. I did not care about anything. All I wanted was to be left lying still. There were days when I scarcely felt any life, when I could not feel the couch under me. My body seemed to be suspended in the air and millions of specks of brown dust danced before me.

One day as I lay so I felt a touch on my wrist. This touch had become familiar since I had been ill. It was a doctor's touch. I opened my eyes and saw a woman, a stranger, sitting beside the couch. Neither in looks nor in dress had I ever seen any one like her in our neighbourhood. She was also beautiful and distinguished.

"How do you feel?" she asked me. Her lips smiled but her eyes remained almost sad. She spoke to mother in German, gave her a card and went away. I spelled out the printed name on the card, Lillian D. Wald, 265 Henry Street. Again I translate from the little book, though it was a long, long while before I wrote what follows: "Miss Wald comes to our house, and a new world opens for us. We recommend to her all our neighbours who are in need. The children join clubs in the Nurses' Settlement and I spend a great deal of time there. Miss Wald and Miss Brewster treat me with affectionate kindness. I am being fed up. I am to be sent to the country for health, for education."

The morning before I was to start Miss Wald herself went with me to get me a hat. We did not go to a millinery shop but what I now think must have been a sort of a class in the little Henry Street School. She asked for a hat that would stay well on my head in all kinds of weather. In the afternoon I washed all my clothing. How I worked! Mother said I looked like the old Rahel. I went to bed and made her promise to call me early. But when she stood at the couch in the morning it was as though through a mist that I saw her face. Later in the day I saw even more indistinctly. First I saw Miss Wald moving about the room, then Miss Brewster. On the table there was a red flower in a glass of water and a little white unfamiliar bowl. Mother saw me looking at it and brought it to me. "You see," she said trying to interest me, "it is jelly and when you feel better you can have some."

Still later the Settlement doctor sat at the couch and mother was weeping bitterly.

In a week I felt well enough to go about again. But now the doctor and Miss Wald thought that I had better go to the hospital first and get quite strong. And so it was that I missed the opportunity of the education, for it never came again.

This was a "piece work" shop.

XLIX

IT was not an easy thing for my people to send me to the hospital. For the very word filled us with fear. How could a helpless sick person be trusted to strangers! Besides, it was quite understood that in the hospital patients were practised upon by hardened medical students and then neglected. Whenever we saw any one miserable, dirty, neglected, we would say, "He looks like a 'hegdish'" (hospital). And so we saw our neighbours all about us borrow and pawn but keep their sick at home. And when once in a while we saw a person taken to the hospital we looked after him mournfully as if he were already carried to the burial grounds. It was also an open acknowledgment of the direst poverty.

And so Miss Wald had a great deal of reasoning and persuading to do and my parents had a great deal to overcome to consent!

Late one afternoon then, with a change of clothing in a little bundle under my arm and a letter from Miss Wald in my hand, I started out for the part of the city we called "uptown," as strange to me as if it were in a different country. And now a great experience was to be mine. Never again could I look upon the life I was leaving in the same way, for I was to have a glimpse into a different world.

As I rode along in the Grand Street and Third Avenue surface cars I asked this one and that one about my destination and was glad to hear that people knew about the place. I felt a little scared, I did not know what I would find. At last I stood before the building of the Presbyterian Hospital and then before the clerk's desk.

"Your name and address," he asked. I gave it. "Can your father pay?" I had never yet been confronted by this question and my face burned. After a moment I had to admit that he could not.

"What does your father do?"

"A tailor."

"How much does he earn?"

"Eight dollars, sometimes ten."

"How many are there in the family?"

"Six beside myself."

"Take a seat, please."

Soon a man came and I followed him through wide halls where our footsteps echoed. We went up in an elevator and I was taken into an immense room with two rows of white beds and in each bed a pale face. Then I saw a nurse, like the nurses in the Settlement, and I felt reassured at once. She led me to a chair at an empty bed, put two screens about me, said hurriedly and without looking at me, "Undress, please," and went away. I felt bewildered. "She could not have meant that," I thought and I sat still. At home the only time we went to bed was when we could not stand on our feet. But I was well now. I also realised that the nurse could come and go as she pleased and there was nothing but a screen between myself and all those faces that I saw in the beds. The more I thought over it the more impossible it seemed that I had caught the right "English words." But what did she mean? I sat and blamed myself for not having been more attentive. The English spoken here and by the nurses in the Settlement was so different from the Yiddish English that I knew. But I soon forgot all about it as I looked around at the snow-white bed beside me and at the little table with a glass top and at the screens forming the walls of a small room. And I thought with joy, "This is going to be my room and these are my things." Over the bed there was also a large window which I claimed at once. The light from the setting sun was streaming in and the muslin walls of the tiny room were coloured rose. I was looking about me and out of the window and reality was slipping further and further away. Presently I saw as in a dream a small round toed boot push one side of the screen away a very little, and the nurse came in carrying a small tub of water. And when she saw me sitting there just as she had left me she put down the tub on the table, placed her hands on her hips and looked at me and sighed, and her eyes said very plainly:

"Well! What kind of a being is this anyway?"

Half an hour later I lay flat on my back, and my wet hair was spread out on a towel over the pillow. When the screen was taken away I saw that mine was the last bed in a row of ten, facing ten other beds.

A few days later when the clock struck two, visitors began to come in. I saw that they were all Gentiles and mostly Americans. All the women wore hats; they came in quietly and their faces looked calm. I sat up and watched the door. I scarcely dared to hope that my mother would come, that she would be able to get away, but she did. She stopped in the doorway and looked eagerly from bed to bed. Her face was flushed and she wore her little shawl on her head. When she saw me she almost ran over the highly polished floor and I was afraid she would fall. All the people stared at her and then at both of us when she sat on my bed. Her face was covered with perspiration. If I had had difficulty in finding my way to the hospital, what must the trip have been for her who could neither speak nor understand a word of English.

I had wonderful things to tell her (and much she could see for herself) about the cleanliness and the care patients received and about the food which I thought fit for holidays, though I could not at once like it for our foods are more highly seasoned. The meat and juice which the doctor ordered I had not touched because it was "trafe" (meaning that the cattle had not been killed in accordance with the Jewish law). But mother told me that I must eat everything and get strong. "You are not here for pleasure," she said, "take it as you would medicine." And so it was that I now had to break the vow I had made to myself when I came to this country, not to eat trafe meat.

Mother went away happy and reassured, and I remained still happier than she.

L

THE first person with whom I made friends (or rather, who tried to be friends with me), was the assistant house doctor. He was not at all good-looking but he was big and strong and good-natured. His small grey eyes twinkled merrily under his light bushy eyebrows. The first time he spoke to me was when he came to take a drop of blood from my finger. "We want to see," he said, "whether you have blood or water in your veins," and he laughed. "How do you feel?"

"Fine!" I said. He gave my hand a slap and watched to see if it would get pink. "You will have to feel a great deal 'finer' before you can leave here," he said. He tightened his lips and nodded at me as much as to say, "You might as well make up your mind to it." I was not at all grieved to hear this. Indeed I should have been grieved if it were to be otherwise. For I already loved it here. The second time he came I had a book which my mother had brought me to read. He sat down on the edge of the bed, took up the book and looked at the first page, then he turned to the end, and he looked in the middle. His face became more and more perplexed. "I cannot read a word of it," he finally said. "What do you call this?"

"It is Yiddish," I told him.

"Read a little." I read.

"Why!" he exclaimed, "It sounds like German."

I tried to explain to him that Yiddish had many German words, though they were pronounced somewhat differently. I tried to explain it in English and I had to guess at many words. And so to make sure that it was clear I also explained it in German, for like every Jewish person I made some claim to being able to speak German.

"What else can you speak?" The doctor was looking quite merry again.

"Russian," I said, "in the peasant dialect of the village from which I come."

He looked about the ward and asked the Russian word for table, chair, plant, window, bed. I told him and he tried to say each word after me. He had his mouth all screwed up and he pronounced the words almost like an infant. I could not help laughing and he laughed too. His hearty laugh sounded through the whole ward and many of the patients took it up and laughed with us, not knowing what it was all about. "What a merry people are the Americans," I thought. We took things more seriously. But very often he was serious too. He would sit on the edge of the bed with his arms folded and ask me to tell him about home and the shop.

One day I saw him coming into the ward accompanied by a beautiful woman. She wore a bunch of violets tied with a purple cord. As they came along there was a sound like the rustling of leaves and the air about my bed became sweet.

"Ruth," the doctor said, "I want to introduce you to a friend."

I had never dreamed there was anything like her beauty, her blue-black hair, her blue-grey eyes, her teeth, her smile. But though I was so ignorant of life I understood at once, somehow, that much of this woman's beauty was due to the care she had received all her life, and her mother before her, and perhaps even her grandmother. It was so clear that every root of her hair, almost, received special attention.

She came to see me often and brought me roses. Once she brought a big box full of pink ones with thick green rough looking stems. She laid a full blown flower on my lap and went to give the rest to the other patients. As she left my bed I wiped hot tears away. I had wanted a bud because it would last longer. But the next moment I thought of myself with contempt that it should mean so much to me. Most of the time she came accompanied only by the doctor; once she brought a friend, a charming young girl of twenty-one who told me she had just come home from college. She plied me with eager questions, about home and the shop. Even if I had known how to express myself, what could I tell them? I felt ashamed before these women that seemed to know nothing that was ugly or evil.

Very soon I had still another friend. At four o'clock in the afternoon a professor used to come in. He was tall, slender and bald. His small face was round and pink and so jolly that I would feel myself begin to grin the moment I caught sight of him or heard his voice. One afternoon he said, "I am going to bring a friend to see you. She is very unhappy; will you try and cheer her up?" I said yes without knowing what I was saying, with all the doctors and nurses looking on and listening, for they were making their rounds.

The next afternoon he came in with a young woman dressed in deep mourning. He introduced her and went away to join the troupe of doctors waiting for him at the first bed. She was as charming as my doctor's friend though not quite so handsome. But what I chiefly noticed and felt was her deep sorrow. Though she made an effort to appear cheerful I could see that she was weighed down by grief. It was in her eyes, in the expression of her face, in her every motion. She told me

that her mother had died recently and then she sat quite
still looking about the ward. But I knew that she did
not see the things at which she was looking. After a
while she asked, "Would you like me to read to you?"
I thought that perhaps in this way she would forget
for a while, so I said quickly, "Yes." The next time she
came she had a book with her. All I remember of it
is the name, "Under the Red Robe." I was not in the
main ward now but in the annex where there were only
ten beds occupied by patients that were the least sick and
had to remain long. Beside my bed there was a fine
window facing Park Avenue. And at this window my
friend sat down and read. Her voice was agreeable and
she read steadily. I was thinking as I watched her face
that she seemed very much interested, when suddenly the
book slipped from her hands, she laid her head on my
pillow and wept. I looked at her a moment, then moved
my face close to hers and wept too.

One day after she had gone the patients whispered to
each other, and the nearest to me asked, "Do you
know who that woman is?" Of course I did not. "She is
a daughter of one of the biggest millionaires in the
United States. You are very fortunate to have such a
friend." Then she said, "But it is wasted on you." She
was a grey-haired woman with a toothless mouth and she
mumbled to herself about "throwing pearls to the swine."
But I thought, "What strange things happen in America,
the daughter of a millionaire and I crying on one pillow." Then I wondered why I was receiving so much
attention. I did not know that the part of the city where
I was living was called the East Side, or the Slums, or
the Ghetto, and that the face of the East Side, or the
Slums, or the Ghetto was still new and a curiosity to the

people in this part of the city, a sight to cheer any unhappy person.

But the daily life in the ward I found quite as interesting as my new friends. Having a fondness for "looking" and dreaming and, I am afraid to say, for idleness,
the life in bed exactly suited me. I heard many of the
patients complain about the food and the attendants and
that they could not sleep, that life was dull and they
longed to be out. But not I. I found every one kind
and not a moment was dull or monotonous. There was
so much to see and every minute something new seemed
to happen. To begin with the early morning at five
o'clock, when our little night nurse brought us each a
basin of water and woke us to wash, I would see that
her face looked paler than it had been in the evening, her
cap a little askew, her apron not quite as fresh, and her
smile not so bright. But she hurried, hurried to make up
as many beds as possible before the day nurses were to
come. She was so sweet, so sweet, this little nurse. There
was such a warm touch in her small roughened hands.
At seven o'clock the day nurses came in looking fresh
and rested. I would watch each one going to her task
with something of a soldier's regularity. If the breakfast happened to be up they came in at once carrying
the trays of food. Then our ward, so quiet a minute before, was filled with life. The doors swung back and
forth, there was a clatter of dishes, a smell of coffee, and
the dull pat-pat of the nurses' rubber soled shoes on
the floor as they came tripping in, each carrying two
trays, the upper resting on two cups. The good motherly
nurses brought their trays in looking neat and the food
was hot and tempting, while the careless or indifferent
ones came straggling in late and the food was cold and
spilled over. After breakfast there was a hustle and

bustle of tidying up, and a sweeper came in. She was a big, stout woman with dark, angry eyes and a bang of oily iron-grey hair that curled all about her forehead. When she took a dislike to a patient she would bang the broom handle against the bed as she swept under it. I used to lie waiting and quivering at the thought of her coming.

By nine o'clock not a safety pin was out of place, the patients lay back fresh and clean, and the doctors came in to make their rounds. I would prop myself up against my pillows, smooth my bed clothes, and watch them going from bed to bed. The nurses lined up on one side, the doctors on the other. They looked so different from us, the people I had been accustomed to see all my life. They were tall, healthy men and women, so well dressed with such fine quiet manners! And I wondered how they lived outside of the hospital, what their homes were like. These two were Americans. All Gentile English-speaking people were Americans to me. These looked so different from our Americans on Cherry Street. Did they too hate the Jews? Since I had been here I had not once been made to feel that there was any difference. And I, as I was growing to know and understand and love the people all about me, was losing my intense nationalism.

On Monday afternoons a missionary used to come into our ward. She was dressed in black and I always thought of her as being long and narrow. Even her features were long and narrow. She would give out the Hymn Books and then stand in the doorway between the annex and the main ward and lead the singing. She had a loud, shrill voice that could be heard above the voices of the patients. After the singing as she collected her Hymn Books she talked to each of us. She would ask, "How do you feel?" But she never stopped to hear the answer. In the same breath she would begin to talk about Christ. The first time she bent her tall black form over my bed I felt very uncomfortable and when she began to talk about Christ I felt miserable. Finally I said, "I am a Jewess," and now I thought she would go away at once. But to my surprise she walked around to the other side of the bed and only now began to talk to me earnestly. My face began to burn. I saw that she wanted to convert me and I on the other hand thought it a sin even to listen to her. Finally I contrived to put my fingers into my ears and make it appear that I merely had my hands over them. And now I lay still and looked at her. Her lips moved rapidly and gradually a red spot appeared on each cheek, and a tiny white bead of foam worked itself into each corner of her mouth. After a few times I felt that she could never convert me and I no longer put my fingers into my ears.

When mother came again I told her about everything else but I did not mention the missionary. I thought, "I am perfectly safe and they will only worry at home." But danger came from where I least expected it.

Besides the missionary another religious person used to come into our ward. First he would come in the afternoon to distribute pamphlets. He was a quiet, elderly, distinguished looking man with longish silver white hair. He nodded to each patient as he laid the pamphlet on the bed within easy reach, and only stopped to talk to the elderly women. I noticed that he did not talk about religion at all. He asked them how they were. He was not smiling but his pale, quiet face looked kind and sympathetic. One day as he laid the magazine on my bed he stopped and glanced at my card.

"Are you a Jewess?" he asked in his quiet way, look-

ing from the card to my face. I said, "Yes." He smiled.
"It is a good religion," he said earnestly and went
on to the next bed. When had I ever heard any one
praise our religion? The words had a strange effect on
me. I sat up and watched him as long as he was in the
ward. I thought, "to this man I would like to talk." At
the end of the day when the sun was going down and we
were finishing our supper, he would come again to say
prayers. As he came in with his long, even stride his
person invited peace and quiet. If a nurse were in the
ward she would sit down for a moment and we patients
handled the dishes less noisily. He would stop in the
great doorway between the annex and the ward and turn
the pages of his Bible slowly, very slowly, that we might
have a chance to finish. Little by little it grew quiet, the
last sounds came more and more softly, the shifting of
trays, the tinkle of a spoon on a glass, a sigh. Then
came his earnest mellow tone, low, yet filling every corner
of the wards, "Our Father who art in Heaven."

After he was gone I would lie quite still, still hearing
his voice; his words were on my lips. One day I sat up
and took the Bible from the box in the bedstead and
looked at it without opening it. This was the first time I
had touched it and I felt guilty and uneasy. Then I
thought, "How could it be a sin to know this man's religion?" and I opened it. There had always been a mystery about this Bible as well as about the people who read
it. The mystery about the people was almost dissolved
and now about the Book too I could see nothing mysterious. It had a musty smell like any other book that was
old and little used; here and there the pages stuck together
with a bit of food. I put it back into the box. The
next day I took it out again, opened to the first page and
picked out the words that I knew. Those that I could

not read I spelled over to the next patient and she told me how to pronounce the words and the meaning. I read every day and soon I was able to read by myself. And as I began to understand it I became more and more interested. Finally I thought about it constantly. I wanted to understand the Christian religion. I was so eager to know and understand it, that though I felt so timid and sensitive I began to talk about it, ask questions, ask for explanations and soon I gave the impression that I wanted to become a Christian. One day my doctor's friend asked, "Ruth, do you really want to become a Christian?" I looked at her. "Oh, no!" I said. She laughed merrily. "I thought not."

No, I did not want to "become a Christian." And yet I felt dreadfully troubled.

In the meantime daily life in the ward became even more interesting. After weeks and weeks in bed I was at last allowed up. And when I again learned to walk I enjoyed helping the nurses. I learned how to make beds beautifully. I used to bring the patients water. I combed their hair. I rubbed their bed-ridden backs with alcohol. I often remained for hours at a fever patient's bed and applied ice compresses. I was happy to learn all these things. I determined that if any one should be sick after I returned home, I would attend to them just as I saw the patients here attended.

So three months passed. It was a bright day in June when I bade farewell to all my friends in the Presbyterian Hospital. When I came out of the building I looked up at the windows. I thought of the life to which I was going and a feeling of dread came over me. Then I remembered that it was three months since I had seen the children and I turned and walked quickly to the Third Avenue car.

LI

ALTHOUGH almost five years had passed since I had started for America it was only now that I caught a glimpse of it. For though I was in America I had lived in practically the same environment which we brought from home. Of course there was a difference in our joys, in our sorrows, in our hardships, for after all this was a different country; but on the whole we were still in our village in Russia. A child that came to this country and began to go to school had taken the first step into the New World. But the child that was put into the shop remained in the old environment with the old people, held back by the old traditions, held back by illiteracy. Often it was years before he could stir away from it, sometimes it would take a lifetime. Sometimes, too, it happened as in fairy tales, that a hand was held out to you and you were helped out.

In my own case it was through the illness which had seemed such a misfortune that I had stirred out of Cherry Street. But now that I had had a glimpse of the New World, a revolution took place in my whole being. I was filled with a desire to get away from the whole old order of things. And I went groping about blindly, stumbling, suffering and making others suffer. And then through the experience, intelligence and understanding of other beings a little light came to me and I was able to see that the Old World was not all dull and the new not all glittering. And then I was able to stand between the two, with a hand in each.

The first thing that I can recall after I came from the hospital, is a feeling of despondency. The rooms seemed smaller and dingier than they had been. In the evening the lamp burned more dimly. And there was a general look of hopelessness over everything. It was in every face, it was in every corner of our dull home as well as in all the other homes that I saw. It was in every sound that came in from the street, in every sigh that I heard in the house. I saw the years stretching ahead of me, always the same, and I wept bitterly. I had never been so aware of it all.

In the shop where I found work now it was as at home. As I looked at the men I could not help comparing them with those other men. To the little insinuating jokes and stories I listened now, not with resignation as before but with anger. "Why should this be? Why should they talk like that?" And I was filled with a blinding dislike for the whole class of tailors.

But I did not give my entire thought to what I saw about me. As the days passed I became aware that I was waiting for something, for what I could scarcely say. Away in the back of my head there was this thought, "Surely this would not end here. Would this be all I would see of that other world outside of Cherry Street?" And I waited from day to day.

In the meantime I filled up the days at work with dreaming of that other life I had seen. I thought a good deal about that fine old man the minister. His words and his voice had remained fresh in my mind. Of course I must not breathe a word at home about him, about the New Testament. This necessity for secrecy soon led to other little secret thoughts and actions. It soon occurred to me, "Why should I not read the New Testament if I want to? Why should I not do anything I like? If four months ago father thought me old enough to get married, then I am certainly old enough now to decide things for myself." So I stopped consulting mother and began to do little things independently. It was not hard to do this for during the three months I had grown away from home a good deal and now with the thought of my experience in which they had no part, every day I was slipping away little by little.

Mother noticed and her eyes looked troubled but I did not understand their meaning. Father had tightened the reins of authority and I only tried the harder to writhe myself free. My only thought now was of myself and the world outside of home and Cherry Street. But underneath all this perversity and selfishness I can see now, as I look back, a deep longing to see, to know, to understand.

In the Settlement I was not so often now. Miss Wald saw that I came home looking well and at once found work. So she thought she would leave well enough alone. Besides, I had told her about my friends in the hospital, so perhaps she thought that she would stand aside and give the others a chance.

The Settlement was, of course, included in my mind in that outside world of which I dreamed. But I felt too timid to go there often even on invitation without a "reason," some one of the reasons for which the Settlement seemed to be established.

One day, however, when I was thinking of the New Testament, it occurred to me to go to the nurses and ask for it. Where would I get it if not from them? They were Gentiles and they would surely have it. And I started at once with that new something in me that was defiant of all the old life.

I found Miss Brewster in the little basement and asked her for it timidly and with great uncertainty. For it was hard for a Jewish girl, brought up as I had been, even

to utter the words, "I want to read the New Testament."
The thought of becoming a Christian was nowhere in my
mind, but this would be the first real step beyond the
boundary.

Miss Brewster looked at me silently and as if she did
not quite understand and I felt still more uneasy under
her observation and explained eagerly, "I want so to read
it." She finally said, "I am afraid, Ruth dear, we can not
give it to you. You see your father would think, 'True,
the nurses have been kind to my daughter but they have
led her away from our faith.' And that would never
do for the Settlement. Do you see?" I was beginning
to feel a little guilty. What she said, the way she said
it and looked at me made me feel that I was wrong to
act in secrecy. Again she observed me for a long moment, then she put her arm around me and said pleasantly, "Come!" We walked up the little staircase to
the sitting rooms on the first floor. She put me into
a deep chair and then she knelt before the bookcase. She
hummed cheerfully as she looked from shelf to shelf, and
I sat and watched her. Her every motion to me was
new and interesting and charming. She represented the
people I wanted to know, the new life I desired.

She finally held out to me a tiny volume and said with
a smile and in that rich voice of hers, "Here, Ruth, is a
sweet love story, read it." And I took it away with me.
The name of it I do not remember and though it was
not the Bible, for the time being it satisfied me. Indeed
just at present it did more than that, it filled me with
joy, for, strange and stupid as it may seem, it had not
occurred to me that now I could read anything. I felt
so proud that I could read an English book that I carried
it about with me in the street. I took it along to the
shop. I became quite vain. Often as I looked about me

while walking through the street it seemed to me that now I did not belong here. I did not feel a part of it all as I did formerly. But very soon something happened which showed me that indeed it was here that I belonged. One day a letter came from my doctor's friend. This was the thing for which I had been waiting and this too was the first letter I had ever received. But I could not read it. The children could not read it either except a word here and there. They pored over the crisp blue paper while I stood over them anxiously and then they handed it back to me. "It is written in a 'fancy' handwriting," they said. And then like any poor illiterate old woman I had to run to a drug store and ask a clerk to read my letter to me. I felt ashamed before the clerk at not being able to read. I determined to try and learn a little from the children and again go to night school when winter came.

LII

My education, if it can be so called, began in the following manner and continued in the same painful unsystematic way all through the years. Self consciousness and timidity were a hindrance and I was always ashamed of showing my ignorance. But we were all ashamed of showing our ignorance. A girl who could not read and write would do anything to hide it. We were as much ashamed of it as we were of our poverty. Indeed, to show one was to show the other. They seemed inseparable.

My education, then, began in this wise. An informal talk was to be given on Shakespeare at the Nurses' Settlement and Miss Wald or Miss Brewster, I do not remember which, urged me to come and I promised. The lecture was in the sitting room in the East Broadway house. From the doorway I saw about half a dozen women of the type that we looked upon as "teachers" sitting in easy chairs and discoursing in low tones. And at a little table, on which there was a shaded lamp, one woman sat with some papers before her. As I took in the atmosphere, so foreign to me, and the type of people, I was at once sorry that I had come and I glanced into the corners for an inconspicuous seat, when an over kind lady came over and fairly forced me into a chair at the little table, right opposite the lecturer, and put a volume into my hands. I felt the light full upon me. It was on my hands, it shone into my lap, it seemed to shine right into me, showing my ignorance.

The evening passed in perfect misery and I heard little more than a buzzing of voices with every now and then such words as "Shakespeare," "plays," "new edition," "old edition," "a later edition," and then, "You can get it in the library."

I breathed with relief only when I came out into the street. But by then I was glad that I had gone and glad that I had remained. And now as usual after it was all over the things I had seen and heard came back to me distinctly and I reflected over them. Shakespeare, this was an old friend. I remembered the men in Mr. Cohen's shop discussing Shakespeare's plays. Evidently Shakespeare wrote that book that had been in my lap. I felt proud of this new knowledge and I walked home with a feeling of superiority over myself of the day before.

I do not know how but it was now that I found that there were such things as free libraries and I joined the one at the Educational Alliance. I felt greatly awed when I looked around from my place in the line to the librarians' desk and saw the shelves and shelves of books and the stream of people hastening in and out with books under their arms. Nevertheless I held my head high. Couldn't I read now? And if I could read the whole world of knowledge was open to me. So I imagined. When my turn came at the desk I said to the librarian, "Please give me the best thing that Shakespeare wrote." She looked at me questioningly. "Do you want his plays?" I reflected, the word play suddenly suggested to me entertainment and I wanted something serious. "Is that the best?" I asked. She shrugged and smiled a little. She was a pretty Jewish-American girl. "I don't know which is his best," she said. It surprised me to hear her acknowledge her ignorance so frankly. She asked again, "Do you want his life?" I thought the story of a person's life must be interesting, but no doubt

it was hard to understand. Perhaps I had better begin
with a play.

"A play," I said.

"Which?"

"Any."

She brought me a volume and when I was out in the
hall and alone I stopped and read the name slowly—
"Julius Cæsar."

I pored and pored over my book for two weeks. I
put it away and went to it again and tried to understand
it. But all I could get out of it were words here and
there. I could not get any meaning out of any of it.
I felt heart sore and humiliated. I think it was then that
I fully realised how little I knew, how ignorant I was.
I decided to be guided by the librarian. Her frank
acknowledgment that she did not know which of Shakespeare's plays was the best made a deep impression on
me and I decided that I too would be frank with her.

The next time I stood before her desk I said to her,
"I can read just a little and I do not understand much.
Will you give me a book?—any book—like for a child."
She brought me "Little Women."

LIII

FATHER did not take kindly to my reading. How could he! He saw that I took less and less interest in the home, that I was more dreamy, that I kept more to myself. Evidently reading and running about and listening to "speeches," as he called it, was not doing me any good. But what father feared most was that now I was mingling so much with Gentiles and reading Gentile books, I would wander away from the Jewish faith. This fear caused great trouble and misunderstanding between us. Of that period this is the first outbreak I recall.

One day my brother, the one who had once dreamed of becoming a great Rabbi, and who was still very religious, on looking through my library book found the word Christ. At once he took the book to father and pointed out the offending word. Father became terribly angry. Then his fears were well founded. I must be reading about Christ! He caught up the book and flung it out of the window. And when I looked out and saw the covers torn off and the pages lying scattered in the yard I turned into a perfect fury, as on one or two other occasions in my life. I wept aloud that I had a right to know, to learn, to understand. I wept bitterly that I was horribly ignorant, that I had been put into the world but had been denied a chance to learn. Father and mother stood staring at me. "Wild talk," they said. Surely! And no one was more surprised at it than I myself. I could not have told when these thoughts first began, whom I was blaming, who was to blame!

After this there were long periods when father and I did not talk to each other.

But little by little as the weeks were passing I was again becoming quieter and more submissive. Again my health was breaking down and at the end of two months I was almost in the same condition as before I left for the hospital and I was again falling into despondency and indifference. About this time the doctor from the hospital surprised us with a visit and when he saw that I was again run down he told me to come to the hospital and rest. "Come whenever you feel ill," he said. And so before long I was back once more.

During the weeks when I had again grown so pale father was gentler and kinder to me. He was not home when I was starting off but mother and the children stood at the window and watched me go. Mother's face was so full of sorrow and I too wept. But this time I was glad to go from home.

LIV

THE winter was divided between the hospital and the shop. When I was well I worked; when I felt sick I went to the hospital. And here was my chance. I was hearing good English, I was reading and with the trait of my race for adaptability I was quickly learning the ways of this country.

But at home and in the shop life became harder and harder. Once or twice I tried other work. I tried domestic service again. I went to take care of a baby and a house but my mistress found it more profitable to put me to sell newspapers at the newsstand which she kept. It was near a saloon in a wretched neighbourhood and I soon left it. The second place was good but here I had to light the fire on the Sabbath. Now I was no longer pious. I observed very few of the rites but there were some of the laws that I could not break. To obey them seemed bred in the bone. While I was in the hospital, of course, I ate the meat that was there but I was conscious all the time that I was eating trafe meat. And to touch fire on the Sabbath I could not bear. Then, too, besides, when I was leaving for this place of service mother begged me not to break the Sabbath. In her own words, "I would rather walk barefooted than that you should earn money while breaking the Sabbath." So I left this place too.

Then I went to work for a tailor who was a member of father's society. He told us he was working in a suit establishment on Fifth Avenue and Thirty-eighth Street. The suits were valued from fifty dollars up and he needed a girl to help him with the lighter work, pinking ruffles, felling lining and so on. Here I went gladly. I thought, "It is uptown and they are working on silks." I pictured an ideal shop. But I soon found that it was the same thing. I saw finely fitted up offices, beautiful salesrooms and fitting rooms, but we, the tailors, were huddled together into the dark basement. The men joked that we were pressed together like herring in a barrel. The tailor who sat next to me once said that he was surprised at his own decency. He wondered that he was not a worse animal than he was. I soon left the shop in disgust.

One day when I was leaving the hospital, after a lengthy stay there, the doctor's friend said, "This will not do. I can't imagine what those places are like where you work that you get run down so quickly." She looked thoughtful for a few minutes, then she added, "I am going to find you work myself." She said this as though now she was going to settle the thing once and for all. She took me into her carriage and we started. I could not help smiling at this unusual and pleasant way of looking for a job.

On the way she explained to me that she would take me to the establishment where she was having her suits made. She was a good customer and Mr. S. would surely find work for me among his tailors. The carriage stopped before a fine brown-stone building. But when I looked out my heart sank. This was the place on Fifth Avenue where I had worked. It did not even occur to me to tell her about this shop. What was the use and what could I say to her? What one heard in a shop I felt was not to be talked about to anybody, especially to one who knew nothing about shops.

She left me in the carriage and went in to inquire while I sat and prayed that there might be no work for me. When she returned she said that there would be work for me in a few days. But I never went to this place, for little by little I became indifferent to work altogether, at least to the kind of work that was within my reach. What with the long periods of idleness after each job, the months of inactivity in the hospital, the natural apathy due to the illness, the miserable conditions in the shops, I lost all taste for work, I lost my pride of independence, I lost my spirit.

LV

In the spring, a year from the time when I first went to the hospital, my health was poorer than ever and my friends there began to look upon me as a problem, and finally to send me to various institutions for recuperation. The illness had procured me that freedom from home for which I had longed. But though I was so free, now less than ever my destiny seemed in my own hands. The illness and my friends seemed to steer it and I did meekly whatever I was told. I asked no questions. I offered no resistance.

At first, as to the hospital, I carried a change of clothing wherever I went. But I soon realised that I did not need it. We were provided. In some of the institutions we wore blue, in some grey, in others checks or stripes. In some of the places my companions were old, in some young, in others mixed. And when I put on my wrapper I felt that I became a part of the rest of the dependents, a part of the house, a part of all that I saw about me. This troubled me, but little by little I became used to it.

LVI

WHEN the warm weather came I was to go to a place in the country called White Birch Farm. I was in the hospital when the doctor's friend told me about it and also that she was sending out another girl, Irene, who was not strong and that I must be friends with her and take care of her. Then one day, just as I was leaving the hospital, I was called to the office to see the doctor. He said in his cheerful kind manner, "You are going to the country and I think this will take you to Grand Central," and he pressed a half dollar into my hand. After this I neither saw nor heard and scarcely knew how I left the building. When I was outside I stood still. In my hand was the half dollar, the first direct gift of charity to myself. My face burned. "I can refuse it," I thought. "I can take it right back—but then, I must refuse everything else, the help, the going away"—and going away had become a necessity. I could no longer stand the mournful looks at home, and I was by now used to having a bed all to myself. When I reached home and told them that I was going away mother cried bitterly: What would be the end of all this going away, of staying away from my own people, what would it lead to?

The next day at Grand Central I was met by a lady, with her was Irene and when we took our seats in the train I realised that I was going further away from home than I had yet been.

LVII

WHITE BIRCH FARM (there were no animals except
a white bull dog and none of the ground was tilled)
turned out to be a summer house run for needy city children sent in batches of about sixteen every two weeks.
The house belonged to a doctor—who, I heard, was a
very kind man. He bought the place for the purpose
and he was supplying all the money to run it. The house,
which was white, large, and had green shutters, stood
close to the road. Across the road there was a barn,
greyed by time and weather, and beyond it thirty acres
of ground for the children to play on. On these grounds,
down one hill and up another, there was a small wood
they called the Grove and at the foot of it a brook ran.
There was a dam and a good stretch of the water was
deep enough for swimming and diving.

The house was in charge of Miss Farly who brought
us down. Besides her, and Irene and myself, there were
two coloured women as help. The children had not yet
begun to come. The house was being prepared for them.
I was helping but had a good deal of time to myself and
I walked about outside. I did not go far from the
house. I felt troubled. There was the great quiet. The
fields lay so still. Yet life seemed to be teeming and
the air was filled with silent voices.

Then it began to appear as though the things were
coming out of a dream. It was all so strange yet
familiar.

In about three days I went further from the house
and walked among the trees. I walked in among some
low bushes. The leaves touched my face and I stood

still. The quiet seemed to surround me and every now and then there was a twit, a rustle, and overhead the sky shone blue. There seemed to be all this and I alone with it. I felt my body quivering with strange feelings, strange thoughts came into my mind.

In the house too it seemed as if I were living in a fairy tale. There was a dining room and a sitting room, and off the porch a little writing room. Upstairs there were bedrooms. Irene and I shared a small one. From the window in my corner I could see some fine old trees, a bit of road, a field, and in the distance the side of a house gleaming white.

There was nothing of the "institution" about this place and I soon recovered my spirits as well as my health. My face became brown and rosy. The sun bleached my hair, and again I began to find pleasure in whatever work I did but that was also perhaps because I loved Miss Farly. I was often jealous of her, at which she laughed, scolded me and looked pleased. I worked well but it seemed to me that this summer I did little more than play—or else even work was play.

I saw here modern, orderly, systematic housekeeping. There was time for everything, room for everything, money for everything that was necessary. The thought did not come to me that all this was possible because there was means. I only saw the facts. Miss Farly was a trained nurse and a woman of education. She could also do things that I had only seen men do, or that I had not seen done at all. She could paint; she could calcimine; dressed in a linen walking skirt and a shirt waist, and a paper cap I would make for her, she would work for hours at a stretch, studying directions as she went along and her fair face was flushed with the exertion and the pleasure. She could do wonders with a grocery box,

a few yards of cretonne and some brass-headed tacks.
And I would be helping her. There again, then, was my
chance. In the hospital I had learned how to take care
of a sick person, of a sick room; and here I was learning
something of modern housekeeping. Miss Farly also
had excellent taste for shape, design and colour. And
this too I was learning—or else, seeing things, I knew
what I wanted.

From the children I was learning their games. They
were from the ages of seven to twelve; I was seventeen
but now I too was twelve. I ran races with them. I
played wolf and when the boys played baseball and were
"short of men," they would magnanimously take in Irene
and me and I was as happy as could be when I managed
to make "a home run." We played in the grove, we
swam in the brook—I learned how to swim and dive.

I loved the spot near the brook. The trees here grew
close, bending into an arch over the water. The sun pene-
trated only in spots so that here it was greener and fresher
than anywhere else and the air was sweet and moist
and cool. The water over the dam fell with a rustle and
the children's voices in the grove sounded far away. I
loved to sit here on one of the rocks and dream.

On rainy days and evenings we played in the basement.
The walls here were rough and whitewashed. There
was a large fireplace and a few benches. Of an
evening then we would hang up some lanterns, make a
good fire and draw up our seats. Some of the boys
played on their harmonicas, the girls sang the latest
songs and I sang Russian and Jewish ones.

It was with reluctance and at a great deal of urging
from Miss Farly that I began to sing. I expected
laughter and ridicule from the children. And I was not
wrong. But Miss Farly made an example of the first

boy who tittered by sending him out of the room. After that it was quiet whenever I sang and little by little they became used to hearing me.

The children were descendants of many nationalities, Irish, German, Italian, American. The Jews had not yet begun to come. They would only begin with me. Some of the children were rough, like the roughest on Cherry Street. Many of the children were very poor. When they sat down at the table it was evident that those who had been receiving little bread had also little manners. They ate greedily as if they would make up for the time when they had not had enough. Soon I also learned to tell which children had never seen the country before. These usually greeted the great outdoors with a whoop and a yell and a busy time began for Miss Farly and her two aid-de-camps, Irene and myself. The boys began to run about wildly, scurrying over fences and ignoring all boundaries, climbing trees, tearing down whole limbs, filling their pockets with green apples, filling even their stockings and trying to smuggle them up to bed to take home. And the little girls would begin to pick hastily everything in sight, not stopping to distinguish between flowers and weeds and pulling all up by the roots. But after a day or two the boys began to play more quietly and the little girls would select their flowers and content themselves with few, knowing that the next day they could pick again.

Sometimes as I watched them, I tried to picture our Cherry Street children scattered over the fields. And on the following summer I did see them there, and my own sister and brothers were among them.

Miss Farly treated Irene and me very much like the rest of the children. She counted us in among them when asked how many there were at the house and we ate with them. But otherwise, in the house as well as out of doors we were her companions. Often then while the children played in the fields we three would sit on the piazza sewing, and Miss Farly would talk to us confidentially, particularly to me—for of Irene and myself I was the more interested because to me it was all so new. I would perhaps lead up with some remark or question on the subject that still troubled me, religion, and she would explain to me as simply as possible many little things of Christianity, of the various denominations, and of the differences between them. And as for her, I don't think she had ever known any Jews intimately before, so she was as curious about me and my people and our customs as I was about hers. I would explain to her as best I could our life as Jews and some of the laws, many of which seemed trivial on the surface but many of which had good reasons, either moral or physical. So we would converse; nor did she make me feel that there was any difference because I was a Jewess.

But twice the most serious question came up between us—the question that so often has agitated the whole world, that has often no doubt filled even the kindest Gentile heart with doubt and suspicion, that has made Jews all over the world band together and appeal to God and men against the false accusation—the question of the Jews' needing the blood of a Christian child for the Passover. This question was by no means unpopular at the time. Somewhere in Europe a child had been found murdered and a Jew was accused and was being tried for his life.

The first time this came up among many other matters, she merely wanted to hear my explanation of it; it was quite understood that she did not believe it. I felt my face flush. What could I explain? I could not express myself well enough in English. To myself it was quite clear. All our laws tended to point against it. No Jew himself may kill even a fowl but must take it to the one certain man who has studied the laws in regard to it and made it his profession. There would perhaps be one such man in a whole town. Ten miles my little grandfather used to walk to have a rooster killed that we might have meat in honour of the Sabbath even if we had to go without it all the week. For weeks and weeks we would be without it altogether because it was inconvenient to go. And yet we would not kill! Even the little children knew that this law was necessary so that each individual might not become hardened to the habit of killing, also because a professional hand would save the animal unnecessary suffering. How could it be possible then that we needs must kill a little human child!

Within my own knowledge and remembrance there was just this——. One warm afternoon in the spring when I was a child in our village, our little old great aunt from the next village came running. Her white close fitting cap was all awry on her head, her face was pale, her lips dry and covered with dust. "Children!" she cried at the door. "Fast! fast all of you, large and small. In a town not far away Jewish blood is flowing like water. A Christian child has been found murdered and they say the Jews have killed it for the Passover." And she ran on to warn the one or two Jewish families in the next village and my mother shut the door carefully and put the supper away for the morrow.

The second time this question came up between Miss Farly and myself was years later. It was a cold evening in September, the children were all in bed and Miss Farly and I, perhaps Irene too, I do not recall, were in the sitting room. There was a good fire in the grate and we felt friendly and congenial as we sat reading. Then, I don't remember how it happened, but Miss Farly picked up a large new volume bought recently I think, and began to read to me a poem right from the beginning of the book which appeared to be a sort of an introduction or opening poem. It told of a garden where there was sunshine and flowers and where two little boys, neighbours, one fair, one dark, were playing. Into the garden the windows of the two neighbours opened. Through one window the fair-haired mother often looked out and saw the sunshine and the flowers and heard her child laughing. At the other window the dark-haired mother often stood. After this I remember only my impression. The fair-haired child disappeared. Its young blood was used as a sacrifice for the Passover. I have the impression of the mother's agony—of the garden still in bloom—of the sun shining—but only one little child playing, the dark one.

It was a well written poem. It would touch any heart with pity and horror.

When Miss Farly was through she sat quite still, keeping her eyes on the page. Her face was flushed. After a moment she said, without lifting her eyes, and her voice was quiet and strange with controlled emotion, "This might have been a custom you know—Perhaps it is not a custom of all Jews—The children would not be apt to know about it." I was dumb with horror and was silent. What could I say? After all the years of her knowing me so intimately what could I say!

That night Miss Farly and Irene and the two coloured women and all the children were together and I felt alone, a stranger in the house that had been a home to me. In that hour I longed for my own people whose hearts I knew.

But after all we were living in the nineteenth century. And so in a day or two all was as usual. I gave her my affection and she was glad of it and she seemed as fond of me as she was fond of Irene.

So that first Summer passed and the month of September came. I thought this month the most glorious of the whole summer with its golden rods and the trees and the little creepers along the stone walls, turning scarlet, the brisk walks on crisp days, the daily dip in the brook, the sting of the cold water and then the feeling of sweet cleanliness. And indoors in the evening there were the open fires, the harmonica music, the dances, the songs. And when the children were gone to bed the pleasant chat with Miss Farly in the pleasant warmth of the room scented with the odour of sweet fern drying on the hearth.

Then a chilly day came. The last batch of the children were with us. Miss Farly began to pack away little bundles for the winter and from home a letter came asking me whether I knew that the Day of Atonement was approaching. Yes, I knew.

Then for a day or two again new life, like the breath of midsummer, swept through the house. Word came that the doctor, who had just arrived from Europe, was coming to spend a day or two with us. So I was to see the man who so generously had been supplying this family of twenty people for three months.

For a day we cleaned and polished and then we were ready to receive him. He drove up from New Haven late one afternoon. And I saw from where we had gathered near the road to meet him, a mature, well-built, handsome man such as I had learned by now to associate with the professional type—"like the doctors in the hospital." He sat still for a moment with the reins in his hand as if he were tired and the picture of us suited him and he wished to hold it for a moment. He smiled at the whole group of us. His face was all kindness and gentleness and in his eyes there was a look of childlike inquiry which a little later I understood was due to imperfect hearing. His gentleness showed itself in his every act, the way he handed the reins to a boy who came to take the horse, in his greeting of Miss Farly and Irene, in the courtesy he showed the little ones who after staring at him for a minute, began to sidle up to him shyly. Mathilda, the cook, came to take the ice-cream he had brought, which stood in the tub packed with salt and ice and was very heavy, and he hastened to help her. When a little later I came into the kitchen for something Mathilda said to me, "Ruth, does you know a gentleman when you sees one?" I was puzzled for a moment. Then I understood. The doctor had helped her as he would have any other woman, regardless of her colour!

He stayed with us two days. During the day he came walking with us, and in the evening, when we hung up our lanterns in the basement and laid a good fire, he sat on the bench among the children and attended with the greatest interest to our performances, and we all distinguished ourselves. The little Italian boy who performed acrobatic stunts was more like an eel than ever and the boy who played on the harmonica and who, his admirers assured us, was so musical that he could play on the piano alike with his hands or toes, this time performed on the harmonica with his nose. Irene led the Virginia reel and Miss Farly made me sing my songs. The doctor applauded and laughed heartily and Miss Farly, who often had to suppress the boys' shouting and stamping, whispered aside with a smile that the doctor made more noise than any of the children.

When he was going away he thanked the children. He said with his kind smile that he had had a very nice time; he said it as if he were the guest and we were his hosts.

And when I went home I knew that the next summer I would come again.

He and Mother carted over the furniture on a push-cart.

PART FIVE

PART FIVE

LVIII

It was hard to get used to the old life again when I came home. It was all stranger than ever, the home, my people; their ways. The children's faces looked lean and a little pale in spite of the sunburn from running about in the streets. Our couch now stood supported by a grocery box; the kitchen looked like nothing more than a black hole; the meals were chance and meagre—oatmeal gruel for dinner. I had good teeth and digestion and I craved substantial food, meat and potatoes. I craved variety.

Once when I had first met Miss Wald, and was feeling downcast as I was leaving the Settlement to go home, she urged me to tell her the cause. But I did not know what to tell her, how to put our dull existence into words. She was thoughtful for a moment; then she gave me some money and said with great earnestness, "Will you do something for me? Will you go and buy a good, good supper, you all?" I had wondered then what a meal had to do with one's outlook on life. I knew better now.

In the shop where I found work soon I felt more and more disgusted with conditions. I found the life almost impossible. My sister and I were working together in a large new loft. Half of it was occupied by cloaks and the other half by a contractor of skirts and capes. Sister and I were working on the skirts and capes. There were seven of us at the finishers' little table, besides sister and myself two other girls and three men. The room was not bad to work in, for there was plenty of light and

273

though the table was small those of us who did not mind stretching out for the scissors and thread could sit a little distance away and so have more space. But it was in other ways that life was made impossible. There was one man in the shop, the designer and sample maker of the cloaks, to whom the other men looked up. He wore a white collar and a coat at work and thought himself clever and witty. Whenever he was not busy he would come and amuse himself by telling obscene stories and jokes. He did not like me, for when I had first come I had managed to gather courage to ask the boss whether we girls could not sit at a separate table. The news of this unusual request soon spread and I began to be looked upon as one who put on airs. "The tailors were not good enough for her to sit with." One asked me: "Do you expect to make the world over?" So it was quite understood that here was a girl who must be downed and the designer, soon learning what I was most sensitive about, sought to do it with his jokes and stories. And whenever I saw him coming the blood in my temples would begin to beat like a hammer.

One Friday he came, placed himself where he could see my face, and began in his leisurely way, sure of being listened to—"I was at a wedding last night." There was a burst of laughter. The men foresaw what was coming. And he, encouraged by the effect he was making, continued after a moment of significant silence. He talked as he had never talked before. He talked of the most intimate relations of married people in a way that made even the men exclaim and curse him while they laughed. We girls as usual sat with our heads hanging, and I was aware that sister's face almost touched the work in her lap. His eyes were on my face and they were hurting me. I was thinking that I could not even hide by merely pretending not to hear as the others did. Suddenly a feeling of rage shook me. "Why did we pretend? Did pretending cleanse our minds from the filth thrown into them?" Then I felt that if I could only stand up, if I could only stop pretending at this moment! I could never quite be a part of the filth I had absorbed. The blood beat so in my head that I was half blinded at the thought of showing myself so openly. Then I rose, and scarcely knowing what I did, I flung the cape from me; its purple silk lining caught on a nail, in the wall opposite, and hung there—and I cried to them half sobbing, "You have made life bitter for me. I pray God that rather than that I should have to go into a tailor shop again I may meet my death on my way home." All this seemed to have taken a long, long time and I gradually realised that it was very still in our corner of the shop and that now it was the men who sat with their heads hung and sister was standing close to me. I took my coat, gave her her little shawl, and we went out. In the half-dark hall her face as she turned it up to me was pale and her lips trembled. "You go home," she said. "But I am not going. It is not as hard for me because the men think I am too young to understand." And I could not make her go with me. She would not lose the half day, she would not lose the place. And she went back into the shop and I went down into the street.

I walked away from the building and turned and looked at it. I was leaving the shop! All sweatshops! When the idea had come to me I could not have told but the thought of going to look for a job in another sweatshop was somehow out of the question.

I sauntered along through the street. What now? Housework was the only thing left to me. I shrank from it. My experience had showed me what my life might mean as a servant, a drudge in some one's dark kitchen, sleeping on chairs, eating at the washtub (since the Corloves I had learned that eating at the washtub was the general rule), being looked down upon as an inferior for whom anything was good enough. A year or two of this and I would be coarser and cruder, the life would grow upon me, I would lose all sensitiveness, I would cease to care.

Suddenly I wondered why I should not go and talk to Miss Wald about the shop. I had confessed to her about so many other difficulties, our own and those of our neighbours, and she had always helped us out. Perhaps she could help here too. We had come to feel that there was nothing she could not do. But the next moment I thought with shame of letting Miss Wald know to what I had been listening in the shop, of letting her find out what my mind had been fed on. "But my little sister is sitting there and listening and I am ashamed to talk to Miss Wald—another woman!"

During the next night and day I fought it out with myself. Beside the sense of shame there was the obstacle of not being able to express myself well enough in English. It was so easy to be misunderstood and misconstrued. People, busy people, listened to your stuttering and blundering, and finally brushed you aside. And this would be particularly hard to tell. However, I was sure of one thing, that Miss Wald would listen to me patiently and try to get to the bottom of what I was saying. But would she think it possible? Would she believe me? Or perhaps this thing that appears so horrible to me is not so horrible after all.

Sunday morning at ten o'clock I started for the Settlement. Miss Wald was not yet down, she had worked hard the day before and had been up late; would I go

up to her room? I found her mother with her and another woman. Miss Wald moved a chair for me near
to her couch and introduced me. At the sight of the
strangers my mind became altogether confused and I
heard their voices as though in a dream. I heard her
mother ask: "Is Miss —— French?" Miss Wald
laughed. "Why, because she is blonde?" So the French
are dark, I thought. My mind fastened on this as though
it were very important and I kept thinking, "So the
French are dark!" Then I thought that the strangers
must be wondering why I was there. The thought also
came that I could still go without saying anything about
the shop. But suddenly I leaned over and whispered to
Miss Wald that I must see her alone. She glanced at me
quickly, laid her hand on mine in my lap and pressed
it affectionately as she talked to her visitors.

At last they were gone. They seemed to have gone
quite suddenly. What happened after that I could never
remember except a look of horror in Miss Wald's face
and the words, "Why, Ruth! they always told me—they
assured me that—Oh, that place is not fit to work in."

LIX

MONDAY morning at eight o'clock I went to the Nurses' Settlement. As the outcome of my confession to Miss Wald, I was to learn how to make shirtwaists in their little shop.

And now I was to know Miss Ann O'There, the woman who made a great difference in my life. The shop was on the top floor in the East Broadway House. To get to it one had to pass a gas-lit anteroom. I climbed the stairs and stopped before this room. My heart beat violently. I was entering on a new life. What was there for me now? As I opened the door I was surprised, then delighted. Before a large table a woman stood, cutting. I had already met her and she had made a deep impression on me, and now when I saw her I knew at once that she was my "boss."

A short time before this she had come to cut out gym suits for the gym class to which I belonged, and show us girls how to make them. She had noticed me because I could baste faster than any other girl. So I basted still faster and observed her. I saw that her ways were so gentle and quiet and she bent over each girl as if she had known her a long time. The suits were made in two or three Friday nights, and the last night she came down stairs with a group of us girls, and as she was bidding us good-night I watched her with regret. Then I saw her glance at me and I was sure she would come and talk to me. She did.

"Where do you live?" she asked. When I told her she slipped her arm through mine and walked with me a little ways.

I had made up my mind that she belonged to a family that were rich and accomplished.

"How then could she be so splendid?"

She learned how to sew, perhaps, that she might be able to teach girls. Then I learned from some one in the Settlement that she was a working woman, of working people, and a champion of labour.

This morning she greeted me in her quiet gentle way. Then she opened the door and we went into a little room where three girls were bending over sewing machines.

"This is Miss ——," she said, and I was amazed. This was like coming to a sociable and not a shop in which to work.

She gave me a seat and showed me how to make buttonholes in a scrap of blue gingham.

Many times that day she came to look at my buttonholes. Her long slim hands touched mine tenderly, her eyes were saying kind things. I could scarcely believe that I was not dreaming. Nevertheless I felt discouraged. For years I had been working for money and now I was sewing on rags!

The little shop turned out to be more and more like a shop in a dream. I was reading at the time a book translated from the Russian called, "What Is to Be Done, or The Vital Question," by Cherneshefsky. In this book there was an ideal sewing shop and I felt as if our little shop too was out of a story.

We all sat in a group in the centre of the little attic room where the best light fell. On my right there was a shelf with some materials, on the left was the door and behind it a little gas stove which we used at lunch time.

The older of the three girls we consulted in regard to

the work when Miss O'There was not in. Then there was Margaret, who was fifteen. She was tall and slim and pretty and her grey eyes were bright with fun and laughter. She had never yet worked anywhere. Fan was a Jewish-American girl of sixteen. She had come from the sweatshop, her life at home was hard, and she worked as if she had never had time to learn anything right. She read greedily, even in the street as she walked to and from work, and she knew how to drive a bargain. Her people were in dire poverty. Perhaps it was this that taught her the art. At any rate it would take a clever pushcart pedlar to get the best of Fan.

After a few days a machine came for me and I was taught how to make shirt waists. And now while I was learning how to make a shirt waist I was also learning something of the meaning of things or many things that had seemed without meaning. Miss O'There took my measure and said I was to be her shirt waist model. The fitting room was a few steps below, where everything was covered with blue denim and we called it the "little blue room." And in this room, with her mouth full of pins and while pinning me into a shirt waist, she would talk to me. With a few words at a time she slowly opened my mind to one thing after another. And I, when I found that I could ask questions, that it was neither improper nor would I be thought a fool, became as greedy as little Fan in her reading. There were so many things that I wanted to know. I wanted to know about our race, about myself, about the Irish on Cherry Street, about the shop. The questions went tumbling all over each other in my mind and in my speech. But she interpreted each one. I did not need to worry about my English. She looked at me, and she seemed to understand me better than I understood myself. And I too soon learned to understand her. I became sensitive to her every motion and expression.

It appeared that there was a reason for everything. Things were not thrown into the world in a haphazard way. She told me something of the history of the Irish people, of their joys, of their sorrows, of their humour, of their bitter struggle to free themselves. And gradually I lost my fear of the Irish on Cherry Street. She explained my own race to me. She explained the shop. What a revelation! The men's conduct in the shop could be explained! "Just look," she would say, "what are their lives? You know, sweating from early to late, some haven't even their families here. Talking? It is perhaps the only joy within their reach. I suppose it is a kind of joy, and when you work like an animal you live like an animal." So I began to see tailors in a different light. The new world she opened to me did not make me sad. On the contrary, it had been far more sad to see things happen and not to understand.

All this time the life of all of us together in the shop was continuing as in a dream. It was like a dream to be working only from eight o'clock until five with an hour for lunch. For lunch one of us three young girls would get off a little earlier and make cocoa for all. We each paid ten cents a week toward it and two cents a day to Fan for the fruit which she bought. And it was like a dream to sit down to a prettily set table with blue dishes, and bright silver, which Miss Wald placed for our use. I did not at once fit in with this new life. I would sit a little distance away from the table and brood. I longed to be with them, but something seemed to hold me back. At five o'clock when we stopped work one of us three younger girls had to sweep up. When my turn came I told her with tears that I did not want to sweep. Sweeping was housework and housework out-side of your own home was degrading. You were looked down upon, you were a servant. And so she would talk to me and would reason with me as my mother had done when I was a child. "No work was high or low," she would explain to me; "all work is honourable if honestly done."

Then I developed a feeling of deep jealousy. I could not bear the thought that all the other girls were as much to her as I was. Having found her I wanted to keep her all to myself. But soon she drew me into the group.

On Saturday Fan and I did not work at all because it was our Sabbath. Now I would have been willing to work for my religious scruples were gone. But my parents would on no conditions consent to it so I was off both days and Fan too, but the rest worked the half day. And after it, on many mild afternoons, we all went to the park. Always it was wonderful to me to hear Miss O'There explain things. There was always some-thing new in the way she saw them. Always there was a touch of seriousness under everything. She treated us all as if we were her little sisters, and taught and guided us. We led a sweet life.

We received very little money, a dollar, a dollar and a half, two dollars a week. At this I wondered for I did not know what this little shop meant, that it was established to teach me and the others a trade, and that what little money we did receive was merely meant to encourage us, or help our families. I did not know. Perhaps it would have been better if I had known. I might have tried harder for its success. Having been trained to work under the lash of a whip, it is a question whether I was fit to be left entirely to my honour. What was true of me was I think true of the other girls too.

At any rate, one day when I had worked at the shop about a year, Miss Wald and Miss O'There were locked up all afternoon in the little blue fitting room. At five o'clock we learned that the shop could not pay for itself. We all wept at the news. And soon we were scattered all over the city, placed at work for which we were best fitted, or wherever there happened to be an opening. I had kept with some neatness the materials on the shelf in our little shop, so I was placed as a stock keeper in a Fifth Avenue dressmaking establishment. I had great difficulty to keep my job with the few words of English I knew how to read and write. But the work fascinated me because I had to use a pencil instead of a needle. Using a pencil meant "education"! So I begged Madame to be patient with me. Here I learned some new words and a little spelling while labelling the stock.

We worked regular hours. But often the girls had to stay overtime, for which they received twenty-five cents supper money. We worked from eight until seven. We entered the brownstone building through the basement, felt about in a pitch-dark closet where we hung our clothes, and stood about in the dark hall adjoining the kitchen and peeped in curiously at Madame's coloured domestic help hustling about, until we heard the bell upstairs tinkle for us.

The dressmakers were three sisters. The oldest was a large woman with grey hair, stern face, and an uneasy self-conscious look in her eyes. She had charge of the waist lining. She kept her girls about her in a group and her face never relaxed for a moment to any of them. The youngest had charge of the waists. She was small and pretty and I never heard her speak harshly to a girl. The middle sister was Madame K. She was good looking and she had a tall, slender, pretty form. When she came

into the room all the heads bent lower over their work.
It was then that the uneasy self-conscious look came into
the grey sister's eyes. Yet I did not think Madame K.
unkind. She was the only one who, it seemed to me,
understood how really difficult for me was the work I
was doing. While she was often impatient and spoke
harshly she was also sometimes kind. After I had worked
a couple of weeks I asked her whether I was doing any
better; I was anxious that she should not be the loser by
having kept me. "Why, yes," she said in her brisk manner. Then she looked at me and her busy fingers, which
were draping a piece of silk, stopped for a moment.
Madame K. rarely took time to look at any one. "Why,"
she said, "you are a queer little thing!" She said it as
if she were seeing me for the first time.

Her admitting that I was doing better meant much
to me. It helped me keep the job as long as I did, for
I had to put up with hardship and a great deal of humiliation. I missed the congenial spirit of our little
Settlement shop, all for one and one for all. Here it was
more as in the sweatshop, each one for himself. I had
not made friends with any of the girls. All but one of
them were Americans. When I made blunders they
could only stare at me, and I thought them proud and
unkind. This one girl was Irish and when I had learned
to understand her and her brogue I liked her. She
worked on the skirts and she often came into the stock
room to baste on a large table that stood there. She kept
her book of measurements open before her. I glanced at
it curiously one day. "Do you know how to write these?"
She caught me up.

"Not these things," I pointed to the fractions.

"Well, you better learn," she said. "One of these days

Madame will call you into the fitting room to write the measurements, and if you don't know how——"

That day I spent the half hour lunch period writing fractions. It was in this way that I liked best to learn because I could see the use for the thing I was learning.

Of the greatest interest to me here perhaps were the garments. From these I tried to get an idea of the wealth in the world and the lives of the wealthy people. As light and as flimsy as some of these garments were, their expensiveness was evident and suggested to my imagination heaps of gold coins. Everything seemed an occasion for the wealthy and there was a garment for each occasion, a dinner gown, a tea gown, a morning gown, an afternoon gown, an evening gown, an opera gown, a ball gown, a street gown. Some of the customers fitted two and three at a time. When did they wear them all? What else did they do beside attending balls and dinners?

At fitting time it was my part to take the garment from the girls and carry it into the fitting room to Madame K. So I soon began to know many of the customers by sight. Their looks and bearing did not suggest simple homes. I pictured mansions and hosts of servants. My reading helped me in the picture making.

The stock room was a little dark room that served also as a passage between the work room and the fitting rooms. A heavy portière hung at one door, hiding the work room from the fitting room. Looking into these two different rooms was like looking into two different worlds. In one, the work room, the girls sat with their heads bent, muscles tense, faces dull or absorbed, stitching silently. Here it was always silent, for either one of the sisters was always there, or both. The faces and the clothes of the girls suggested their life, the life that

I knew. In the other room, through the portière, many hours of the day one woman or another would be standing before the long mirrors gazing at herself. Beside her Madame K. kneeled with the long train of her black silk dress spread behind her on the green carpet. Here there was always a light babbling which I could not help overhearing. There were often little bursts of confidences. "I know I looked well last night, because the women were asking me whether I was not growing fat." Usually it was on clothes. "Yes, I like my hat and it was a bargain this time. It was only sixty-four dollars——"

"Sixty-four dollars!—Father would have to work six weeks for sixty dollars. I received four dollars a week." It came quite natural to figure it so. But I felt no envy and no resentment.

I worked here until Christmas or rather over Christmas. Christmas Eve two of the girls had to stay over time to finish a gown. That night I sat in the little darkened stock room and waited to pack it; downstairs I knew the coloured man was waiting to deliver it. From where I sat I could see the whole workroom, dark except for the one corner where the two girls sat bending over the white satin gown between them. One of the girls was weeping. I had often thought her proud, but now she did not look a bit proud, she looked so human and loveable. Tears were running down her little straight nose. Whenever the tears came she would turn away a little that they might not fall on the small pink roses she was stitching on to the hem. She reminded me of the many times I had been felling sleeve lining until late at night after the other workers were gone.

LX

AND now I went to the factory to make use of the trade I learned in the Settlement shop. Miss O'There found me a place. I learned that to find a job it was not necessary to go from factory to factory. Instead you read the advertisements in the newspapers. And strange enough, the printed names and addresses turned out to be of "real people." Miss O'There, who came with me, inquired for me. Yes, shirt waist makers were wanted, and I was "taken on."

I followed a forewoman through long aisles of sewing machines till she placed me at a machine in the middle of the loft and showed me how to work the treadle. It was run by steam power. I pressed my foot, there was a terrific noise, and I did not hear the forewoman go. Then something made me turn my head and I looked up and found her standing at my machine. So it was all day.

She brought me a bundle of work and told me to make up a sample waist.

I worked very carefully. I measured the centrepiece with a tape measure I brought. I made dainty French seams and stitched with a small round stitch. I felt confident. In our little Settlement shop I had worked on silks, French flannels and fine chambray. This was ordinary material.

Shortly before noon I finished the waist. I was not mistaken. The forewoman looked pleased as she examined it. She turned to me. "This is beautiful!" she said. "But, my dear girl, working like this you won't earn your salt. Do you know what these waists pay?"

I shook my head. "A dollar and a quarter a dozen." I was dumb with surprise. She looked at me a moment. "What you need," she said, "is speed! I'll show you how to work!" I rose and she sat down at the machine. She lengthened the stitch to three times the size, her back bent over, her eyes fastened on the machine, her hands flew, and the machine whirred. She seemed to become one with it. I remembered this picture later. It was the typical picture of a sewing machine operator.

I worked a few days, then I was sent away. I was not worth the machine and space I occupied. In my place they could have a woman turning out a dozen and a half waists a day. So now I went from factory to factory trying to acquire speed. I worked a day here, a few days there, till they found me out. It is as hard to become a botcher as a good worker and I was often discouraged and despondent. The thought, "What is it all about—what is it for?" came rather often. To turn out a good piece of work had been a satisfaction. Its place now was taken by: "How many more waists can I do to-day than yesterday?" But how long can this kind of thing satisfy one?

At last I came to the immense shirt waist factory of F. Brothers. Here I had applied as a tucker in the hope that by specialising I would do better. The forewoman soon noticed, no doubt, that I was not a tucker and needing "a hand" on one of her special machines, she asked me if I would like to try it and told me its merits. A "hand" who could earn a good day's wages would have hesitated to accept. But what had I to lose? I had not yet earned three dollars a week as a shirt waist maker. If I had not had my people and my home, where would I have been now? And besides, I was always eager for new experiences. It turned out to be an eight

needle tucking machine. I was at once delighted and
fascinated by it. A machine that could make eight
tucks in almost the time that it took to make one! The
strain on my eyes was terrific. I had to watch eight
needles instead of one, but then, I told myself, I would
earn several times more than I would have otherwise!
"What a wonderful inventor! What a wonderful machine!" I soon learned, however, that I was paid no more
than if I were making one tuck!

But the machine continued to interest me, and I was
doing here better than I had yet done. So when there
was an opening I brought my sister and settled myself
down to stay. Sister was put to make shirt waists at
the extreme end of the block long loft and I in a group
of several other eight and five needle tuckers, stood in the
middle of it. And now all day long I sat feeding white
lawn and eight pin tucks came out. All day hundreds of
yards of lawn slipped over my table and fell into a large
basket. At first I dared not lift my eyes from the
needles. In the evening my eyes smarted and my back
ached. But when I learned to understand my machine I
did not have to watch so closely. I could tell by the
sound it made when a needle grew dull, when a thread
broke, when a stitch slipped. Every different trouble
made its own different sound. And as I watched my machine from day to day it seemed to me like a human being.
When I did not take care of it, oil it, clean it, it did not
work properly. I began to love my machine and in my
mind I called it my partner because it helped me to earn
my six dollars.

We were piece workers. Some of the girls who could
work without lifting their eyes earned more than six
dollars. That was how my sister worked. But I could
not do that! Indeed, I did not want to. I did not want

to become like my machine. So while I fed it the lawn I listened, and looked about a little and thought over what I saw. From where I sat I could see the whole floor from end to end. I saw hundreds and hundreds of girls bending over sewing machines. The floor vibrated, beat steadily like a pulse with the steam power. The air was filled with the whirr. I had to keep my head low to distinguish the noise of my own machine and we girls shouted and watched each other's lips when we talked. But we did not talk much! Right in front of me at a big table stood a large stout woman with a red handsome face. She was the head forewoman. All day long she stood or sat at the table draughting patterns, drinking beer with her head bent under the table, and watching us. There were also assistant forewomen, and foremen and assistant foremen, and superintendents and assistant superintendents. They were all watching us. The "bosses" we only saw once a day pass through the aisles. One was round shouldered with a little black beard and a cross eye. He walked through quickly with his head bent and a preoccupied look on his face. The other boss was straight and tall and he wore a grey French beard. He walked leisurely with his head in the air and looked about.

One day we heard that one of our bosses had gone to Europe. When after some months he returned to the factory there was a celebration. The steam power was turned off and the assistant forewomen announced that downstairs in the salesrooms there was cake and wine and music. But few besides the forewomen went down. We remained sitting at our machines talking to each other. Our own voices sounded strange to us in the quiet and we felt self-conscious.

Soon the forewomen returned and each one of us

received a sealed little envelope with her number on it. We were all called here by the numbers of our machines. My machine and I were 93.

In the little envelope each one of us three hundred employés found a little trinket in Roman gold.

When the head forewoman returned her face was redder than usual and beaming with joy. She had received a curiously made ivory cross. She called us to her table and showed it to us. She raised her hand for attention and we all pressed to the table. She cried, "It is no wonder they are so prosperous. They are so good to us! God is blessing them!" Some of the girls looked at her in bewilderment and listened doubtfully. The year before, two weeks after the gifts had been received, the prices had been cut, a quarter of a cent on a yard of hemstitching, five cents on a hundred yards of tucking, twenty-five cents on a dozen waists.

It was a one-window store.

LXI

I was eighteen when I met L. V. I had come home from work, had supper, and sat on the stoop looking into the street when suddenly a small dog jumped into my lap. I stood up so quickly that he fell like a bundle at my feet. Then I saw that he was on a chain and tugging at the end of it was a small, dark young man. He slapped the little dog. "I am so sorry!" he said. I saw that his eyes were not serious. I said I was all right. I brushed my skirt and sat down again, and he raised his hat and led the little dog away.

The little animal I knew belonged to our neighbour in the front, a middle-aged, childless woman who repaired wigs for her living. "Who was the young man?" None of our men raised their hats like that and from the few words of English he had spoken I understood that he was not only an American but a person of education.

He came back in a few minutes and stopped near the stoop and I knew that he would talk to me and I sat there. The dog soon made it possible. He kept pulling at the chain toward me. I had sometimes stopped to pat him. "Does he know you?" the young man asked. I said, "Yes." So we began to talk. He told me that he had come from Chicago to visit his aunt.

The next evening when I came out on the stoop he too soon came and again I let him talk to me. I had never before spoken to a young man to whom I had not been introduced. Yet this seemed all right and I spoke to him as if I were in my own house. To the house I did not ask him. It was nothing unusual to receive "company" on the street. In fact it was often the only place. It was hard to entertain guests in the one room. For the little dark bedroom was filled with clothing and folding cots and the extra bedding and other things, and the little dark hole of a kitchen was out of the question. So there was really only the one room. And this was the living room of seven of us. Here we slept, and washed, and dressed, and ate. We had to make great preparations to receive a stranger. Now it was not as when we were little. We felt conscious of the inevitable dirt and the dinginess and the broken up furniture and felt ashamed.

So we met on the stoop. L. V. told me he had been to many places. And I was proud to tell him what I knew of life outside of Cherry Street. I told him of the people and White Birch Farm. He showed surprise to meet any one here who knew anything outside of the old customs. Our common knowledge outside of here was at once like a relationship between us and seemed to separate us a little from the rest.

My parents saw me talking to the young man and they smiled at each other. The aunt also saw. Then one day I noticed that my mother was no longer smiling and she told me that L. V.'s aunt felt it her duty to tell us about her nephew. "He was really not a bad young man, but he got in with the Christians, with the missioners!" the aunt explained. At this my heart began to beat so quickly that it pained. I felt a foreboding of coming trouble. Soon I learned that L. V. was baptised and that the missionaries were training him for their own profession.

By now L. V. was coming into the house and I continued to see him as before. But to my parents now there was all the difference in the world. A Jew who forsook his own religion, his own people, was worse than a Gentile, worse than a heathen. He was an "apostate." He was a disgrace! Supposing the neighbours learned who the young man was; that their daughter went about with an outcast! For he who forsook Judaism for another religion belonged nowhere. He may be baptised a thousand times to the Christian he is still "The Jew" and his own people can only pray to God to have pity on him. If, then, it should become known that their daughter associated with a "meshumad" (apostate), the whole family would be disgraced. And what would her chance of marriage be! And marriage was all important. As a specimen of a daughter I was a disappointment. First there had been the illness, then disobedience and queer notions, and what kind of an influence was I for the children? Clearly, then, it would be a blessing if I were married. And then, too, I was already eighteen. And it was really high time, the two younger girls were coming up very fast.

As to myself, I felt bewildered. Between my parents and the young man and my own feelings and ideas which seemed all tangled up, I could not easily distinguish one thing from another. To break friendship because his ideas happened to be different seemed narrow-minded. And I did not want to be narrow-minded. I also felt that my parents must allow me to judge for myself. And they must trust me. But they would do neither. Father, as of old, wanted me to submit to him in the old custom. His opposition antagonised me now more than ever. I fought against him with all my strength. Mother hinted that I drop the acquaintance with L. V. but I ignored it. Father commanded and I refused. Of course, they could do nothing. They even had to smile that neighbours might not guess. But what trouble there was within our four walls!

In the meantime I learned to know L. V. better and better. He talked religion just as the woman missionary in the hospital had talked. It sounded like a lesson learnt by heart. Then, too, there was a certain lightness about everything he said. Always the eyes lacked seriousness and the lips almost smiled as if life were a joke. I felt dreadfully troubled.

One Saturday he came to our house with a young man friend of his and introduced him. I little thought that day to what his introduction would lead later.

It was late in the afternoon and our candlesticks which we placed on the table Friday night still stood there. We would not touch them until it grew dark and at least three stars were out. Only the very orthodox Jews observe this custom. But in our house father made us all observe it, no matter what other customs were neglected. L. V.'s friend noticed it with surprise. He said he had not been to such a strictly orthodox looking house since he had come to this country ten years before. I could see that he looked at us all with pity. Knowing L. V.'s ideas on religion, he understood what trouble we were all in.

I had never seen L. V. before with other people except with those of my own family. He and his friend discussed politics and religion. And I sat and listened and watched them. They were so different. L. V., as always, spoke jestingly about everything. The friend was serious, yet he could jest too. He was very outspoken, almost blunt. I liked him.

When they were gone mother looked at me with her pleading eyes and said, "Now, do you see the difference?" Something within me seemed to harden in a moment. And I said, "No, I can't see any difference."

What would have happened I cannot tell, but he

soon left for Chicago to prepare to go to a theological seminary out West and we began to correspond. And now an unexpected joy came into my life. Writing! And here again, as with the other things that I had learned, it seemed accidental. It is to this correspondence that I owe a great deal of what I learned of writing in English. With the help of the children I could read and write script myself now. All day long then at the machine, I thought over what I would say, and looked forward to the evening when I could write. This to me was not like writing a sentence which no one would ever see. The thought that what I wrote would be read and weighed and thought about filled me with excitement. So I wrote and re-wrote my letters using up a great deal of paper. Months passed, and one day I was filled with joy and pride. I realised quite suddenly that I had learned to read and write well enough to do the corresponding myself.

In the spring L. V. returned to the city to start West. One day he told me that he loved me and asked me to wait for him two years. I thought of my parents and I could not help weeping at the suffering I must cause them. But I also thought it right for me to do what I thought was right. I saw my life so empty without the letters. "Surely, that was love." And I promised to wait.

He went away and again he began to correspond. How joyfully I greeted the first letter that came! I knew and loved every line and curve of the simple, clear handwriting. I spent a great deal of time in copying the phrases that pleased me. I gave these letters most of my time and thought. I almost lived for them.

In his letters, L. V. sometimes told me of boyish escapades, flirtations, but as long as letters came noth-

ing mattered.   Sometimes when I thought it over it
seemed queer that it did not matter.   Sometimes, too, I
tried to think of myself married, but I could not picture
myself married to him or any one else.   I liked the com-
panionship of men, but the thought of marriage often
filled me with fear, even with disgust.   So the sweatshop
left its mark.

LXII

FATHER felt relieved when L. V. was gone. Upon the correspondence he chose to look as "nonsense." He thought if he showed he looked upon it—the correspondence and the promise to wait—as nonsense, it would soon, in my mind too, be "nonsense," and come to nothing.

But it was not at all so. I arranged my life now, or it arranged itself, in some sort of a systematic way. This was the end of June; I soon left for White Birch Farm. Since that first summer I continued to go there every summer though my health was better now. I had many little responsibilities there by now, and both Irene and I felt a part of the place, and it was so that we were looked upon by the doctor and Miss Farly. Not to go there now that I was well never occurred to me. I even thought that it was fortunate for my people that I could go. Since I was no comfort to them, the less I was home the better. And as for me, the very thought of that sweet, quiet life out there was a joy.

When winter came I went back to my tucking machine. In the evening I wrote my letters and read a good deal. I went out little. I wanted passionately to be "true."

On a Sunday or an evening during the week I would go to see Miss O'There, who lived in Brooklyn. I would walk to and across the bridge thinking over all I wanted to talk to her about. But often when I came near the little house my courage failed me. I was in constant fear of meeting strangers, and I would turn and walk back. One night what I feared happened.

Once when I came and she opened the door for me, I

heard voices, laughing and talking. I wanted at once to run away. I knew that some of the girls who were visiting her were teachers, and some were still attending normal college. I thought, What have I in common with them? What can I say to them? What can they have to say to me? And I mumbled that now that I had seen her I would go home. She looked at me, and there was a twinkle in her eyes. I could never hide anything from her. The next moment she begged me earnestly to meet the girls.

"Stay and make friends of them."

And I begged her, "Not yet, wait till I learn a little more."

"But they too will be learning," she said. "Do you suppose they will stand still? Come, you will learn from them. And, Ruth, you too might have something to teach them."

The next moment she opened the door. "Meet my friend," she said, and I saw five girls of about my own age stand up. Through the years each one has become so dear to me, and I do not know where to begin and what to say. I can tell of that first evening only. I did not get their names, but in the course of the evening each one did something different and it was so that I remembered them later. Three of the girls were sisters; the eldest, an athletic-looking girl, with a wealth of brown hair and a hearty laugh, played the piano. The next sister, who bubbled with enthusiasm, sang Scotch songs and the youngest, with fine dark eyes and her hair still in a braid, read aloud from "Margaret Ogilvy" by J. M. Barrie. The fourth girl had a sweet voice and sang German songs. And the fifth, a quiet girl, would every now and then say something in her quiet way and there would be a burst of laughter. But they did not perform all evening. They also talked. They talked about the theatre, the opera (foreign language to me). They talked about school and college. The labour champion was there, they talked about labour. There seemed to be no end to their knowledge and their plans. They even talked in a dreamy way about taking a trip to Europe when all the girls should graduate and earn money. Miss O'There was with them in all their dreams and her white-haired mother was as young as the rest.

After this the girls would hunt me up and make me join them. One of the sisters helped me to a little more systematic study.

Besides these girls there were my old friends, the women I met through the hospital, whom I would visit. Most of them were unhappy in some way or another, and tried to forget. They and their lives still fascinated me. There was one who lived in one of the most beautiful homes there are in the city. She gave me the New Testament, which I still have, and would talk to me of the "Simple Life."

There was another, a very charming woman. I used to hear her friends say of her with a great show of enthusiasm: "Those big rough men at the church are like putty in her hands." She felt she knew the working people's lives. Yet she used to invite me to come and see her at the queerest hour, six o'clock, when I would be coming from work. I could no longer listen without criticism, and it was often hard to go from their homes to my own.

But there was one whom I loved to visit. She was twenty-five, and she was a mixture of three different nationalities, German, French and American. She was so good and so beautiful that it seemed she inherited only the best qualities of the three nations. She showed frankly that she knew nothing about the working people and that she was curious. She could never stop wondering at my going out alone at night. She had never been out without a chaperon. She would often urge me to put on a veil.

"At least," she once said, "put it on when you come to your own neighbourhood."

I laughed at her and assured her that I was safer in my own neighbourhood than in hers.

"In your neighbourhood," I said, "there are so few people in the street and the houses stand so dark and still."

To her, I, too, would talk frankly. And we often got into arguments. She defended her people and I defended mine. She talked of refinement and culture. I was at a loss. What was refinement and culture? She explained to me simply, "When for generations you live in a beautiful home, you are surrounded by beautiful pictures, you listen to beautiful music, you eat good food, you are taken care of. Do you see?"

I said that I saw, but it was all so puzzling.

"It seems to me," I said, "that when a man, my father, works all day long, he ought to have a beautiful home, he ought to have good food, he too ought to get a chance to appreciate beautiful music. All day my father is making coats yet his own is so shabby, and my mother, if you ever saw her hands! Why should she know of nothing but scrubbing and scrimping? Why should her children go without an education?"

Then her pretty forehead would pucker up; she moved closer to me, if we were on the couch, her hand would clasp mine.

"Yes, it does seem so," she would say thoughtfully. In this way a part of the two years passed in something like a peaceful way. Then father noticed that I had not the least intention of dropping the correspondence and he felt ill treated and became bitter. "Good God," he complained to mother, "was it possible that the girl meant to keep up that nonsense?" He commanded me to drop writing the letters. I refused, and our troubles began once more. Now he fairly burnt me with his anger and I thought him cruel and was more relieved than ever when summer came and I could escape to the country. Father hated to see me go there. He was in constant fear that I would forget whatever little there was in me that bound me to my race. And this year, it was the second, my father whom I remembered so gentle, cursed me as I was leaving and I went from home for the three months without a word of farewell to him. Mother ran after me into the hall. She suffered more than any of us from these ruptures. She begged me not to leave my father without a kind word. But I would not even look back. She turned back into the house weeping and I went into a strange hallway and wept too at all our misery.

When I returned home in the autumn I could not hold out against father, and I finally had to give up the letters, but of L. V. I heard through a friend. What those letters really meant to me I only now understood.

The letters out of the way, father gave me a few weeks to forget and then began to consult matchmakers. Several nights a week now on coming home from work I would find a matchmaker and a young man. Father no longer kept a secret my friendship with L. V. He was in terror about it. He began to consult friends and relatives and they all seemed to combine against me. Wherever I went to visit now I was sure to find a young man, and the relative or friend acting as matchmaker.

The younger and seemingly more enlightened friends would argue. "What are you waiting for? You are wasting your best years. You are losing your best chances." A lawyer we knew, a very nice man, who married money to establish an office, said, "There is no love!" And still others spoke with pity. "You are chasing after a shadow! This is not the age for religion. The young man is a mercenary, he is not sincere, he is being supported by missionaries. He is selling his soul for an easy life! There are others like him."

And father would demand, "What do you want anyway? The young man you saw last night is worthy ten of your kind, with your queer notions. He has fifty tailors working for him. He will give you a home with carpet on the floor, a servant and a piano."

I would answer. "I promised to wait."

But sometimes there were moments when I was tempted. A home! A piano! But was this all I wanted? And what was love? Now I knew that I still did not know.

With all my troubles I went to Miss O'There whom I gave my every thought, and she even in her affection never failed to tell me the truth. These moments were always painful to both of us, for I was so often wrong.

One night in the spring when I came to her—it was the end of the second year, and I was complaining of the old life and customs and father's treatment—I suddenly noticed that she was all upset and I stopped talking quite abruptly. I suddenly felt guilty and uneasy without knowing why.

"You are always complaining about your father," she said, "his selfishness, his narrow-mindedness, his hardness. And soon summer will come and you will go away to the country. Every summer, no matter where you are, what you are doing, you leave your work and you go away while the rest remain here sweating. Do you give a thought how your family lives here without your help?"

I felt horrified. I never saw it in that way before. She went on.

"You say he is scrimping, he demands your board whether you work the week or not; he lives for money. One has to live for something. His ideas? Right or wrong, according to him, you have been a disappointment. He had placed all his hopes in you, his oldest daughter. Who knows what this disappointment may have meant to him?"

So I gave up White Birch Farm. At first life seemed hardly worth living. All day now lost in the clattering noise of the machine there was nothing to which to look forward. Now it would always be so, feeding, feeding the machine. And then the night. The nights were the worst.

I had forgotten what it was like in the hot summer. There were five of us, the two boys in one cot and we three girls in the other, in the one room filled with the odour of cooking, of kerosene oil, the smell of grimy clothes, of stale perspiration, the heat of the body; at first as I lay with my two sisters in the sagging cot, with an unconscious limb of one or the other thrown over me, I wept. Then I thought, Why need it be so? Why? And later little by little I became used to it and at my machine I would live certain moments in the country over again. I would imagine myself in the grove. I heard the children's voices. Under the trees were the red and green benches I had helped to make. I walked down to the brook and sat on the rock from which I used to dive and listen to the quiet. I smelt the grasses growing on the edge; I felt the cool, moist air on my face,

I sat perfectly still. From far out came a familiar shrill, cheerful call "Bob-White!" And I was not so unhappy. I saw that I could still visit White Birch Farm. I was helping my people and my friend's approval meant much to me.

In August it was slack in our shop. It was slack in all trades. Miss O'There urged that I deserved a vacation, so I packed a few things and went to White Birch Farm, and was heartily welcomed. Again I was in my little room with the pale, blue walls and the window looking into the green trees. Again I played with the children in the shade of the grove. I bathed in the brook, I wandered about in the fields. But what was it? I could not find the joy of the other years. Wherever I looked I seemed to see Cherry Street. I could not shut it out. I saw the children on the hot and none-too-clean sidewalks, the fire escapes littered with bedclothes, overheated sickly infants, tired out women. The sight of the beautiful green fields irritated me. And I went home in spite of Miss O'There's letter urging me to stay, of the forewoman's letter telling me that there was still no work, in spite of Miss Farly's arguments. I felt strangely glad to be home and share the good and the bad with my people.

LXIII

ONE day in the third year I met L. V.'s friend. I had seen him twice since the first time he had been introduced. Once during the first year he came on receiving a letter from L. V. asking him to come. Because he was L. V.'s friend I too looked upon him almost as a friend. I felt no awkwardness in talking to him. I asked him that night to come again. But he never came. And I never saw him until I met him now in the street. I was so glad, he was L. V.'s friend! To him I could talk of L. V., whose image was growing more and more vague in my mind. And the more vague it became the more I wanted to think and talk of him. His friend guessed how it was. He watched me curiously, and smiled as if he were a little amused. We walked about and we talked. We talked of books we had read. He was a Russian and he had some education in that language. English he had picked up in some such way as a hen gathered food, a crumb here and a crumb there. He was extremely well read in both Russian and English.

I asked him to call. But again I never saw him until we met once more by accident. And again we walked and talked all evening. This time, when he was leaving me at my door, I did not ask him to come and he asked me quite suddenly in his blunt way, "Why?" I felt confused and did not know what to answer. He bent and looked at me and then threw his head back and laughed. I left him abruptly and went in. The next night, to my surprise, he came up to our home! He stayed all evening and talked to father about his work

and father looked pleasanter than he had been for a
long while.

After this he came often and brought books.

Once almost two weeks passed and he did not come.
Then we met, by accident, as I thought. It seemed to
me he looked thinner and I asked, "Were you ill?"

"Oh, no!" he said, and added, after a moment, without looking at me, in his blunt way, "It is just this, I am
not ready to get married."

I stared at him a long minute before the full meaning
dawned on me. I felt my face flush. I was indignant.

"So sure is this young man."

He noticed my discomfiture.

"Oh, you know how these things end," he said. "At
least I do," he smiled.

I felt calmer by now and decided to deal with the
young man.

"By all means this must end, if you feel there is danger
for you. Of course," I assured him, "there is none for
me."

To my surprise he looked anything but happy, at which
my spirits rose.

"Let us say good night at once," I said cheerfully.

"I see," he said crossly; "you are only too eager."

I laughed and we walked in silence for some moments.
Then an idea occurred to me at which I could not help
laughing.

"I have a bright idea," I said. "Let us be friends.
But as soon as one of us feels the least bit of danger
for himself he must tell the other at once."

"That is brilliant," he said in Yiddish, and laughed
too. "But remember if it should be you!"

"I'll tell," I assured him, and laughingly we parted.

'And now we saw each other often. We would go to

lectures, often we would go for long walks and talk nonsense. He said I was too serious and teased me until I had to laugh. One day he asked me to go to the theatre with him, but of course I would not go. Besides, he had once said that women generally liked men for what they could get from them. I was very touchy on the subject of my sex and I meant to teach him to have a different opinion. I would not take anything from him, at which he looked miserable and I thought it an excellent punishment and a good lesson. Then a time came when he began to demand to know what I had for supper and would insist on my coming to a restaurant. He said I looked hungry and I would be indignant and accuse him of trying to "boss" me. If I had allowed myself now I would have been happy. But how could I? When I thought of L. V. I felt miserable and guilty. He had not returned at the end of the second year. But now it was almost three years and he must surely soon come. What would I say to him?

When he came I explained as well as I could.

One night in the spring a year later, D. C. and I were taking a long walk. It was windy and we walked with our heads a little bent. I thought that he scarcely talked, and he had remarked that I was so silent. At ten o'clock we stood on the stoop before our door. He was still silent. Suddenly I could not have told what came over me. I said: "I think our friendship better cease here." No sooner did I utter the words and he looked at me than I remembered the agreement we had once made in jest and I could see that he too remembered it. I felt panic-stricken. I rushed to the door, pulled it open and ran through the dark hall,—the gas was already out. I ran up a flight of stairs and there I stood, panting. The next moment I heard the door open, a quick footstep in the hall and my name:

"Ruth!"

I pressed my hand to my heart. He had never called me Ruth.

"Please come down!" came from the foot of the stairs.

"I can't," I said.

"Just for a moment."

"I can't."

"I want to see your eyes."

"Not to-night."

"To-morrow then?"

"Perhaps."

"Good night! Then I'll wait till you go in."

A moment later I called: "I am in. Good night!"

I found the house dark when I opened the door. From every corner came quiet breathing. I felt the way to my cot. Sister, too, was asleep. I sat down beside her, and sat still for a moment. I could almost hear my heart beating. Then I remembered that sister once wondered how it felt to be happy. I touched her face, "Wake up!" I wanted to tell her that I knew.

LXIV

THAT summer work was slow in father's shop, and as he had at last saved a hundred dollars he thought, "When could there be a better opportunity to try business?" So the fall found us established in two rooms in the back of a little grocery store and the whole family was bent on making a success. Sister was behind the counter, as she was the most competent and modern and really showed a knack for the business and father and mother did the rougher work and looked on. Now it was necessary and they must learn the modern ways, learn from the children. Father shook his head at this sadly, "What a strange world!" he said.

At first the pennies came in so slowly that there was great fear for the long saved hundred dollars. But little by little business began to improve. Indeed, how could it be otherwise? Sister, who was so good and kind and sweet tempered, would wait on a little girl buying two cents' worth of milk with a courtesy as if she were buying a dollar's worth. And father and mother and the younger girl and boy would, any of them, climb five flights of stairs at six o'clock in the morning with five cents' worth of rolls for a customer who bought nothing else. So trade was coming their way. The store soon became one of the most successful in the neighbourhood, and sister became very popular. The women told her their troubles, the children saved their pennies in her care. When she would pass through the block, from everywhere children would come dancing up to her, calling her name and greeting her affectionately. Every one loved and trusted her.

But there was one trouble about this store. It threatened to absorb her whole life. As neither father nor mother could write or keep accounts she was completely tied down to the store. Father, who was happy to be making a living independent of the tailor shop, found it hard to see how she should care for anything else but the store. Nevertheless he began to learn how to write. Of an evening then, when business would be slow, he would sit down at the counter with pencil and paper and try to copy the letters or numbers we would write out for him. After poring over his slip of paper for a while he would look up, his forehead covered with perspiration. Then he would lay down his pencil to rest his stiffened fingers and sigh, "It is hard to learn at my age, children, it is hard to learn."

The boy, nineteen years old now, the one who had once dreamt of becoming a great Rabbi, was not in the store. He was bringing home the laurels.

Though he was earnest and studious, at thirteen he still had two years of public school ahead of him, since he had begun late and what education he had was foreign. So, as he was of an extremely independent nature, and also perhaps because he wanted to see something of the world, he had made a great plea to be allowed to go to an agricultural school instead. There, he heard, he could finish his elementary education and earn his living by working in the fields after school hours and at the same time learn a trade. He would be an agriculturalist. And it was from that school that he graduated two years later. He was placed by the school with a Gentile farmer. It was Passover and he thought of home and felt lonely and strange. And one day he walked off to the station, carrying his little trunk on his shoulder—both were very small, the trunk and the boy—and for the present this was the end of farming.

After this he worked as a grocery boy, a drug store boy, a boy at a newsstand, a delivery boy on Wanamaker's wagons and through it all he had his troubles. He was so honest and outspoken that as he went along he made as many enemies as friends. Above all he disliked pity and patronage. One day while working on Mr. Wanamaker's wagon he delivered a ninety-eight cent parcel. The woman who received it at the door gave him a dollar and told him to keep the change. He said, a little huffily, I imagine, that he did not take "tips" and held out the two cents. She looked him up and down and shut the door in his face. So he laid the two pennies at her door and went away. Two days later there was a complaint of discourtesy against him and he was discharged.

Because of his independence he was often in trouble but he managed somehow. He paid a certain amount into the house and the rest he saved always for some purpose of study. He often got into debt to the house but as soon as he would get work he would pay scrupulously every cent.

During an interval of out of work he had learned bookkeeping and typewriting and this was his work now. While doing this he was also making Regents counts. And it was at this time that he took a Civil Service examination and was appointed clerk in the Bureau of Education in Washington. His dream was to earn enough money to go to Columbia University.

He realised his dream, and it was while in his last year at the university that he won the second prize in the "World Work" contest on "What the School Will Do for the Boy of To-morrow." From the material side this money came now as if in answer to his great need. He had nothing with which to pay his last year's tuition, and he was worried and discouraged. But far greater than the value of this money was the honour, for so we felt it to be. Mother had tears in her eyes. Her boy was at the great university! Her boy's article was valued second to that of a superintendent of Industrial Schools! And father looked on at us silently unbelieving; then he said, "Ah! After all this is America."